FEAR OF CRIME IS THE
AVERAGE AMERICAN'S #1 CONCERN.

But no one product or method will make you safe.
Personal safety is a multi dimensional discipline. To be
safe you need first an awareness of the danger and a
healthy level of common sense. Then you need a *system*
of protection tailored to your individual needs.

   We'll show you the face of the enemy, and what
criminals are *really* deterred by. We'll show you unarmed
combat techniques developed on the street, in the
prisons, and in police academies—techniques that work
for real instead of in theory.

   You have a right to fight back against crime.

   In this book we'll show you how.

                                        Massad Ayoob

QUANTITY PURCHASES

THE TRUTH ABOUT SELF-PROTECTION

Massad F. Ayoob

BANTAM BOOKS
TORONTO · NEW YORK · LONDON · SYDNEY

> The opinions in this book belong exclusively to the
> authors, and do not necessarily reflect the opinions
> of the publisher.

THE TRUTH ABOUT SELF-PROTECTION
A Bantam Book / October 1983

ISBN 0-553-23664-4

Published simultaneously in the United States and Canada

Bantam Books are published by Bantam Books, Inc. Its trade-
mark, consisting of the words "Bantam Books" and the por-
trayal of a rooster, is Registered in U.S. Patent and Trademark
Office and in other countries. Marca Registrada. Bantam
Books, Inc., 666 Fifth Avenue, New York, New York 10103.

PRINTED IN THE UNITED STATES OF AMERICA

O   0 9 8 7 6 5 4 3 2 1

CONTENTS

"You must either conquer and rule, or serve and lose. Suffer or triumph, be the anvil or the hammer."
—Johann Wolfgang von Goethe, *The Grand Master*

INTRODUCTION

Neither I nor Bantam Books take the position that citizens should violently fight back against criminal depredation. That should be the individual's decision, the individual's option. However, you don't have that option until you know how to resist with maximum force and maximum safety to yourself.

Some of the self-protection measures presented in this book are totally passive. Others involve application of lawful, countervailing violence to a degree that may predictably cause death or crippling injury to the attacker. With power comes responsibility, in this case, the responsibility to know the prevailing laws on the use of deadly and non-deadly force by private citizens in self-defense.

The self-defense techniques and weapons options presented here should be used *only* after you have studied under responsible supervision from a professional instructor. Practice in the home or by the untrained could cause grave injury or death.

The fact that you have picked up this book shows you to be concerned about being victimized. No protective measure works 100%; else, a hundred armed policemen would not be murdered in the line of duty in this country every year. Yet possession of true defensive and protective capability—from locks and alarms to trained hands to properly selected dogs and protective weapons—will be an incalculable advantage in protecting you and yours.

What you will learn in this book may give you, or cause you to acquire, power you did not possess before. I, and Bantam, ask only that you handle and treat these powers with commensurate responsibility.

Massad F. Ayoob
Concord, New Hampshire

January, 1983

I. UNDERSTANDING THE DANGERS

1. THE FACE OF THE ENEMY

You're reading this book because you're afraid of criminals. Your fears are justified. If you haven't been confronted by a criminal yet, you don't know just *how* justified you are.

To understand the criminal mind, try this purely hypothetical experiment. Take a human embryo; breed it in a ghetto environment where the only people who are successful and enjoy creature comforts seem to be the pimps and the drug dealers and the stickup artists. Give that child only a half a chance of getting even the most menial job (at this writing, the unemployment rate for black youths nationwide is fifty percent), in a world where the only cheap entertainment is TV, where the upper-middle-class life-style this child can only hope to partake of through criminal enterprise is glorified. What do you *expect* to end up with?

You're born with intelligence, but not with ethics. If crime has become the recognized avenue for success because most of the others are effectively choked off, then it will become ethically acceptable to that organism.

When that human organism commits a crime, throw it into a prison system where a whole different dimension of life exists, a world of predatory animals who dwell within a hierarchy based on who is the strongest, the most vicious, the most ruthless—a world inhabited by those whose stock-in-trade is crime. These people can teach that young and malleable young organism how to make a hundred grand a year dealing dope, or a thousand dollars an hour stealing cars or burglarizing homes. Our young organism, if he has a quick mind, can learn enough to pursue his new trade in a couple of weeks, but there's no one out there who would fund him through trade school for a couple of years to learn a middle-class skill acceptable to middle-class society.

In the seething world behind the prison walls, there is one criterion only: "Look out for Number One, and fuck everybody else." If you don't, they'll rape you anally, or crunch you in your house (beat you in your cell) to steal a few packs of cigarettes, and move themselves another step up in the food chain hierarchy of prison life.

This is the culture and the habitat where criminals breed. They regard human beings who conform to society as a resource, to be harvested like corn or complacent livestock for their bounty. In fact, a common term street people use for straights is *whitebread*.

See them in their prison environment, and you can't help but feel sorry for them. There isn't one of them who won't seem like a victim to you when you talk to him in the visiting room, because there isn't one of them who *isn't* a victim. Call it genetic defect; call it society, but *something* victimized them and robbed them of the rich sensitivities law-abiding citizens enjoy.

But sympathizing with a criminal in the prison visiting room is like sympathizing with the timber wolf caged inside its bars at the Bronx Zoo. It's safe enough there, but you don't want to meet either of them in their natural habitat.

Veteran prison guards and cops will tell you, "Look, save your sympathy. They're animals." You respond with outrage and think the guards and cops must be animals themselves for feeling that way about other people.

You'd be stupid. Cons themselves will shrug and tell you, "You act like an animal if you're treated like one."

But I don't think of them as animals. Spend time

with animals and you can learn to relate with them. To most of you, criminals are as alien as supernatural beings.

The best analogy is with werewolves. We all know that werewolves are mythical creatures that exist only in the minds of the scriptwriters; they make you tingle with excitement in the movie theater, but you don't have to fear that one is going to bite you on the way home. Most people still feel that way about violent criminals; until they meet one, they simply don't exist.

You might say I believe in werewolves. If so, it's because I've met them. I've worked with detectives who convicted killers solely on the basis of teethmarks they left when they bit their victims' breasts off. I know a convict who killed at least one teenage girl by shoving a gun barrel up her vagina and pulling the trigger. He was convicted for one brutal sex murder, although the cops are convinced that he's guilty of others that they just can't prove since he's a psychopathic killer who is so good at covering up his hideous murders.

He can't bring himself to tell me, "I didn't do it." He just sits there across the slate-gray steel desk in the prison office and says, "I've always maintained my innocence."

His eyes are slate-gray too, and he has learned to stare people down like Kipling's Mowgli staring down the wolf pack, and he can't keep a mocking hint of a sneer off his face when he speaks of the crime he was convicted for.

One senior guard at the prison where he is serving his life term says of him, "He's a model prisoner. We've never had any trouble with him, and we probably never will. He's bright and articulate. And he is possibly the single most dangerous human being in this institution."

He says he was railroaded on circumstantial evidence. The cops think he's a psychopathic killer who is so good at covering up his hideous murders that they'll never convict him for more than the one. He's bright and engaging and informative to talk to, and when I'm alone in a briefing room with him, I keep my hands free and my chair back from the desk so I can move fast, just as if a strange Doberman had walked into the room.

The kind of werewolves I've met carry their fangs in their belts or their pockets (almost never in holsters, so they can ditch their weapons immediately with no evidence attached to their persons). They react less to full moons than to bellies full of alcohol or a couple of days doing speed or three weeks without sex or three days without money.

Psychiatrists call them sociopaths. Sociopaths don't really care about other people one way or the other. They see people as a resource, as food as it were. They will steal your belongings the way you devour an ear of corn, feeling good afterward for having sated their appetite, and with absolutely no regard for the feelings of the cornstalk that grew the bounty and left it where it could be harvested.

Being a sociopath isn't necessarily bad. There are times when society deliberately trains sociopaths since they can serve extremely useful functions. If a conglomerate has just taken over a marginally profitable firm and has to clear out a lot of deadwood, they'll send in a personnel executive who can be ruthless about firing people who don't produce. He hasn't spent fifteen years at work and at play with the people he's firing, and if it occurs to him that this loss of their jobs will be the most shattering act in their lives short of the death of a child or parent or spouse, he sloughs it off. He is doing it impersonally, for the greater good of the corporation.

In wartime, every soldier on the battlefield has been taught that the enemy is subhuman or nonhuman, a target to be destroyed in return for recognition (medals, favored assignments, and promotions for those producing the highest body count). The tragedy of the foreigner's death, of the widowhood of his wife, and the orphaning of his children, is ignored. The soldier kills wholesale for the greater good of his unit, and is rewarded by his own survival and that of his nation.

That soldier's own generals will send him to die, because they know that there is a certain "acceptable casualty rate" when the death of one's own compatriots is accompanied by strategic victory. The general sends his men to die for the greater good of the service, and the head of state who commands the general endorses this act for the greater good and survival of his government and his society.

The dead soldiers on their own side are ciphers. The dead soldiers on the other side are bodycount and victory, with tangible rewards in terms of national riches and security and of forestalling the advances of Communism/Capitalist Imperialism (pick one). In corporate head-rollings, the suffering jobless disappear from sight, and all that remains is the relief and good feelings of those who still have their jobs and are still occupationally alive.

The sociopathic outlaw who commits crime against another person feels those same justifications. He does it for the greater good of himself; the suffering of his victims doesn't concern him. He is isolated from it. He feels he has his own problems that drove him to this life-style; the agony he causes for others is simply *their* problem.

The average person could not identify with murdering for profit. The sociopathic criminal will do so with no more compunction than the manager of your local MacDonald's makes his order for the week's hamburger. Each is doing what he perceives his job to be, and if some living thing dies for it, that is a problem for the thing that dies, not for him.

Consider a young man whose street alias was Ronnie. Ronnie is twenty-nine, an affable guy with a raffish air about him. Everybody who chats with him likes him. I chatted with him in the state prison where he's going to be for quite some time, because Ronnie has done a lot of sociopathic things in his life.

Ronnie tells me about how he makes his living as a professional burglar and car thief when he's "outside the walls." He knows I can tell when he's lying, but he doesn't lie because, even though he knows I'm writing this book, he thinks you're too stupid to take his advice and even if you do, he can defeat any auto theft alarm now made and a majority of the residential alarms, anyway.

Ronnie is a nice guy, when he's in prison. You don't want to know him when he's outside. Ronnie has stolen about 1,400 cars in his life, and burgled more than 300 carefully chosen homes. He steals expensive cars for about $1,000 turnover apiece—"It's no harder for me to steal a new Cadillac with an alarm than a five-year old Plymouth without one," he says flatly—and he averages $5,400 per home burglary because he hits carefully selected, fancy houses, and takes everything there.

A security guard caught him stealing a car once, and Ronnie put an automatic pistol in his face. Ronnie meant business and the guard knew it, so Ronnie left with the car and then sold it.

Ronnie is one of many burglars who gives the lie to the myth that this type of criminal doesn't carry weapons or hurt anyone. "I never did a job without a gun in my belt," he says, "and if anybody had ever tried to stop me, I would have killed 'em." Fortunately, Ronnie cased his jobs well, and the only time in 300-some hits that he encountered the residents, he found them asleep and sneaked out with his gun in his hand.

He's a stone professional, our Ronnie. He likes "old money" houses with old-style alarms installed years ago, alarms that he can put out of commission with two pennies. (No, I won't say how, but it does work.)

In all of those home hits, Ronnie went up against about twenty dogs. Some were lapdogs, and he just fed them out of the homeowner's refrigerator and went on his way.

I'm not scared of dogs. I can always shoot 'em or hit 'em over the head. If you throw pepper in their face or Mace 'em, they're helpless, 'cause their mucous membranes are all on the surface, and spraying Mace on the dog's nose is like shooting it right down a human being's throat.

Ronnie always had a piece of pipe and a gun, though, and he told me about the worst deal he had with a dog. "It was a Do-vey," he said, mispronouncing *Doberman*.

I was halfway in the window and the damn thing came right at me. I smashed it right in the middle of the head and it fell down. I don't think it died afterward; it just sort of laid there the whole time, but it was breathing when I left. I'll tell ya, though, if I ever get out of prison and get my own house, I'm going to get *two* of those Do-veys. Ain't no way ya can get 'em both at once, and they *do* come at ya.

Ronnie was always ready to use his gun to kill anyone who messed with him. He preferred a Smith & Wesson 15-shot 9-mm automatic, bought on the black market from a thief in Providence, Rhode Island, who stole it at a time when Ronnie could prove he was in prison. If he got caught with the gun he couldn't be tied to the theft; if he killed someone and ditched the gun it couldn't be tied to him either. He was never stupid enough to carry a gun he had stolen himself. He always sold those.

I asked Ronnie what he would do if he faced an armed homeowner. "If neither of us had drawn yet, I'd draw and shoot him. If I had my gun out and he went for his, I'd kill him. If he had the drop on me, I'd wait till he turned away, and then I'd pull my gun and shoot him." What if, I asked, the homeowner didn't give him an opening? "I'd let the cops come and take me back to prison," he said. "I'm not stupid enough to get myself *killed*."

Ronnie does not mince words about his willingness to use a gun. He was once imprisoned for attempted murder when, in an argument over a young girl, he shot another street person seven times with a .357 Magnum revolver, pausing only to reload. Incredibly, his victim lived, though he was paralyzed for life.

I know who Ronnie is, but Ronnie doesn't know who I am. He thinks I'm just a street-smart journalist. We both have a rough idea where we stand, though. If Ronnie comes into my house when I'm there, he'll either threaten me with death or actually kill me, since I sure won't be inviting him over for a drink. And if I ever come home and find Ronnie there, I will violate every rule I teach and shoot him down on sight.

He is the wolf, and I am the shepherd. It is one thing to grieve for the loss of natural ecology for arctic and timber wolves, and quite another to be responsible for the sheep that they kill.

Timber wolves are wild and free and they love their families, and if you could get to know them you'd like them. All that is true of Ronnie, too. I feel sorry for the wolves in the zoo and for Ronnie in prison. But I know that their instinct is to kill my sheep, and if they try to, I'll destroy them, just as they would me if they got the drop on me first.

Pogo said, "We have seen the enemy, and they is us." That's something that crosses every citizen's mind when he gets bitten by someone like Ronnie and decides that it isn't going to happen anymore. But we don't *want* to be like them.

Those who want to ban guns make the point that burglars kill more homeowners than vice versa. That's only because burglars come in ready to kill anyone who messes with them, like Ronnie, and some of them have a bit of rogue leopard in them and kill just for fun. Homeowners, by contrast, don't kill unless they have absolutely no choice. When a Ronnie runs, they don't shoot him in the back, the way Ronnie might do to them. Ronnie isn't afraid of silver bullets or garlic or anything else except either two Dobermans at once, or a gun held on him that doesn't waver and that he knows is going to go off if he turns mean.

One convicted rape-killer told me, "You'd have to be out of your mind to move on a woman with a gun. Of course, a lot of your really psychotic rapists *are* out of their minds." He didn't want to discuss the likelihood of a woman who froze on her gun, versus a dead psychotic rapist. Perhaps he identified too strongly with the latter. I asked him though, how his wife would defend herself against people like him while he was in prison and unable to protect herself. He shrugged and said, "She's careful about strangers, and she's got a shotgun. *She's* pretty safe."

These predatory people don't think like you. They *aren't* people like you. They are a different breed.

Talk to doctors and psychiatrists and lawyers and probation officers. These are all people who understand the criminal mind. They'll be reluctant to talk about the full depths of what they know until they know *you* a lot better, because they think you'll say, "Come on, there really aren't beings like you're describing except on TV and in the movies."

But if you could look into your city's list of registered holders of pistol-carrying permits—as a number of city newspapers and magazines like *New York Magazine* have— you'll find that these doctors and psychiatrists, these probation officers and lawyers, are among the highest occupational categories of people who carry guns for self-defense.

This is because they work every day with the sort of people we are talking about. They have seen the face of the enemy and they are indeed frightened. They arm themselves with guns because they also know what fends off the sociopathic werewolves from our city's streets.

Call a Doberman breeder and ask him how many of his clients are doctors and lawyers and judges. It's not just because they can afford the money, or they'd be buying Lhasa apsos.

Those of us who have dealt with hardened criminals know them better than anyone else. We also, even more than the bleeding heart pseudopenologists, understand just what a rotten hand they were dealt even before they got to prison, let alone after they got out again to hunt.

I have been friends with criminals; I ran with them as

a kid. Later, because I was lucky enough to get out of their mold before it marked me, I became a police officer. Then I arrested criminals. Since then, I've spent a lot of time researching them.

I can empathize with the wolves and the werewolves, however. They follow their nature, the way they were bred, into an environment and a shape they didn't choose for themselves. They are predatory and carnivorous and protective of their own. But if one of them gets out of his cage and comes after me or mine, I know that the only effective way to stop him is to shoot him. I know that, and the wolf knows that, and if the wolf senses that it's going to go down that way, it's probably not going to come after me or mine at all.

2. WHY YOU HAVE BEEN MISINFORMED ABOUT SELF-DEFENSE

Polls tell us that the fear of crime is the average American's Number One concern. A multitude of industries have arisen around this "fear boom." K–9 guard dog kennels, locksmiths, alarm purveyors, karate instructors, and private firearms academies, are proliferating. Many are being opened by quick-buck artists who have a very limited grasp of the dynamics of human violence and the methods of controlling it.

Many people in the protection field will tell you that their discipline or their product is the "one true religion." They'll imply that only their burglar alarm or only one of their Dobermans or only their method of self-defense training will make you safe.

This is totally false. Personal safety is a multidimensional discipline. To be safe you need an awareness of danger and a healthy level of common sense. You want good locks and state of the art alarm systems tailored to your individual needs.

You want to learn what makes criminals tick because a basic truth of human confrontation is that you can never defeat an enemy you underestimate; there are even martial arts techniques specifically designed to work for weak defenders against strong aggressors. You may even wish to arm yourself to the level of a firearm's deadly force.

You need a *system* of protection, because each individual consideration—locks, alarms, dogs, guns—only works within its own narrow band in the whole threat spectrum. The lock *should* keep an intruder out, but a skilled criminal can breach it. The alarm *should* scare the criminal off or at least alert you to his presence, but he may not fear it or he may know how to nullify it. If he has penetrated that far, the dog *should* be able to fight him off or frighten him away, but hardened criminals know how to deal with dogs, too. Extensive training in the martial arts *should* enable you to fight off an assault, but it won't do much for you if you face multiple assailants or deadly weapons. A gun *should* be your salvation against otherwise imminent death at the hands of a criminal, but there's very little else it's good for, and it can't keep you safe just by being in your night table drawer.

When you study the field of self-protection, or as professionals call it, Threat Management, you have to go beyond the reams of misinformation that have been written by people who have never been in the position of having to protect innocent life, people who have never been attacked on the street, or by people who have never actually met a violent criminal and gotten inside his head.

The people who know how to protect themselves best are those in law enforcement, because it is their job to know. They know criminals are afraid of being hurt. Criminals fear police dogs and people with clubs and heavy flashlights. Above all, they fear cops because cops have guns to kill them with.

If you go back mentally over every article you ever read about self-defense in a newspaper or general magazine, you'll recall that they told you that any weapon more formidable than a rat-tail comb or a squeegee of lemon juice to squirt into a rapist's eyes, was too dangerous for you to carry. They may even have told you that formidable dogs were too dangerous to keep.

They probably told you that the best thing to do, when confronted by a dangerous criminal, was not to resist. If you can't deal with it, then compliance is certainly your *option*, but it is not written in stone. You also have the right to fight back.

In this book, we'll show you how.

We'll show you the face of the enemy and what criminals are *really* deterred by. We'll show you unarmed combat techniques developed on the street, in the prisons, and in the police academies—techniques that work for real instead of in theory. Because most violent criminals are only deterred by two things—big, vicious dogs and armed people who appear resolutely prepared to kill or cripple if the assault isn't broken off—we shall place those alternatives into perspective for you, and help you determine whether a protection dog or a firearm is really suitable for *you*.

We'll show you some ugly realities of street violence as well as the criminal justice system as it works in America today. Some of what you read here will be depressing. Some of it will make you feel naked because it will strip away the false confidence that some of the "conventional wisdom" of self-protection may have instilled in you.

I'm sorry about that, but it's better for you to learn the truth here, now, in time to prepare a different protection plan, than for you to find out the hard way in the course of a violent assault.

But it's not all bad news. Learning effective self-protection is like building muscles in a weight-lifting gym. You have to break down the old fatty tissue so that the new, hard tissue can grow bigger and stronger. Once we strip away the flabby myths, we'll give you hard, street-proven advice on how to take care of yourself the way the professionals do.

The techniques we'll teach you, and the equipment we'll recommend, aren't just for strong young cops. They'll work for any law-abiding citizen, old or young, male or female, in shape or flabby. They were designed to, because the cops who use them also range from young to old, male to female, in shape or not.

It's a serious commitment, one that goes beyond reading this book. This book is designed to raise your consciousness to the reality of self-protection against street criminals. It's not an instant guide to toal safety in ten easy lessons.

Few police officers will have any objection to my teaching these things to you. All the advice is defensively oriented, and none gives away proprietary knowledge about police strategy. My experience has proven that America's over-worked, underpaid cops get into their profession because they want to help people, and they're generally elated when one of their citizens is able to fight off a vicious criminal.

Some of the things you will read in this book will be hard to cope with. So is life. Crime against the person is a hard act done brutally by hard people who can be stopped only by hard measures. It's like radiation therapy to treat cancer: an ugly and painful thing to go through, but less ugly and painful than the otherwise-inescapable alternative.

In medicine, the term is *toxin-antitoxin:* poison against poison. In real life, if the criminal who attacks you has not been deterred by locks and alarms and walls and barred windows, you are given the same choice as a cancer patient: Resort to "treatment" that will be unpleasant for you, or suffer a fate far more unpleasant. *Toxin-antitoxin* has been proven on the street as well as in the hospital: Ultimately, if all the preventative measures fail, criminal violence can only be dealt with through countervailing violence, lawfully and judiciously applied. Only tough responses answer tough problems.

Some of what we'll be talking about will cost you money. Because we understand that many of you have limited funds, we'll give the best alternatives. But the ultimate question really, is what self-protection is worth to you—not so much in dollars, but in terms of personal commitment.

3. THE CRIME WATCH CONCEPT

Many Americans, to help avert the rising tide of crime, are turning not to vigilante justice, but to organized efforts to spot crimes in progress in time to summon the duly constituted police authorities.

With names like Crime Watch, Community Watch, and Citizen's Patrol, these unarmed citizens have no authority but the universal power of citizen's arrest, and no uniform except for a common T-shirt, Windbreaker, baseball cap, or beret.

Perhaps the most highly evolved of these groups is the Guardian Angels, founded in New York City some years ago by Curtis Sliwa. Loved by the public, resented by many in law enforcement, the Angels have put together an undeniably excellent record of deterring crime and capturing muggers and rapists. Part of their popularity is that they deal only with crimes of violence; Sliwa told James Gordon of the National Association of Chiefs of Police, "You can walk by me with a whole wheelbarrow full of cocaine and I'm going to say, 'That's none of my business.' But if I see a man trying to steal a woman's pocketbook, I am going to grab that guy."

Members of the Angels tend to be black and Hispanic youths from the slums of New York. They show a deep commitment to their work. It is not uncommon for them to get hurt either since they don't carry weapons. They are trained in karate, but the real-life applications of empty hand fighting against guns and knives are limited, indeed.

Sliwa is interested in seeing more cities around the country adopt the Guardian Angels concept (Boston and Atlanta had mixed reactions when test groups were fielded there); more information is available from the Guardian Angels, 982 East 89th Street, Brooklyn, NY 11236.

While the Angels' existence is only grudgingly accepted by their city's police establishment, there are many similar but less-flamboyant groups that operate in close cooperation with the police. Contact your local police department's Community Resources Office or Crime Prevention Bureau and ask if there is a volunteer Community Watch program already functioning in your neighborhood.

Many Community Watch programs do not involve any sort of patrol. An excellent system in Hazelwood, Missouri, enlists citizens (especially the retired and the infirm) as "observers," who are taught how to spot a burglary in progress or how to identify suspicious actions; they keep their eyes open and call the police when they see something fishy.

The Hazelwood system also includes "safe houses," conspicuously marked by decals on doors and windows. Residents of those dwellings, checked out beforehand by the police, will give sanctuary to any woman or child being threatened or chased, and actual incidents have already proven that the concept works.

The Hazelwood police program is a model of citizen involvement. In addition to the crime watch and safe house functions, volunteers (after a background check, of course) are taught how to analyze a home or business in terms of locks, alarms, lighting, and architectural security. These people help others in the community to "harden their perimeters," leaving more officers free for patrol tasks.

Community patrol groups have often been formed from CB clubs. Almost always forbidden to carry guns, they stay in radio contact with police headquarters and patrol highways in search of stranded motorists. Essentially, these volunteers act as eyes and ears for their local police. Trained in first aid, they will intervene *only* to save the life of an injured victim, and are normally strongly discouraged from attempting to apprehend violent criminals.

For those who don't have such an operation in their community at present, information on how to organize one and coordinate it with the local police is available through the National Crime Watch Program, American Federation of Police, 1100 N.E. 125th Street, North Miami, FL 33161, to the attention of Chief Gerald Arenberg.

Another option is joining the Auxiliary Police in cities where they are allowed. This is an actual branch of the police department. The volunteer cop is either sworn or nonsworn.

A *sworn* auxiliary police officer has full and autonomous arrest powers—that is, he can take action on his own command, up to arresting a suspect and transporting him to the detention center—and he is armed with a firearm. The sworn auxiliary also functions alone at times. A *nonsworn* volunteer can perform arrest-type duties only at the specific command of a full-time police officer, whom he must always accompany, and will usually be forbidden to carry a firearm.

Illinois' police officers once experimented with auxiliary troopers statewide, but use them now primarily on the dispatch desk and they carry no weapons. In most police departments, however, auxiliary officers carry the same gun and wear the same uniform as full-time patrol officers. They are normally distinguished only by a slightly different badge and shoulder emblem. An auxiliary police officer is sometimes paid by the day or hour, though they are required to donate generous amounts of free time. They are employed frequently at civil disturbances.

In some communities part-time sworn officers are known as Special Police, not to be confused with security guards who sometimes have similar titles. A department's special police officer may work regular tours of patrol duty by himself. In most states he will have a minimal level of training as mandated by the Police Officer Standards and Training Council. In many small communities these part-time officers are the backbone of the whole police force; New Hampshire, for instance, has some 115 communities where even the chief of police works only part-time.

New York City's auxiliary police officers, however, are not allowed to carry guns even if they have private pistol permits; they have only handcuffs and a baton. The Los Angeles Police Department, on the other hand, arms its auxiliaries with .38 revolvers.

Taking the Community Watch route is one thing: You are the eyes and ears of the police, and can do your thing from a safely remote distance. To enter the fray in a uniform is something else entirely. You are most definitely putting yourself in harm's way. When you ride with a regular police officer you are caught up in his routine, and when he answers a deadly danger call, you're right there with him. Your uniform makes you just as much a target of a criminal's gun as the career police officer is. Violent crime by armed and dangerous felons is a "lethal threat management mission," and you can't control that threat without the proper tools. Among these tools is a legal gun you've been trained and authorized to use.

If you wish to formally join the war on crime, I would earnestly suggest that you do it at either the mildest level or the strongest, as a member of a Community Watch Program or as a sworn, armed, and trained part-time police officer. Anything in the middle is ultimately going to put you into a situation you won't be prepared to cope with.

You wouldn't try to perform a tracheotomy on a choking man by cutting a surgical hole in his throat to allow him to breathe, unless you had extremely advanced emergency medical training, and the proper tools. The results can be just as tragic and fatal when an untrained and unarmed civilian "plays police officer" in a violent crime situation.

4. UNDERSTANDING THE COPS

Whenever the subject of crime comes up among civilians at a gathering I always hear stories of how the responding police officers were cold and unfeeling toward the victims. I especially hear that from women's groups; many members of such groups have never actually spoken with a police officer at a crime scene.

I used to take those stories seriously. Then I became a police officer. I was twenty-three years old, with a college degree, one of what used to be called The New Breed. I really bought that Boys' Town line that goes, "There's no such thing as a bad boy."

In police work, I got a very quick education on the street. I think the turning point came the night an armed robbery suspect vehemently told me as he was being led away, "Pig, I would'a blown your head off if I coulda grabbed my gun the second you stepped outa that *po*-lice car!"

It was the first time in my life a human being ever told me that he wanted to kill me, meant it, and would have if he could have. And, to my greater horror, I heard myself answer, "I know. That's why I got out of that police car with this shotgun pointed at you."

I no longer believe that there is no such thing as a bad boy. I changed my mind after I met and interacted with and interviewed, human beings who were evil. There's no other word for it—evil. I never lost my sense of compassion for them or for their loss of human dignity—I never arrested a person I didn't feel sorry for—but that compassion has been tempered with control.

I'm sorry for you and the things you felt you had to do, but you won't be allowed to do those things to me or to anyone under the mantle of my protection, and that's why my gun is pointed at you, and that's why you *will* be very docile as we put these handcuffs on you.

I don't know if you can understand that but it works.

In police work you learn up front that becoming emotionally involved with a victim of a crime is *verboten*. It is the antithesis of professionalism. The police officer is taught to be emotionless and totally objective. He has to be. If he catches the perpetrator of a crime, he may well have to interact violently with that person, and if a lawyer can say later that the officer's aggression was due to a need to avenge what had been done to the victim, that officer's career is ruined and so is the credibility of every man and woman wearing the same uniform.

Besides, when you're a police officer it's easy to desensitize yourself to violence; you see it all the time. After the first few weeks the sight of blood no longer bothers you, and if you're on the job long enough, you stop throwing up when you find the dismembered, rotting corpse of a child. Yet, there's something in the human being's natural parental instinct that causes a definite emotional response when a child is hurt, and you just never totally block it out. I have taken my share of dead people out of wrecked cars; most of the time it's just another chore at the accident scene, but when it's a child tears come to my eyes. Every other cop I've ever discussed this with feels the same way. So do pathologists who do hundreds of autopsies a year.

The cop, therefore, learns to be calm and dispassionate when he talks to the victims and the victims' survivors and the witnesses. *He has to,* partly because it's his job, and partly because he sees so much human tragedy that he would go insane otherwise.

The most common myth though is that police officers don't care about rape victims and take the side of the rapist because they're chauvinists. That's completely untrue. Do police officers ever take the rape victim's story with a grain of salt and wonder if she's making it up out of spite or for some other reason? You bet they do, for one very good reason: They've seen it happen.

I personally witnessed two such cases as a cop. I hadn't been on a year when my partner and I were given a warrant to serve on a man suspected of rape; a 14-year-old retarded girl swore that he violated her. I was fully prepared to punch this guy's face in if he even slightly resisted arrest. Later, I was glad that we didn't find him; the girl admitted the next day that she had fabricated the story because she feared she was pregnant by her 15-year-old retarded boyfriend, and thought her parents would punish her if they knew the truth. It just didn't occur to her that her lie could destroy an innocent human being.

In another case we worked day and night trying to find a man who had "abducted and raped" a 45-year-old woman. We stopped looking when the woman, feeling she had gotten in over her head, told us the truth about what had happened. She had picked the guy up in a bar, they drove out on a country road, and had consensual sex; she then made disparaging remarks about his sexual performance. At that point, he slapped her in the face, ordered her out of his car, and left her there to walk home. She reported it as kidnapping and rape.

These false reports constitute a very small percentage of all reported rapes. Tragically, because they still do occur, police officers have to ask those seemingly brutal questions: "Did you date him? Did you offer to have sex with him? Was money discussed? Had you had sex with him before?"

Don't blame that on the cops. Blame it on the small percentage of neurotic women who make false reports to get even with boyfriends who've dumped them or to cover up an illicit affair.

I also hear a lot about how "The cops won't do anything when your husband beats you. They just tell him to behave and they probably side with him anyway."

Wrong, wrong, wrong. More police officers have been murdered responding to domestic disputes than were killed handling armed robberies in progress during some years. There exists a classic syndrome, one every rookie cop is warned about long before he leaves the police academy.

You, the cop, go to a house where a guy is beating his wife. He gives you a hard time, maybe takes a swing at you. You fight back. Now, guess who's on your back, trying to gouge your eyes out or brain you with a frying pan? Right. It's the wife, who moments before was the victim you thought you were protecting.

It's not hard to understand. However rotten her spouse is to her, they share a home, and now this blue-clad authority figure has invaded it. They will instinctively bond together against him, and that instinct will be fueled by the social reality that the cop's very presence there is an embarrassment to them: How can they face their neighbors again?

Even if the husband has savagely beaten the wife, she may come even to his aid with physical force if he gets into a fight with the cop. Clinging to her pathetic fantasy that if she fights by his side, he'll love her again and appreciate her again and stop hitting her, she'll join him in attacking the cop, *and the cop knows it.*

The cop also knows that most abused women aren't going to press charges. Except in states where special laws have been passed to protect battered women, a cop can't arrest someone for assault unless he has actually witnessed assault; he can make an arrest only if the victim swears out a complaint. As he explains that, the beaten wife looks nervously at her husband, who is glaring at her, and she often decides that she doesn't dare.

Often, too, the victims are overwhelmed when they face a complex criminal justice system they don't understand. They worry about shame; they worry about publicity; they worry about revenge that the person who hurt them may take once he's free on bail.

The officer knows that and he is not about to make a "false arrest" without grounds. He can be sued personally as well as through the department if that assault victim fails to follow through on the charges, and he has his own spouse and family to think about. Is he going to ask some hard questions before he places that person under arrest? You bet he is. In that context, do you think that makes him hard and cold, or does it just make sense?

ON THE STREET

If you fear that you may ever be involved in a violent encounter on the street, an encounter that you choose to take control of with physical force, you must understand that the police officers who arrive on-the-scene will deal very harshly with you.

In my deadly force courses for civilians (open only to people who have pistol permits and who furnish me with a letter of reference from the chief of police in their community), I make a point of explaining that when even the most law-abiding citizen is involved in a violent encounter—whether it involves fists and feet or knives and guns—he has to expect to be treated like a criminal suspect by the responding police officers. Too many people think that if they punch a mugger or hold an armed robbery suspect at gunpoint, the cops are going to rush up and pat them on the back and say, "Great work, fella!"

They won't. Those police officers may have no way of knowing who is the Good Guy and who is the criminal. More than likely, they've been called by someone who said, "There's a violent streetfight going on outside my shop," or, "There's an armed robbery going on here, people with guns!"

You may have just outfought a couple of muggers. You may be a woman who has just used a weapon to successfully subdue a rapist. You may be even an off-duty cop who has just witnessed a robbery while shopping at the 7–11 store for a pack of cigarettes, and drawn your gun. You could be a panicky homeowner who has called the cops after hearing a noise downstairs, and then grabbed your hunting rifle and gone down to check it out yourself.

In each of those scenarios you are a citizen doing something you have a legal right to do, but you will be caught up emotionally in what may be the most cataclysmic moment of your life. And, in each of those scenarios you will feel a sense of righteous indignation if a cop intrudes and brusquely gives you orders as he would a common criminal.

But the cop, in fact, is *not* going to say, "Great piece of work." The cop *is* going to say, "Police! Don't move! Drop that weapon [if you have one]!" Go back to the scenarios. The patrol officer has been told that some people are fighting in an alley and now he sees *you* standing over two fallen muggers. Does he assume that you are a violent attacker harming an innocent citizen? Of course. He has to. And he'll treat you accordingly.

You are the rape victim who fought back. All the cop has probably been told is, "Unknown trouble at Fourth and Main." Now he sees you there pointing your pistol at a prostrate man. If he's been on the job for a while in a heavy-action precinct, he has seen a lot of men who were murdered by women. He *is* going to "throw down on you" (draw his gun and point it at you) and issue the standard challenge, "Police! Drop that weapon!"

You are the off-duty cop in a district where you're not known, standing there in your blue jeans and T-shirt holding your snub-nosed .38 on two armed robbery suspects in the 7–11. When the alarm went off, the responding officers knew they would come up against a violent armed criminal, threatening others with a gun. And when they see you they're going to think, "Look! There's one now!"

You're the homeowner out stalking prowlers. Your wife called the police from the bedroom and said, "Come quick! We have intruders in our house!" Those cops are prepared for anything—they know that despite the common beliefs, most burglars *do* carry deadly weapons, and they know that in some parts of the country, every second house contains at least one firearm of some type.

If the burglar didn't have a gun going in, there's a good chance he's got one going out, and as the officers pull up near your residence they see *you* stepping out of the back door with a gun in your hands. Are they supposed to know automatically that you're an indignant homeowner protecting his domain?

Whenever the private citizen fights off criminal violence with his own righteous, legally justified, countervailing violence, he is doing a very good impersonation of a violent criminal. All the cops see is a man or woman beating somebody else up, or a man or woman threatening someone else with a gun. *You have to understand that*

*they have no way of knowing that you're the Good Guy; they must
assume that you are the Bad Guy.*

Cops won't shoot you down or club you into the
ground. They *will* however, order you to halt and they *will*
order you to drop any weapon you may be holding.

Now, let's flash back to *you*. You've just been through
what may have been the most traumatic moment in your
life. You have successfully asserted your right to protect
yourself as an American citizen. You're going to be feeling
awfully righteous and when the cops bark at you, "freeze!"
everything inside you is going to tell you to turn around
and yell, "Stupid cops! *I'm* the *Good Guy* here!"

Don't. About half the time cops know change accordingly
when they confront a violent armed criminal and issue the
challenge, the criminal will turn on them and try to kill them.
They have been trained to deal with that. Most of that
training centers on shooting the suspect in the center of his
torso. If the suspect is unarmed, however, someone they
reasonably perceive to be a mugger or a streetfighter beating
up an innocent victim, the cop will very likely smack him
down with a blow delivered via a twenty-four-inch hickory
nightstick, a heavy PR–24 baton, or a clubbed flashlight.

There are times when you, as a victim or complainant,
will interact with the police on matters less serious. Let's
say that your car is stolen. Do you take it as a personal
affront when the investigating police officer doesn't exactly give you a shoulder to cry on?

If so, consider this fact, well-known to police officers
and insurance underwriters, but less well-known by the
public: In 1981 an estimated twenty to twenty-five percent
of all car thefts reported were in fact cases where the
owner of a car he couldn't afford to gas up or pay for,
"sold it to the insurance company." That is, the owner
dumped the car someplace or set it on fire or paid someone to steal it, and then filed a "stolen auto" claim and used
the money to buy a car that was more affordable in terms
of gas mileage.

That figure is not hypothetical. It comes from the National Auto Theft Bureau, a nonpolice organization set up by insurance companies to monitor the truth about stolen cars. *The cops are familiar with this procedure*; that's why they don't get all misty and brim over with sympathy for everyone who tells them, "Gee, my Continental Mk. Four just got stolen out of my driveway."

Don't take it as a personal affront when you've just been pulled over for a traffic violation in the middle of the night, and, in your side-view mirror, you see the officer unsnap the safety strap on his revolver holster. Cops know that an extraordinarily high number of their brother officers killed or wounded each year are shot during "routine" traffic stops. A dope dealer who just made a score or an armed robber fleeing the scene of a holdup, tends to drive faster and more erratically than the average motorist. When the cop pulls him over for a ticket that guy is thinking, "They've already got an APB [All Points Bulletin] out on me! I'm not gonna let this cop arrest me so I can be put in jail for life! I'll shoot him *dead* first!"

Every cop on the street knows of cases where this happened. A friend of mine, a midwestern highway patrol officer, got shot in just such a scenario. Do cops come up to your car ready to shoot you if you pull a gun on them? Damn right. Is that paranoid? You may think so, but you haven't been a cop and you've never had to spend a midnight shift pulling cars over, cars that contained unknown people and unknown potential violence. After two in the morning a good percentage of automobiles on the road are driven by people who are drunk. When cops stop them they find that as many as one drunk driver out of every six, attempts to violently assault the arresting officer. Are the cops ready for violence when they pull *you* over? Yes, and now you know why.

The police officer won't be your salvation when you need him because he can't be. It is generally recommended in law enforcement that there be one full-time police officer for every thousand citizens. But each of those officers works only 40 hours of a 168-hour week. Some of them are supervisors, managers who never get onto the street themselves. Some are detectives and investigators who don't get involved until after a crime has been committed.

All of them have to spend a lot of their time in court and behind a typewriter doing paperwork. A routine drunk-driving bust usually takes the arresting officer off the street for two to three hours cutting his shift of "sentinel duty" nearly in half. When you look at police work in real life, you know that each cop is responsible for protecting *several* thousand people at a time, probably over a distance of ten or more square miles if you live in a rural or suburban area.

Police work is *re*active instead of *pro*active. Despite all the publicity given to "team policing" and "crime prevention," the police are generally called in only after a crime has been perpetrated. This may be cold comfort to the victims but you can't blame the cops for it.

Criminals *know* that there aren't enough cops to be everywhere; they deliberately strike areas where the cops either don't patrol often or have already patrolled for the evening. Often they even make a fake distress call to lure the police officers to a part of the community far away from where they actually plan to strike.

Cops know they can't be everyplace at once. That's why most street police officers leave a loaded gun at home where their wives can reach it, and if you don't take that as fact, just ask the head of your local police patrol officer's union about it.

In using self-defense against violent human threat, your karate, your gun, whatever you fall back on, is only an emergency, short-term defense to allow you and, if necessary, your loved ones, to get clear of the danger and call the proper authorities to deal with it. The proper authorities are the police.

But in such moments, you'll have to be extremely careful to act in such a manner that no one—cops, witnesses, or criminals—is going to mistake you for anything other than a law-abiding citizen.

5. MAXIMUM UTILIZATION OF YOUR POLICE

We have just explained how to properly interact with responding officers at a crime scene (one that you have hopefully controlled). Let's look now at services you might not even know about—how to take advantage of free police services that can help protect you and your family and your home.

Home and business security checks. Many police departments offer, through their Crime Prevention Bureau or Community Relations Division, the service of sending a specially trained police officer to your home or place of business to do a security analysis. Some forward-thinking police departments have even trained selected civilian volunteers to perform that function.

Within a week or two of your request, at a mutually agreed-upon time, an officer will go through the premises, showing you door by door and window by window, how to better secure the place against intruders. They normally won't make brand name recommendations or steer you to a specific locksmith or alarm installer, but you *will* have had a professional and personalized security survey at absolutely no cost.

Operation Identification. Begun some years ago, Operation Identification works through participating law enforcement agencies which lend engraving tools to citizens in their community. The tools are used to engrave the homeowner's Social Security number or driver's license ID number on inconspicuous metal parts of TVs, stereos, cameras, guns, and other "stealables." Mark them inconspicuously on the revolver frame where the grips cover the number, or inside the film door of your 35-mm camera. This way, a criminal isn't likely to spot the marking and grind it off. This also keeps you from losing resale value if you later decide to dispose of the items yourself. Decals then go on your door saying, Property Inside This Home Protected by Operation Identification.

Operation Identification has only been a partial success. Professional burglars know when they see that sticker that they're going to lose money trying to fence any items they steal from that residence because their fence will say,

Jeez, Lefty, I gotta go to the trouble of grinding this number off this thing, and while I've got it in my possession with the number still on it, the cops could arrest me for possession of stolen goods. I can only give ya a nickel on the dollar for this stuff.

Amateur burglars don't know what Operation Identification is all about so it doesn't deter them, but at least you have a chance of getting your stuff recovered. Any burglary detective can tell you countless stories about the person whose thousands of dollars worth of goods were recovered after the burglar was arrested, but lost them anyway because the owner couldn't identify any of it as his own in the police department's Property Recovery Room. This alone is worth going to Operation Identification.

The only reason Operation Identification doesn't work better than it does is because citizens are so complacent. Even if they know their community's police offer the service, they fail to take advantage of it. One could make a good argument that compacency in the face of predictable danger is contributory negligence. Call your local police department, ask about Operation Identification, and follow through by engraving your valuables. If your local police department doesn't offer Operation Identification, contact your county sheriff's department or the nearest post of your state police. Failing that, check with the Kiwanis, Lions, or Rotary clubs in your area; they frequently offer this service.

Support your local police. That sounds like a trite, redneck, Nixon-esque phrase, but in fact, it's good insurance. Responsible police officers do tend to have a little more appreciation for the feelings of people who obviously do like them. That's just human nature.

Some people buy Support Your Local Police bumper stickers or purchase auxiliary membership in a local police union so that they can have decals on their car windows that a police officer will respond favorably to. Those people are kidding themselves if they think it will save them from getting a parking or speeding ticket. The vast majority of cops aren't for sale at all, and those very few who are, can't be bought cheaply.

But the day may come when you get into a fistfight with some weirdo at the scene of a fender-bender accident and a cop is going to arrive and find two suspects, one of whom is you, and is going to have to make some sort of judgment as to who is the Good Guy and who is the Bad Guy. At that moment, a car window decal that says Auxiliary Member, Fraternal Order of Police, is not exactly going to *hurt.* Just don't expect miracles from it.

Police training. One day in 1979 I got a call from a young woman who lived in the community where I was the police department's weapons instructor. "I've just bought a gun after my husband got held up, and I need to be trained with it. The police chief suggested you." I called the chief back—a bit surprised, since he was one of those rare cops who didn't think anybody but police officers should own guns—and he replied ruefully, "Mas, I just issued her a carry permit. She's the first person I've issued one to since I came up here who actually asked to get trained with the gun. Can you do something for her?" At reasonable cost, I subsequently trained the woman, who became lethally adept with her .38.

That was a fluke, though. Most police departments won't offer a certified instructor to train you in self-defense, unless you represent a professional or retailers' association and specifically ask for training for a group of your members. Even then, you will be expected to pay for the officer's time.

Neighborhood associations, professional groups, and local clubs, can usually get expert speakers from the police department, at little or no cost, to address the membership on matters involving home security, shoplifting, rape prevention, and so on. You only have to call them. The logo on the side of the Los Angeles Police Department (LAPD) patrol cars speaks for America's law enforcement community: They really *are* there To Protect and Serve, and they ususally appreciate the opportunity to help a group of citizens in crime prevention.

II. PASSIVE SAFETY MEASURES

6. SCOUTING YOUR OWN PERIMETER

The key to winning any form of human conflict is to understand the mind of the enemy. This holds true when you play "beat the home invader."

Put yourself in the intruder's shoes. You may not have his unique technical knowledge and street savvy, but you have your own common sense. Armed with that, cruise your own perimeter and look for chinks in the armor.

There are few people who haven't broken and entered their own home at one time or another after misplacing their keys. If you, an amateur, were able to do it, how much easier would it be for someone who does B&E (breaking and entering) for a living?

Start from an outside perimeter and move in gradually. From across the street what can a burglar see that makes your home inviting? Fences and hedges will make him smile because they'll give him cover in the dark, especially if you have trees and shrubs near the windows.

Is your garage locked and windowless? If so, he won't be able to tell if your car is there or not, and that alone could make some burglars sufficiently uncomfortable and therefore abort their mission.

Watch your own windows at night. Are your shades and curtains sufficiently dense to keep an outsider with binoculars from telling whether or not there are people inside or whether there are automatic timers working the lights and the TV?

Burglars know they're dealing with automatic timers if all the lights go on at once, or exactly at 9:00 or at 9:30. Suburbanites tend to be orderly creatures who set everything on certain schedules. Do you know anyone who sets their alarm clock for 6:07?

Set the timers a little more naturally, at 9:03 or at 9:37. Burglars know that most people go to bed after their last TV show, so your phantom light switch should start shutting them off a couple of minutes after the programs change. Time yourself going through the house shutting off the lights, and set the timers just that far apart, in the order of sequence that you would normally go through room by room. That creates a much more convincing impression of someone being at home.

Now move in closely. Can a would-be intruder peer inside past the edges of the curtains? If so, some oversize drapes are in order or perhaps some clips to hold the curtains together against the edges of the window frame.

Now that you're in close, check all the doors and windows from the top of your house to the bottom. We'll go into detail in a separate chapter. When I say top to bottom, I'm not kidding: The roof is usually weak and easily penetrated in apartments and mobile homes; in single-family dwellings, attic windows are often ignored and left with feeble latches, creating an easy entry point for someone who can climb a ladder, tree, trellis, or porch roof.

A lot of burglary prevention experts recommend the installation of front doors with mail slots. Their theory is that this prevents mail from accumulating outside, tipping off people that you're gone for a few days. Personally, I've never bought that. The letter slot allows a burglar to listen inside and determine for himself if there are really people at home, or if you're just faking him out with the old "playing-the-radio-trick." It also is the perfect avenue for burglars to introduce a fistful of poisoned hamburger to kill your dog.

If you're going to be gone for a day or more, have your mail and newspaper deliveries held at the post office. A friend or neighbor picking them up at home is often recommended by "the experts," but if a burglar has you staked out, a stranger collecting your mail and paper is a giveaway in itself. The post office needs three-days' notice in writing. That should include the names of anyone designated to pick up your mail.

Check out the yard. Have your kids left any toys around, or you, any tools? If you leave today and it rains tomorrow, it'll be a dead giveaway: Burglars will figure that if you were home, you would have taken these items in.

Do you have neighbors within sight of your house? Don't be an isolationist: They're part of your perimeter and sometimes better eyes and ears than $25,000 worth of electronic alarms.

But to do an effective job of protecting each other's empty homes you and your neighbors have to come to an understanding. Be sure never to mention to anyone that "the Smiths are away for the weekend." As another chapter in this book indicates, there are more people than you think who make part of their living soliciting or overhearing that sort of information and selling it to burglars.

Make sure your neighbors know your electrician, plumber, and carpenter. That way, if they see an unfamiliar van in your driveway while you're gone, they'll know immediately that something's up.

Should you leave your keys with the neighbors? That's up to you and your own limits of trust. I personally hate to take a neighbor's keys. If the neighbors *do* get ripped off, there's always going to be that nagging seed of doubt, and you'll be living next to each other for a long time. This is one reason why the police will *never* take a vacationing homeowner's keys.

If a neighbor is house sitting or house watching for you, make sure they've read this book. Have them check the place out, window by window and doorknob by rattled doorknob. Better yet, you and your neighbor should have a talk with an officer from your local police department's Crim Prevention Bureau.

House *watching* is one thing. House *sitting* is something else again. Most burglary prevention experts love the idea. I'm opposed to it. Here's why.

The only advantages of a house sitter in burglary prevention are that (a) if someone tries to break in they can call the police before the thieves get away with the loot, and (b) their presence will supposedly scare burglars away.

Objective a can be accomplished by alarm systems. Objective b will be accomplished only if the intruders are cowards. Suppose your home is targeted by a strung out junkie or a sexual psychopath who digs home invasions? The typical choice of a house sitter—your mother, a younger sister home from college for a while, or a good family friend—is usually not the person you want to leave in harm's way.

In some cities, rental agencies and other organizations can arrange to find you house sitters. Some travel agencies will do the same and at least one airline offers a "house-swapping" package where you trade domiciles with another vacationer. If *you* want to give a stranger the run of your home for a week, go right ahead. Would *I*? No way. For one thing, ask your insurance agent how quickly his company will pay your claim if your valuables are ripped off by someone *to whom you gave the keys to your house, even though you didn't know them.*

OK, you've checked your perimeter. You've got an idea where you're strong and where you're weak in terms of location, layout, externally visible signs of occupation, neighbor protection, and entry points. In the succeeding chapters, we'll show you how to "harden your perimeter" without digging a moat, installing an electrified fence, or loosing a pack of hungry Rottweilers on the grounds.

7. COMMON SENSE ABOUT LOCKS

Among many security experts locks are the Number One answer. Those who feel this way tend to be the same people who feel that you shouldn't own a gun or a big dog because you're so incompetent you'll hurt yourself with them. I love good locks. I believe in them. Good locks have protected my own home twice from burglars, leaving only some ineffectual "jimmy" (prying open) marks. I once watched as a good deadbolt lock defeated someone who was trying to force his way into my elderly father's house, before I placed that man at gunpoint and legally terminated his illegal act.

And yet, after eight years in police work and a good deal of time spent learning from the best street cops all over the country, I have to tell you that locks aren't the panacea that so many people would have you believe.

You have a pickproof lock? That's wonderful. The problem is that very few burglars out there *pick* locks. Most of them resort to forced entry, "violently and tumultuously" as the lawbooks put it. It isn't called breaking in for nothing. And there are a lot of locks that will stand up to the craftiest lockpicker but will last only a minute or so when worked on with a slam-hammer.

Locks won't stop the handful of "supercrooks" who study locks and alarms the way professional installers do. However, the majority of burglaries—especially of middle- and lower-class homes—are not committed by television cat burglars who can sneak the Crown jewels out of the Tower of London.

The average burglar, whether he's a junkie, teenager, or chronic loser, isn't going to be the most skillful and well-equipped cracksman in the world.

In other words, *with a good system, you can lock out the great majority of burglars who are likely to prey upon you.*

Let's look first at the standard advice.

An amazing number of burglaries are committed on unlocked premises. There are two kinds of people who leave their doors unlocked, whether they're home or not: Eskimos and fools. Only Eskimos tend to get away with it for long.

It remains a common practice to leave keys under the doormat, in the mailbox, or atop a doorsill. Do you *really* think a burglar, even if he's retarded, is going to overlook those obvious places? You may think you've found some cunning new place to hide your key, but burglars do this sort of thing for a *living*, and your clever hiding place is probably a routine checkpoint for them.

Even if we allow that you've found an ingenious hiding place, *you're going to be placing the key there frequently, and eventually, you'll be observed.*

Who are you leaving that key *for*? Your housekeeper? If she isn't trustworthy enough to have her own key, she isn't trustworthy enough to be working for you at all. Your child? If your child isn't responsible enough to have his own key without losing it, he certainly shouldn't be left home alone.

Is it because *you* have a habit of losing your keys or locking yourself out? Well, I won't make any gratuitous remarks about whether or not *you* should be out by yourself. I *can't*, 'cause I've locked myself out a couple of times. What we will do, later in this chapter, is show you how a proper lock system will virtually guarantee that you can't lock yourself out!

If nothing else I've told you is going to change your

mind, consider this: If you are burglarized and hit hard, you'll be making a substantial insurance claim. The insurance company will send over an investigator, and among other things, he'll ask everyone in the neighborhood whether you leave a key under the doormat or wherever. If he finds out that you do, you can possibly kiss your insurance settlement good-bye. Such stupidities may void burglary claims among certain insurance carriers.

"There exists an amazing syndrome, one we see almost every night," chuckles Walter Rauch of the Philadelphia Police Felony Warrant Squad.

"So many of the guys we go after, being drug dealers and whatnot, have all kinds of locks on their doors, top to bottom. Yet they leave their windows unlocked, even open. The stupidity of that never fails to amaze us ... and we never fail to take advantage of it."

Rauch is a legal burglar, a man empowered by his felony arrest warrants to enter the home of the suspect by whatever means possible. The only thing he leaves with, though, is the individual he came after. The other kind of burglar is going to leave with everything, and often because the homeowner has made that same classic mistake: putting multiple locks on the doors and virtually ignoring the windows.

Like the average citizen, I've always resorted to a window when I've locked myself out. As a landlord, when I had to force access and the tenant had changed the lock, I never met a window that I couldn't penetrate, and only once had to break a pane of glass, to turn the flimsy little latch. We'll show you soon how to toughen up your windows against illegal entry.

Finally, an appalling number of citizens still have locks of the flimsiest types on their main doors. It is common knowledge among even law-abiding citizens that you can "loid" a springbolt lock (spring it open with a piece of celluloid), yet people persist in trusting their lives and their valuables to this sleazy piece of garbage, the "Saturday Night Special" of locks.

Springbolts are used by housebuilders and landlords for one reason: They're dirt cheap. The springbolt is the type that locks automatically, with a wedge-shaped bolt. Trouble is, a celluloid strip, credit card, or plastic-coated driver's license slides in between the door and the frame, pushing the wedgie bolt right back into its channel and popping the door open. It can be done in about three seconds. If you have such a lock in your home try it yourself.

If the home protection experts are unanimously agreed on anything, it's that springbolt locks are an invitation to burglary. I'll certainly buy that. At the same time, I disagree with their universal recommendation that you should remove the springbolt and replace it with a deadbolt.

Instead, I think you should keep the springbolt on there, whether it's part of the doorknob mechanism or a separate unit, and *add* a deadbolt.

Why? Because the deadbolt, while it's a far better piece of equipment, operates at a much slower pace. In a single-cylinder model, you have to lock it from within by manually turning the inside knob, while with a double-cylinder deadbolt, you have to insert, or at least turn, a key. *There may be times when you have to slam that door shut on an intruder with only a second to spare.*

That can happen more often than you think. It can be when a drunk boyfriend is dropping you (or your daughter) at the door, and his clumsy passes are rapidly approaching the level of sexual assault, the so-called date rape phenomenon.

Another scenario is a sudden assault by home invaders or "stranger rapists." In New York City recently there was a rash of murders of elderly women in Brooklyn, all of which fell into the same pattern. The killer followed them home from the supermarket, tagging them by the discreet distance of half a block; he entered their building inconspicuously and let them get inside where they had to go into the kitchen and set their bags down before they could fix the typically elaborate New Yorks locks on their doors. They never got to do that: He went in a few seconds behind them and murdered them.

If you can get the door shut with a quick slam of your shoulder, the springbolt may hold it long enough for you to operate your sturdier protection locks. Considered a "convenience lock" by locksmiths, the springbolt is an "emergency escape lock" in the mind of the self-defense instructor, and you should see it that way, too. *The springbolt augments the high-security deadbolt lock. By no means, though, does it replace the deadbolt!*

A good deadbolt is square edged so that it can't be loided. It goes deep into its socket in the doorframe; the deeper it goes, the harder it is to jimmy the door. If your door is solid (no hollow-core design and no glass) the deadbolt lock should have a turnbolt lever on the inside. If there *is* a window, or if the door is hollow-core, it's only going to take one or two punches from a gloved fist to break through, reach in, and turn that latch open.

Doors that can allow a hand to break in cry out for a double-cylinder deadbolt lock. A key is needed to either lock or unlock from the inside as well as from the outside. It is ideal for frustrating burglars but it presents great danger to the homeowner: If there's a fire, you're trapped inside if you don't have your key.

In my home after the first burglary attempt, I made the decision to go with double-cylinder deadbolts. To cope with the fire hazard, I made sure that my wife and I always had a key in reach. Fasten a large, bright-colored plastic tab to a spare key, and you'll quickly find it. I don't have one in my wallet because a pickpocket who gets it, will now have my address *and* key. Instead, it is on the keyring I keep on my belt. This offers numerous advantages.

As we'll see in the chapter on makeshift self-defense

weapons, a keyring on a leather beltstrap can be a fierce instrument of destruction if you're under attack.

More to the point, the key is always under your hand. I leave my keyring in the belt of whatever slacks I'm wearing during the day, and at night, those slacks are right next to my bed in case I have to dress in a hurry. The keyring is always within immediate reach. Morning is time enough to change clothing ensembles for the next day.

If you need that key in a fire situation, it's going to be dark and smoky. You want to be able to find that key, by feel. Fasten a large, orange plastic tab next to it, and you'll quickly be able to find the key in the dark.

Few women care to carry the masculine-styled belt keyring. My wife has four keys—the double-cylinder deadbolt key, the springbolt key which also activates emergency locks on both doors, and both her car keys—on a flat little spring-steel clip resembling a money clip. Costing only about $1.50 at any locksmith shop, such a unit is ideal for constant, comfortable wear with beltless slacks or skirts. It rides comfortably, unobtrusively, and always in reach on the waistband of the beltless slacks and skirts she usually wears.

An alternative is to mount them on a Kubotan, another handy little self-defense item that we'll discuss in the same section as keyrings. Resembling a slim, six-inch Tootsie Roll, it tucks comfortably and unobtrusively into any waistband, man's or woman's, belted or not. Quick to find in the dark, it doubles as a protective tool if things get ugly when you're opening the door.

I can't stress fire protection too strongly. After all, you're a lot more likely to burn to death in a domestic blaze than you are to be strangled in your bed by the Manson Family. If you go with the maximum intruder protection of the double-cylinder deadbolt lock, many experts think it's a good idea to have a key in the inside lock any time you're at home and awake.

I do that in the daytime, but at night, the key comes out and goes into a *known* and *constant* hiding place, where my wife or I can reach it instantly by feel, if we haven't been able to get to our regular keys.

If you have a front door with glass, make that hiding place at least eight feet away and out of sight, where a burglar can't reach through the broken pane with a bent coat hanger and some chewing gum to retrieve it. We also keep another set of keys on the night table, with a large, orange plastic tag.

Another lock that has found widespread favor among professionals is the 3 M Lockalarm. Here you've got a deadbolt with an inside latch, *and* a battery-operated alarm that can't be snipped off with a wirecutter, nor spotted from outside. Check it out. For a nonglass door it's an excellent choice, and reasonably priced considering what it offers.

The chain lock is a nice added feature on the 3 M, but it isn't much protection by itself. A lot of people have chain locks on their doors, not realizing just how frail they are.

A strong man can pop the chain lock with a shove of his shoulder or a high, flat-footed kick. He can reach in and manipulate it loose with his bare hands if the chain is too long. Even if the chain is the proper length, many homeowners make the mistake of installing the channel track vertically: All the burglar had to do is open the door until the chain is taut, push up on it with a finger or makeshift tool, and slip it free.

Some burglars make a point of fastening the chain lock once they've gained entrance to your home. When you innocently unlock your door and shove it open, both you and the door are likely to make a noise that will indicate to the burglar that it's time for him to split.

When you enter your home, open the door slowly— it's a good idea to try the knob with your hand, to see if it's been jimmied loose or if someone's holding it on the other side ready to pull it open and grab you—and if you open it and see the chain in place, close it smoothly and silently and run, don't walk, to the nearest safe spot with people and telephones.

About all the chain lock—or viewer lock as some call it, because you're supposed to be able to open the door and see who's out there—is good for, is to briefly stall a forced entry. If you're not right at the door, all it does is make the intruder kick the door a second time to force it all the way in. If you *are* right there, it *may* hold him in check long enough to slam the door on his hand or foot, and shut it quickly as he pulls away.

Later, we'll give you more details on what you should do if you've opened your door and suddenly found the Boston Strangler on the other side.

You should have a peephole in your door so that you won't have to open the portal to see who's outside. The peephole should be made of glass (the plastic kind scratches easily and quickly becomes useless, at least in the dark), and it should have a wide angle lens. There are several available. I recommend the French-made Microviseur.

But the peephole won't cover you one hundred percent. You still receive deliveries and that sort of thing, where you have to open the door at least a little way. If you want some added protection at that moment, you can do a lot better than a chain lock. Invest in an inexpensive Racine Door Guard.

This unit resembles the ratchet-type, key-locking units sold as "portable door locks" for motel rooms. It opens to three positions and is almost impossible for an intruder to manipulate. It also resists forced entry with much greater strength than any chain lock.

For maximum security I strongly recommend the Fox Police Lock, a standby of burglary-plagued New Yorkers for generations. It operates on the principle of jamming a chair under the doorknob, but unlike that makeshift device, can't be jiggled loose or forced back. The Fox lock has a steel bar that locks into one mortise on the door, and another steel-reinforced mortise buried (discreetly and with acceptable aesthetics) in the floor. It is all but impossible to kick in a Fox-locked door. The same firm makes a lock that goes all the way across the door horizontally, locking on either side of the frame.

With either of those in place, you've got more security than any conventional lock provides. The door can be locked and unlocked from the outside on some models. Some variations also allow you, when you suspiciously open the door from within, to remove the rod portion and use it as a defensive weapon; it resembles a fireplace poker in size and heft.

The Fox locks are not universally available, however. You can make a functional imitation of it yourself with a tough steel rod and a couple of brackets. The bracket on the door should be A shaped and enclose the head of the rod; the part buried into the floor should be grooved so that the rod comes out sideways to unlock. This makes for a quick exit in an emergency, and also allows you to rapidly and unobtrusively put the rod in your hand when opening the door late at night.

Indeed, it almost requires this; if you just kick it away, it can land on your foot and break some bones.

Gosh, Officer, I didn't arm myself when I came to the door. I just unlocked my homemade copy of the Fox Police Lock, and I was still holding the steel bar in my hand when the intruder forced his way in and came at me, and I just swung instinctively before I realized I was holding it.

I don't normally recommend homemade protection, but in this one case, with Fox locks so hard to come by, it's worth a shot. Make sure it fits snugly, with absolutely no play when it's locked in place; otherwise, an intruder will be able to force it loose.

A lot of people make the mistake of screwing locks

onto their doors from top to bottom, and paying no attention to the condition of the door itself.

Age, wear, warping, and the natural settling of any building, can cause a sloppy fit between door and frame. When this happens, the best locks money can buy won't do you any good.

The door *has* to fit tightly or the rest of your security efforts are wasted. One good thing about the low-rent housing projects constructed in most inner cities is that the high burglary rate there has forced builders to install steel doors and door frames. Thus, homes that may contain little worth stealing are often better protected than upper middle-class Colonials that date from the nineteenth century, with their sloppy-fitting doors that their affluent occupants don't replace since they don't want to impair the quaint originality of their now burglary-vulnerable homes.

Steel is the way to go, if you can afford it and if it's your own house. It's not unattractive and doesn't warp the way wooden doors and frames do, especially when newly constructed (and *especially* in prefabs). And it's a lot harder to jimmy.

Jimmying a door is one of the main techniques used by the run-of-the-mill burglar. In goes the crowbar, the doorframe is pushed a scant inch to the side, and *voilà*, the bolt of the toughest double-cylinder lock pops free of its mortise, allowing instant entry.

To resist jimmying, you need a couple of things: a stout door/doorframe system and locks with long bolts that bury themselves so deeply into the wood of the frame that they can't be pried loose short of someone taking an ax to the door. That could happen, but it's unlikely: Unless you're talking about a house or cabin in the remote boondocks, anything that requires an ax or sledgehammer is something the average burglar wants to avoid, because noise draws attention that can quickly terminate his illicit career.

Choose your lock carefully on the recommendation of a trusted locksmith. There are good ones and sleazy ones. Two that stand out are the American-made Medeco and the Finnish-made Abloy*. Both have specially hardened bolts, and both are virtually "pickproof." Lockpicking may be the least popular method of burglar entry, but I think it will increase, for several reasons.

In general American criminals are becoming more sophisticated and are literally training themselves in their unlawful crafts. There is nothing to keep some convicts from taking mail-order courses in locksmithing. True, they'll never be certified or bonded as legitimate locksmiths, but they don't *intend* to become legitimate locksmiths, remember?

Appallingly, there are still many jurisdictions where locksmiths need not be licensed, and such an ex-con could theoretically move in and set up shop! We'll show you how to get around that when we discuss how to select your locksmith.

There's no way for even reputable locksmithing schools to know with certainty that one of their students isn't a burglar who just hasn't been caught and earned a criminal record as yet. Besides, sleazy magazines are full of mail-order books you can buy on how to break into homes. They give detailed, top-quality locksmith training for this sort of break-in. You think I'm kidding? Pick up a copy of *Soldier of Fortune*, a newsstand magazine that purports to service the needs of mercenary soldiers (and is actually a standby of Walter Mitty types, survivalists, and closet or noncloset criminals). Just take a look at the ads.

You can even order varieties of "pick guns," designed

---

*In addition to its tough internal hardening, the Abloy works on a unique locking concept. Instead of tumblers, the mechanism has a series of discs set at different angles in the manner of a combination lock's innards; these are activated by the special Abloy key which has specially angled cuts. It makes the unit as close to pickproof as conventional locksmithing has yet made possible.

to automatically pick locks. There are no restrictions at this time on the sales of such items.

This makes the choice of a pickproof lock more important than ever. If some criminal picks my lock with his how-to book from *Soldier of Fortune* and his mail-order lock-picking gun, the physical evidence left will be the same as would be left if he had come in with a key or had found the door unlocked.

If he's determined to get in and rip me off he's probably going to do it. And if you think insurance companies just smile benevolently and pay total replacement costs when you say you've had a loss, you probably haven't filed a claim. They are in business to make money, and this means that come claim time, you'll meet them in an adversary relationship: You want them to pay you, but they don't want to unless they absolutely have to, because it costs them money. They *will* send in their own claims investigators who are usually very sharp people. And, if there is any reason at all to believe that you left your door unlocked or with a key in or near it, that could nullify your claim and they don't have to pay you a nickel. If your lock had been picked with no signs of forced entry, it's very likely that at worst, they won't pay your claim at all, and at best, you'll have to fight for your claim in court, an experience that might cost you many years and many dollars.

Therefore, if those who want to rip you off manage to succeed, you want massive, obvious evidence of forced entry such as a busted door, busted windows, or busted locks. Besides, you might as well make the burglar work. If nothing else, consider the fact that burglars who've got a good score are like satisfied customers: They keep coming back. If my systems fail and they finally get inside, I at least want them to leave thinking, "I'm not going through *that* hassle again."

Which brings us back to pick-resistant locks. Medeco is the almost universal choice of American experts. They use a pin-tumbler system different from other locks: The pins twist as the key is inserted, making it all but impossible for a lockpicker to get by with his trial and error probing. Only the proper key will turn all the components the right way at one time.

Several years ago, the Medeco Company put up a five-figure prize to any locksmith who could pick one of their units. The prize stood unclaimed for several years. I'm told that one master locksmith finally defeated the unit with a pick after more than twenty-four hours of work. Medeco is the overwhelming choice of police burglary experts I talk to when it comes to the locks they install on their own homes.

The other top choice is the Abloy. Made in Finland, and using new technology that you'd have to be a locksmith to understand and appreciate, the Abloy also employs state of the art metallurgy for almost supernaturally tough resistance to cutting tools. To my knowledge, at this writing, no Abloy lock has ever been picked, even under ideal test conditions by professional locksmiths.

The Abloy is hard to get and expensive, but worth it. Some locksmiths don't even recognize the name. This is a good indication to shop around for another locksmith.

Is there such a thing as a burglarproof lock? Frankly, no. You can force entry past just about any portal this side of a bank vault. *But the harder you make it, the more likely they'll give up and leave.* If burglars were into hard work, they wouldn't be burglars. They're looking for an easy score, someplace where they can get in and out quietly and quickly, preferably without carrying burglar tools that cops can use against them as evidence.

Your 007 spy types and the people from *Mission Impossible*, can get in anywhere. They have the time and the skill and the equipment. But unless you've got the kind of goodies in your home that can be turned around for a fast $20,000, (that is, a real value of maybe $100,000, since fences pay about $.20 on the dollar for stolen goods), your heavy-hitter professional burglar isn't going to bother with you. Instead, he's more likely to break into a half-million-dollar home and rip off a Picasso or two.

No locks are absolute. They harden your perimeter against surreptitious entry and temporarily keep out someone who's chased you into your house. Ask a fire fighter; these guys chop their way into burning homes every day of the week, and the finest Abloy and Medeco locks do not deter their axes for long. Ask cops, from the felony warrant squad or maybe from the narcotics unit: Despite the locks that every drug pusher in America uses to reinforce his apartment, when the cops pull their raid, they get in quickly.

I've forced my way into more than one establishment the way a smash-in burglar would. When a door is lightly locked you can kick it in with the flat of your foot (I prefer a karate sidekick, right at the level where the door bolt meets its hasp), and as often as not, either the door will swing open or it'll fall down like a drawbridge.

Against solid hardwood or steel doors or doors well reinforced with deadbolts and Fox locks, I know something everyone else in America who ever wore a badge for a while knows: You can break your foot trying to kick in a "hard" door.

Against something like that, *we'll* use sledgehammers and axes like the fire fighters. Indeed, most experienced SWAT teams and narcotics bureau raid units use battering rams for such occasions. These are made, usually, from a six-foot, fat iron pipe filled with concrete, and with handles welded on so it can be wielded by four men, two on each side.

If you lock your door up hard enough to require that degree of forced entry, it's a good bet that 99 out of 100 burglars are going to leave you alone. To harden your door to that extent, you want deadbolt locks, Fox Police locks, a door of steel or at least, solid hardwood, and the hardest, tightest-fitting doorframe you can afford to have installed.

We've already described what makes the Abloy Lock worth its price. The domestic Medeco Lock is in the same ultrapickproof class: Its unique design requires a series of pins to be turned simultaneously to the correct angle, each at the proper height, something virtually impossible for someone not possessing the special Medeco key for that particular lock. The unit has a "false slot/real slot" design to further frustrate an unauthorized person attempting to open the Medeco Lock.

Abloy's Super-Stopper lists for $97.20, while the Medeco double-deadbolt costs $96.00. These are five times the price of conventional acceptable quality deadbolt locks. They're worth it if you've got the money. I can only tell you that almost every locksmith and every felony warrant detective I know makes a point of keeping either Medeco or Abloy locks on *their* doors.

Perhaps the most cost-effective compromise is Emhart's Kwikset deadbolt or double deadbolt, at about $20.00 not including installation, followed by the equally good Schlage deadbolts at suggested retail of $40.00.

I advise against buying cheaper, imported deadbolt locks. They may hold up moderately well, but if damaged or tampered with, or if the keys are stolen, many cannot be rekeyed or repaired by a locksmith. Those predictable servicing needs *can* be handled cost-effectively with Emhart, Schlage, Abloy, or Medeco locks, with more peace of mind to boot.

Now, it's time to look at windows. Experts recommend all sorts of stuff for windows. Holes drilled through the double-hung sashes so that a tenpenny nail can be installed; bolts in the window frames to limit opening space—the list goes on.

But when you talk to burglars, and you've had to break into a few windows, you find that there's only one sort of lock that works, and you find out something else:

Even more than with doors, window security is a function of the strength of the unit itself, and not just the lock.

The only window locks that really work are key locks. The Griptite Sash Lock is the most widely recommended window lock among experts.

If you leave the key in, all the intruder has to do is break the glass, reach in, and turn. He can do this silently with a glass cutter and some tape, or just by taping over a large area of glass and rapping it with his fist. The tape muffles the crash, and when he peels the tape back, most of the broken glass will come silently back with it.

But, if you take the key out, you're back in the fire-danger situation you face with double-cylinder deadbolts on your doors. *Have all your windows locks fitted to work off the same key,* and have that key on your person or within your reach at all times, the way we described with the double-cylinder door keys.

The average burglar doesn't mind silently breaking out one pane of glass to reach for your key, but it's unlikely that he'll smash through the whole window. He needs a quick way out once he's inside, and he needs a portal large enough to hand out big items like TV sets and stereos. In an occupied area, the sound of breaking glass is going to make him nervous. And, as we'll see in the chapter on alarms, he's going to want to be in and out in two minutes *max* if he thinks he may have triggered an electronic sensor that calls the police.

By the time he's spent about five minutes messing with your window, even breaking part of it, and still hasn't gotten in, the average burglar is in most cases, going to start getting awfully nervous. In fact, he might even be nervous enough to abort the mission. This is what happened during one of the burglary attempts on my home. Against your amateurish class of burglar, an apt description of the great majority of them, slowing them down is often all the deterrence you need.

But suppose you live alone on a hundred acres where

there's no one to hear the glass breaking? Suppose you live in one of the inner cities where the crash of glass, like a woman's cry for help, is only a signal to the witnesses to turn away quickly so that they don't get involved? Suppose you've got enough goodies in your house so that a thief will take the risk of smashing out your entire window?

To harden your window beyond a keyed lock, you have to go to a modern, burglarpoof window design. You want steel, not wood, in between those windowpanes, and you want a lot of little windowpanes instead of three or four big ones. They can be in the shape of small squares or diamonds. It looks terrific, unlike most burglary protection expedients.

It also frustrates the burglar who realizes it's going to be an hour's job or more just prying this one window open, steel strut by steel strut even after he's broken the glass. And even if he's a little dim-witted he's going to realize that somebody who cares enough about what they've got inside to install windows like that, is probably also smart enough to have burglar alarms in place. And he's likely to give up. After all, he has the world's supply of houses to pick from out there with flimsy doors and big, easy-to-enter windows.

Finally, you can go to shatterproof glass. We're talking about an expensive substance that is considerably more rugged than the car windshield everyone told you was so superstrong. You can go all the way up to Lexan; if thick enough, it will even stop a .38 caliber bullet and in fact, is widely used in bank tellers' cages, pawnshop cashiers' windows, and taxicab dividers. But for pure burglar-proofing, you'll want Secure-lite by Globe Glass, of Elk Grove, Illinois. Most glaziers can get it for you.

You should have this stuff installed by professionals, and you should tell them that security is your main concern. Cheap putty, as used by many of the contractors who put up houses in volume, tends to dry out and get weak fast. Even bulletproof glass is useless in your window if it falls out when a burglar slaps it flathanded and crumbles the cheap putty that holds it in place.

Secure-lite is too expensive for a lot of people. It is best used on picture windows and glass doors. You probably don't need it if you have your regular windows set in small square-or diamond-shaped panes, with steel in between. Putting in either type of window is costly, but it's an effective selling point when you put your house on the market, and window replacement doesn't usually count in terms of reevaluation and tax assessment. If you do any of your business at home, you should talk to your accountant about writing off these security expenses.

Possibly the ultimate window protection against intruders is an outside steel grille. It doesn't have to look like a Forty-second Street kiosk that's been shut up for the night. You'll never escape the "prison look" one hundred percent, but filigreed wrought iron is considered *de rigueur* in many neighborhoods.

Naturally, a grille is even more imperative with a metropolitan apartment on the ground or basement level.

The trouble with barred windows is that they don't just keep the Bad Guys out; they can keep the Good Guys in, and more than one of the latter has burned to death in a fire when he couldn't escape through his own steel protection bars. J. Kaufmann Ironworks in the Bronx, sells Protect-A-Gard, a steel grille that covers the windows so tightly that a street criminal can't even squeeze his fingers inside to *try* to release the lock.

Yet, for the Good Guys inside, it takes only a touch to operate the swivel that pivots the Protect-A-Gard away from the window, giving escape access in case of fires. It wasn't designed by theorists, the way so many burglar alarms are: Protect-A-Gard was designed by New York fire fighters who watched people burn to death when trapped behind their barred-in windows; they wanted the people they protect to be safe from intruders *and* from deadly flame and smoke.

HOLDING THE DOOR

Maybe it's three in the morning and you've just blearily answered the doorbell. Maybe you've just come home with a bagful of groceries and as you enter your apartment, you hear feet shuffling behind you. Or maybe you've run home with an attacker on your heels and you haven't been able to get the door all the way closed behind you.

When the Bad Guy is trying to force entry and you, the Good Guy, are trying to hold the door, you'll be grateful for those things the security experts tell you are worthless, like a springbolt lock that locks automatically when the door is closed, or like a chain that gives you at least a brief moment before the whole door can open enough to let the attacker's body through.

But I really hope you haven't been foolish enough to open the door for an intruder in the first place. That's what your door peephole was designed to prevent. *If you come to the peephole and there's no one in sight, it's a good indication that someone is hiding in the shadows. Don't open that door!!*

Some experts worry that the Bad Guy will stick an ice pick or a gun muzzle up to the peephole. Be ready to duck back if that happens. This is why we told you to get a *wide angle lens peephole*, not a cheapie or a homemade unit that gives you a narrow field of view. Rattle the doorknob and wiggle the locking latch, not enough to unlock the door, but enough to sound as if you are. If someone is lurking there, they'll probably figure, "This is my chance!" they'll lunge for that knob and come into view of your peephole.

If the door is open and you're fighting to hold the guy back, it's a good bet that he wouldn't have tried to break in if he didn't have superior strength in either physique or equipment or numbers of accomplices. You and your chain, or even your Racine Door Guard, may not be able to hold that sort of power at bay by pure physical force.

Unless the guy is awfully smart, he's going to try to put a limb through that door. Slamming a door on a shod foot, if the guy has any kind of hard leather or thick rubber-soled shoe, may not hurt him too much. If he's got his hand inside, slam the door on it.

He may have already reached in and grabbed your hand or wrist. Don't panic; he has just played into your hands.

Curl your fist toward your belly, for leverage. That way, he can't get *your* wrist in the door. If he has you by the hand or wrist, raise your elbow so that your forearm is parallel to the floor. This forces *his* wrist into a horizontal position.

Now, slam the door on him! When a hand slithers into a door it usually has the knuckles parallel to the doorframe, which means that the ulna and radius bones of the forearm are in an up-and-down position where, if you slam the door, they are somewhat protected by muscle tissue. Slamming the door on an arm in this position is painful, to be sure, but is not likely to break the arm or wrist.

However, if his knuckles are parallel to the *floor*, as they will be if you raise your elbow when he grabs your wrist, the ulna bone is against one hard door/doorframe surface, and his radius bone against the other. When you slam the door, you will probably break one or both bones if you do it hard enough.

You don't believe me? Put this book down and go to the nearest door. Insert one of your hands, knuckles parallel to the doorframe, and with your other hand, *slowly* close the door on it. You'll feel some pain and pressure, but probably not enough to deter you from a serious assault if you were in a state of rage.

OK, now put your knuckles parallel to the floor, and catch that arm in the door again. Feel the instant pain, the almost electrical shock that courses up your forearm? Can you imagine how it would feel if somebody was actually *slamming* the door on your wrist that way?

You want to give your attacker the world's supply of pain. Pain enough to make him instinctively recoil, let go of you, and jerk the offending limb out of harm's way. Keep holding the door tightly on his arm, though. After you've given him a second or two of agonizing pain, loosen up just a little on the door so that he can get his arm out; you'll know the time is right when you feel him trying desperately to pull free. If he screams, that's a good signal, too.

Make sure he's pulling, first. Then, when you open the door just that little bit, his own momentum will jerk his arm out.

This is the time to slam the door shut! Let the springbolt lock in, and then lock the deadbolt, pulling the key out and taking it with you if it's a double-cylinder type. Run for the phone or for a weapon, whichever at this moment is going to save you quicker. For me, it's "gun first, *then* telephone," but you may not be so equipped or so inclined.

What if the guy has his foot in the door? Burglars typically wear soft shoes for silent walking, which give them little protection from the agony of a door being slammed on the joint of their big toe, but that won't do you any good if you've been followed home by a rapist wearing motorcycle boots.

If the door slamming on his foot doesn't hurt him, you might want to ease up just enough to let his foot all the way in. If he's pushing with it, it will usually snap through. *Now, slam the door shut on the ankle.* Even the toughest boots have only soft leather over the ankle area, and catching it in the vise of door and doorframe will still hurt. If you're dealing with a foot instead of an ankle, don't be too quick to release your pressure and let him pull his foot out; people can stand more pain in their legs than they can in their arms. If you've got his leg in the door, wait for one of two cues to indicate that he'll pull the foot out when you loosen up slightly: He desperately attempts to withdraw the foot or he screams.

To shove a door shut in somebody's face takes an awful lot of force. If you're not very big, your best bet is a variation of what football players call body checking: You plant your feet behind you, lean your torso forward, and slam your shoulder into the door at about the level of the lock, which will usually be at chest height.

The quickest way to get a door shut if nothing is yet between it and the doorframe, is to kick it shut.

This technique worked for me once when a bunch of teenagers tried to con their way into my home with the old "we need to use your phone" scam. When I realized what was going on, I opened the door for the ringleader and then kicked it shut behind him, in the faces of his three cohorts who were rushing to follow him in.

The emergency springbolt closed, and I locked the double cylinder and pulled the key while the ringleader put his back to the wall. He was trapped inside, away from his friends, with me and the trained Great Dane that was holding him on point: he hadn't even noticed the .357 Magnum in my hand yet. A *very* quick change of situational dominance. It could have been different—quite possibly, a bloodbath with some shed on my side as well as theirs—if I hadn't been able to kick that door shut and temporarily confound his three stupid friends.

A handy thing to have by—indeed, *under*—your doors is a simple triangular wedge of rubber. It costs a dollar or so at hardware stores, and is worth it. Great for carrying to hotels, too. It won't deter a forced entry much more than a few seconds, but sometimes, a few seconds is all you need to retreat to a safer position and implement an alternative course of action—escape through a ground floor window, for instance.

Motel rooms. For the better part of ten years, I've spent so much time traveling that, at least one year, I could have legally stated my main residence as Holiday Inn, U.S.A.

You hear a lot of horror stories about people getting robbed in motels and hotels, but it hasn't happened to me yet, though I have dealt with one illegal entry and one mugging attempt in a metropolitan hotel's hall.

By all means, carry a "traveler's lock," a variation of the Racine Door Guard; this uses a steel bar cut in ratchets to hold your door in place. You probably won't want to do without room-cleaning service, so if you're not going to leave your valuables at the desk, you'd better put them in the closet (if it has a conventional door) and use your portable lock to secure *that*. You can also use such a lock to secure (more or less) the topmost drawer of the motel room's dresser.

Rubber wedges are good to have under your door. There was one morning when I probably wouldn't have had to pull a gun on a "hotel room invader" if I had been carrying those wedges in my suitcase, the way I do today.

There are several types of people who will rip you off in motel rooms, and you have to understand them to guard against them. First are the ones who'll rent a room, then skate the next morning without dropping off the key. They'll try sometime later to rip off the next occupant of that room.

There are maids or people who work with, and viciously manipulate, the maids. Hotel maids are grossly underpaid and often insulted by hotel guests.

Some of them don't find it hard to let their boyfriends in to plunder a couple of suitcases here and there, or to pick up airline tickets that are readily redeemable at airline check-in counters.

Frequent travelers who have been robbed in hotels often ask me how I manage to practically live in such places and not lose anything. I tell them what I'll tell you now.

Hotel room thieves often get their access through someone else who works there. They aren't going to risk compromising that regular source of income by staying a long time or by busting up stuff *or even by taking anything that a customer can prove he didn't lose on his own.* In each of my suitcases is a pair of regulation police handcuffs, and when I leave my room I put one bracelet on the handgrip of the locked suitcase, the other around whatever piece of bathroom plumbing I can get at. I attach it in such a way that only someone with a key can maneuver around that piping and release the lock.

I've also found, and hotel chain security experts I talk to support this, that you're less likely to get robbed if you tip the maid. You think that's buying safety? I call it only fair.

Most hotel maids are honest working people. Does that mean my tip is wasted? Uh-uh. It means that she appreciates me and keeps a special eye out on my room in return. What a deal!

I know the law enough to play with it, and in states where it is legal for a transient to have an unloaded firearm in his luggage, I bring one. In most states, once you're there in your "domicile" (the motel room) it's legal in some places, to have the gun loaded where you can reach it. However, mere possession of a handgun without an in-state license is patently prohibited—in New York and in the District of Columbia, to name a couple of areas. Again, carefully check the laws of the states you're traveling through.

I was in a hotel room one morning when I got up early to shower and dress. I was getting out of the shower when I heard a rattling on my doorknob. "Who is it?" I yelled.

The rattling on the knob became more insistent and violent. I heard a key go into the lock.

Wet and naked, I dove for the bed, and for the Smith & Wesson snub-nosed .38 revolver that was on the night table. I scooped it up, rolled across the bed, and came up in a kneeling position on the opposite side of the mattress as the door opened. The security chain caught it, and a man's face peered in the door.

What he saw was my .38, the hollowpoint bullets in the firing chambers looking back at him.

His eyes grew wide and then he slammed the door behind him as he fled. I heard two men's feet running down the hall. I put on my pants, and with gun in hand, I hit that door the way I would on the street in uniform. They were gone.

I called the desk and asked if anyone had been sent up to my room by mistake. They assured me that no one had and that maids were not yet checking rooms. Maybe I should have reported the intrusion attempt to the police. Had I done so, I would have probably had a hard time explaining the gun laws of that state to the rookie cop they might have sent. I just checked out, no hassle, with the now-unloaded revolver locked in a suitcase I would legally register as checked baggage when I flew out. I also told the manager that someone with a key had tried to open my door.

It was easier to live with the hope that I had scared that guy and his friend, that they might leave future travelers alone. Two years before in that city, two men had been shot dead when they tried to break in and terrorize a hotel customer: Their intended victim was a southwestern deputy sheriff there for a convention, and he slew them both with his service .38.

Really, hotels aren't that bad. Don't take anything with you you can't afford to lose, and bring a portable door lock and a couple of those rubber wedges. Those cheapie door alarms that hang on the doorknob and go off when jiggled, can be worth their weight in gold when you're traveling. And consider those handcuffs in and on your luggage. They worked for me for quite a number of years.

Locks on the doors and windows of your home? You're a fool if you don't have them. Just make sure you understand that all they are good for is deterrence. You want those criminals to leave proof of their violent, forcible entry for the sake of the insurance company, so that you can get compensated for your losses.

If you have locks, buy the best you can—Abloy and Medeco, or the second-best that your limited funds can purchase. Secure your windows with keyed locks and supertough glass, and remember that solid, hard doors with well-fitted frames, and well-designed windows, are at least as important to burglary prevention. Go with deadbolts on your main doors, the double-cylinder-style as long as you are ready to cope with the difficulties it poses in escaping from a fire in your apartment. Remember that good locks are a deterrent to most burglars, but only a slowdown to others. Nothing gives you total security except a total system that slows down or halts at all entry attempts at the door or window, an alarm that sounds and calls for help when your defenses have been breached, and whatever security hardware you have to protect yourself with when your perimeter has been overrun.

8. TROUBLE WITH ALARMS

The "fear boom" has made burglar alarms a booming growth industry. The demand has prodded both established manufacturers and genius outsiders to dramatically improve the technology of these devices, but it has also enticed a number of people out of the woodwork whose only technical expertise is in making a fast buck at the expense of the consumer. Perhaps more than in any other phase of personal protection, the would-be purchaser of an alarm system needs to be a supercareful shopper who knows how to take a salesman's line with several grains of salt.

It is significant that Webster's New Collegiate Dictionary (7th Edition) defines the noun *alarm* as follows:

1: A call to arms; 2: a. a signal warning of danger, b. a device that signals a warning of danger; 3: The terror caused by danger; 4: A warning notice. (Synonym: see FEAR)."

As a verb, *alarm* is defined as "1: to give warning to 2: to strike with fear 3: DISTURB, EXCITE."

One has to go back to these basics to understand what burglar alarms can accomplish for you in terms of keeping yourself and your possessions safe from criminals.

The device can alarm the intruder, putting him to flight before he carries out his intended crimes, and/or it can alarm you or your protectors (police, security guards, or neighbors) to take action and summon authoritative reinforcements to forcibly intervene in the attempted crime. Ultimately, though, we come back to Webster's first definition: The alarm "calls you to arms."

Altogether too many people think that a burglar alarm alone is all the protection they need. They're kidding themselves. That's like saying that a home smoke alarm will, by itself, keep you and your family from burning to death.

A smoke alarm will only save you if, after you hear it go off, you have the coolness and the plan and the equipment wherewithal to summon your family to a position of safety, shepherd them to an exit door or a fire escape or a safety ladder, and get them clear of the danger. So it is with a burglar alarm: It only protects the occupants of your home if you have additional defenses within that allow you either to escape, or to neutralize the deadly threat of the man or men who are forcing their way into your house.

Don't forget that two definitions for *alarm* in the dictionary are "a call to arms," and "a warning notice." The burglar alarm, then, is not an end in itself in crime prevention; it is only, and literally, the "opening bell" in a combat between the forces of law and the forces of crime.

If the warning bell does indeed "alarm" the burglar sufficiently so that he takes flight, that's fine. It has done its work. Many, many burglars have fled empty-handed when the siren went off as they made their entry.

As many as ninety percent of all burglars are total incompetents who don't know how to circumvent alarm systems and will even avoid a home they believe to be fitted with such a system. They can be convinced of that with fake decals and tape that, as we'll explain later, do a very convincing imitation of the real thing.

The ten percent (and that may be an exaggeration) who are seasoned professionals in the art of criminal housebreaking, are convinced that they can bypass any conventional system. In some cases they're right. I've talked to prisoners who weren't blowing smoke when they told me of alarms they had defeated with a couple of copper pennies in the right place, or one or two judicious snips with a wire-cutter, or a spritz of shaving cream into an alarm bell. (I won't tell you *how* they do that, because this book is not a "beginner's guide to burglary," but any burglary detective or competent alarm installer can confirm how it's done.)

A great many alarm systems are built to prevent "false alarms" by absentminded homeowners. These give you a grace period of, say, thirty seconds to a minute to get to the control box and shut it off before the alarm "activates." Criminals know that, and the smart ones know where to look for those control boxes.

For that reason, if you choose to alarm your home, *don't* put the control module someplace where the invaders are likely to find it. The alarm industry is happy to sell you control units that look like a digital clock or a stereo speaker, *but the burglars know that*, and they run immediately to something like that, to shortstop the alarm.

If you have one of the systems where the control module is designed to be in the master bedroom, it probably has both the delay mechanism built into it, *and* an override switch that allows the owner to deactivate the alarm with a touch of his finger. Do you doubt that a professional burglar who is a "second-story man" (someone who specializes in making his entry through second-floor bedroom windows) can't get to the module and press the counter-command button before the alarm goes off?

In a master bedroom, the logical place to put the control module is next to the bed. If you have it elsewhere, a silent flashing light or a soft buzzer won't be readily apparent when you're awake, or rouse you from a sound sleep.

You want that control panel someplace where it will trigger something loud enough to wake you up, and whether you go with a hookup buzzer next to your bed or just a loud signal on the control unit itself, you can afford to have it hidden in a bottom bureau drawer, on the top shelf of your closet, or in a flush-fitted hiding place behind some baseboard concealed by heavy furniture, or— ideally, if you can afford it—built into a wall behind a picture or removable mirror where *you* know where to get at the controls, but where a burglar probably *won't* find it in time to deactivate your whole system.

Everyone recommends a system that both goes off loudly at the entry scene to scare the burglar, and also sounds at strategic points (the master bedroom, the police station, and the security firm headquarters) to send responsible people in to deal with the intrusion and capture the offenders. I won't exactly argue with that. I will, however, play devil's advocate and toss you out some other possibilities.

If you have decals conspicuously posted that say, Protected by *Silent* Alarm, the burglar is going to have to wonder if he can be *sure* he has circumvented your alarm system once he's broken in. Sure, he cut some wires, and sure, he's been there for over a minute and no alarm has gone off.

If he had reason to believe that your alarm system was tied in with a bell or siren or horn, this would reassure him that he had, indeed, shortstopped your attempts to electronically prevent his breaking in. But if you've given him reason to believe that you have a *silent* alarm, he can't be sure of that. He's going to be nervous. And maybe, just maybe, he's going to be anxious enough to leave *now*, without stealing anything or messing with you and your family.

Signs are available anywhere, but the fact is that in a growing number of localities, the police either discourage the installation of alarms going directly into police head-quarters, or forbid them outright. That's because there are a lot of false alarms for every one real alarm, and the drain on police manpower is awesome. In a big city, it can cost a million dollars or more a year just to send cops to answer false alarms. Even if they still allow the alarms to be connected to police dispatch centers, the cops have learned from bitter experience that most alarms are false, and no longer consider them "high priority calls."

Do you doubt that the true professional burglars know this? It's their *business* to know. When you look at how many burglars are never caught, it becomes obvious that most burglars *do* know what they're doing.

Bell-type alarms on the outside of your home can be silenced by emptying a can of shaving cream into them. Simple horns and sirens can be disabled by cutting a wire. One burglar may see a horn outside your house and think, "Oh, wow, they got alarms; I think I'll try some-place easier." But another, if he thinks he has time and concealment, can simply remove it as easily as the guy from the alarm company installed it.

If you do have an alarm, you are wise to have multiple sound units. One should be inside the house, to alert the occupants to an invasion attempt; locate it centrally, where a burglar who just got in the door won't spot it and rip it off the wall before the delay time runs out. I would also suggest that this unit be concealed from view, so that a "point man" (someone who frequently has reason to be in other people's homes such as an appliance repairman, and has chosen to supplement his income by scouting out the inside, asking the owners about their upcoming vacation plans, and selling what he knows for $25 and up to professional burglars) won't note its location and warn a burglar to rip it out before it blurts its warning.

Place another sound unit outside, conspicuously, where every thief can see it and be intimidated. But for the professional who is not so easily intimidated and knows how to silence that obvious noisemaker, you should have a third unit hidden in your chimney or under your roof gables where he *can't* see it in time to disable it unless he has killed your whole system.

A number of alarms automatically shut off within a certain period of time and then reset themselves. This fact is not known to every street patrol officer or police dispatcher in America.

If the cops haven't arrived in twenty minutes, and the sound has shut off, the nervous neighbor who called in the alert to the police is now going to be even more nervous.

He or she may think, Oh, my God, I just made the first call of my life to the police department, and it must have been a false alarm because the Smith family next door has obviously shut off their alarm. This is so embarrassing. Thank God the cops aren't here yet. There's only one way to keep from making a complete fool of myself: I'll call the police station again and explain that it was only a false alarm and that everything is all right.

Some police departments will automatically check out the scene anyway, but some will be relieved to have the original "complainant" call in and say that there's no "complaint" after all. If you have a burglar alarm with an outside siren, I would urge you to explain the basics of how it works to your neighbors, and tell them that you would appreciate it very much if they would call the cops and *keep* calling, any time it goes off at your house.

Whether an alarm system will work for you depends in part on where you live.

Especially if you live in a rural area, you know that a smart burglar has only to call your police station and say, "I just moved here and I want to know if I can install a burglar alarm directly into your police station." The chief will probably reply, "Sorry, but we don't offer that service."

Your burglar now knows that the cops won't respond automatically if he hits your house while you're gone, unless you have a unit that's phone-wired into a central dispatch center; in minutes it would translate into a call to the local police. He also knows that if your home is out in the boondocks, nobody's going to hear your alarm horn go off if you aren't home. If he's done his homework he knows what he wants in your house and where to find it, and he's going to be in and out in about three minutes. Even if you have an alarm system hooked up to a national network, it's a safe bet that the thief is going to be on his way long before the first patrol car in that rural area even gets within striking distance of catching him. Is that going to "alarm" a professional burglar who works the beautiful countryside?

No, it isn't. But if you live in a metropolitan area, in an apartment building, a siren going off in your home is going to motivate a lot of your neighbors to call the authorities. They don't know if it's a burglar alarm or a fire alarm going off, but they're scared, and they're going to call for professional help.

Even if that city no longer chooses to repond to burglar alarms coming into their police dispatch centers, they *will* respond with great speed to phone calls from frightened citizens. If that burglar has lived in that city for a while, he *knows* that the blaring siren or horn alarm he has tripped is going to bring him a lot of company in a hurry. That could be a couple of squad carloads of cops with drawn .38s, or it could be half a dozen burly fire fighters, some of whom may be wielding axes. He doesn't want any part of either team. He's probably leaving, *now*.

You have to tailor your protective systems to where you are and what you're fighting. In a big city, where there are more burglaries and more people around who can get scared when a siren goes off, a loud alarm is definitely worthwhile. In a remote rural area, it's only going to scare the kind of amateur burglar who might be scared off just as easily with a fake burglar alarm warning decal and some nonconnected alarm tape around the doors and windows. In one community, the thousands of dollars it could cost you for a proper alarm installation would be worth it; in another place, it could be almost a waste of money.

In Los Angeles it has been a long time since you could count on police officers to respond immediately to a burglar alarm in your home. That's why organizations like Westec have sprung up. Westec is short for Westinghouse Security, a firm that offers state of the art, hard-wired burglar alarm systems that are connected to their own dispatch center. When a signal goes from your protected home to the Westinghouse "switchboard," two things happen simultaneously: One employee calls the police and another dispatches Westec's own uniformed, armed, and highly trained guards to your home immediately.

After spending a week or so looking over the Westec operation, I came away convinced that it was the best I had ever seen. The bad news is that it's only available right now in certain parts of southern California, and of course it's not cheap; but the good news is that it delivers an ultimate degree of near-total protection.

When you look at hard wiring versus modular install-ation, and perimeter security versus internal or "area" security, you have another set of debits and credits on the balance sheet of your own protection. Hard wiring won't be cost-effective for someone renting or leasing space, and it generally requires you to pay quite a bit of money for the services of an expert installer. The plug-in systems, while portable, tend to be more complex and more expen-sive item-for-item, and also somewhat more prone to false alarms and breakdowns.

Perimeter security is easier for a professional burglar to breach; he doesn't know what is covered by the invisible rays of the area detection device inside, and is more likely to trigger that inside alarm.

At the same time, an area alarm with a microwave or electric eye or infrared sensor design, is not compatible with a protection dog of any size, or with children who go downstairs to the kitchen after the system has been locked on from the master bedroom after everyone supposedly went to bed. Microwaves are also not compatible with heart patients who wear pacemakers.

Pressure-sensitive alarm units can trigger an alarm when touched (as when the burglar sets foot on the alarmed staircase carpet), or when pressure is released (if a pre-cious painting or vase is lifted from its hanging or resting place).

Pressure-or movement-sensitive alarms on doors and windows can go off by themselves in windy climates, or when the innocent postal worker is knocking on the door, or when your big dog presses its nose to the window to watch a kid taking a shortcut home from school through your backyard.

Sound-discriminating alarms that go off only when triggered by a sound like a window breaking are now available. They work. But they theoretically might also go off if you've left for the weekend and your pussycat knocks a breakable drinking glass off your wet bar, onto the hardwood floor.

If I sound skeptical about alarms, it is because of the many years I spent in law enforcement. Cops tend to take alarms with a large grain of salt because they answer so many false ones. Those of us in the business can also remember going into many burgled homes where the alarm systems were easily shortstopped with wire-cutters or by the professional "power meter burglars" who kill the whole electrical system before they even hit the door.

That's why relatively few police officers invest in burglar alarms for their own homes, and why those who do, insist on units backed up by battery support units. Obviously, units which depend solely on batteries can't be trusted to do the job for you if left alone and untested for extended periods.

I think alarms are useful for people who can afford them. They are an important band in the total spectrum of protection. They can scare amateur burglars away all by themselves, and if you're up against hardened criminals who are ready to terrorize, torture, or even kill your family, the electronic "call to arms" can give you a chance to protect yourself with called-in police, with your dog, or with a gun if necessary.

My complaint with people who sell alarms as being total security systems is the same complaint I have with people who profess that guns or dogs are, in themselves, total protection against criminals. An alarm that tells me only that people have broken into my home doesn't do me a lot of good unless I have the wherewithal to answer that "call to arms" and repel the assault with superior force. At the same time, a gun in my night table drawer won't do me a lot of good if I don't know that my home has been invaded until I wake up in bed with a knife at my throat.

What you want is a total spectrum and if you don't have it all, you may not have *any* of the protection you thought your money was buying when you spent it at the alarm shop *or* the gun store *or* the dog kennel.

The alarm is not an end in itself. It is only one link in a chain of total self-protection. I don't put down alarms; I *have* alarms. But I understand that they aren't the total self-protection the salesmen say they are. They're only what *Webster* said they are: warning signals that announce a call to arms and instill immediate fear in everyone in reach of their unmistakable warning.

Invariably, when it comes down to installing intruder alarms, it comes down to price. Asking, "What does a burglar alarm system cost?" is like asking, "How much does an automobile cost?"

If you don't have much money, you can get around in a jalopy if you shop carefully and schedule your driving habits around its weaknesses. If you'll be relying on it seriously you'll want the best you can afford. If your life-style is appropriate, a $35,000 Mercedes will not be "expensive."

It's the same with alarms. A $10 Radio Shack alarm that slides over the doorknob and buzzes loudly when someone jars it by rattling the door is better than nothing and can't be disconnected from the outside. On the Mercedes side, I know a lot of people who think spending five figures on a hard-wired, professionally installed alarm system is cost-effective for their quarter-million-dollar homes and the treasures they contain. They, too, have found a cost-effective balance.

The average citizen is more likely to spend $260 (1983 dollars) on a Sears Roebuck alarm system, with two-channel receiver and enough transmitters for seven doors/windows. Accessories are modular and can be added.

Elsewhere in this book we discuss "the price of safety." Suffice it to say that you can find yourself very quickly spending four figures to professionally "alarm" the average American home.

You killed a few dollars buying this book. Are you ready

for an in-depth immersion course in the world of alarms, for free? Just look through the pages of your newspaper and call the local alarm services and ask for information.

You'll soon be inundated with sales literature. (One tip right now: The stuff that goes heavy on scare tactics and light on technical facts in the sales brochures, tends to be the stuff you want to avoid, since that's a good indication that the given product can't sell on its own merits.) You'll get demonstrations in your living room that will turn out to be an education in two things: alarm systems and consumerism.

Don't commit yourself to any system until you've seen at least four or five demonstrated, and had a chance to go over all the literature. Installing an alarm system is a big expense, and you wouldn't be doing it if you didn't think that one day, your family's posessions or even their lives, might hang in the balance. Take your time and trust your own analytical mind to select a vendor who (a) can be trusted to do good work; (b) is likely to still be in business five years from now when you need repairs or want modifications; and (c) handles a line that's modular, and can adapt to your security needs as they grow in the predictable future.

9. THE TRUTH ABOUT BOOBY TRAPS

A midwestern farmer, righteously enraged by multiple burglaries on his place, rigged up a "trap shotgun" so that anyone who opened the door of the shed where he kept some of his most expensive equipment would be shot.

Sure enough, a burglar forced his way in. The shotgun went off, crippling him for life. He never denied being a burglar; but when he sued the homeowner, the court ruled in the plaintiff's favor.* Not only did the farmer not have the right to kill to protect property, the judge announced, but the act was reckless: What if a child had run into that shed to fetch a baseball that had been batted through its window? The civil court judgment against the farmer was so huge that he had to sell his farm to pay it.

I can empathize with the person who has had his home violated and seeks both revenge on burglars in general, and a painfully deterring experience for the next burglar in particular who chooses him for a victim. But booby traps are not the way.

The court judgment of *Katko* v. *Briney* has been upheld again and again in high courts. You do not have the right to kill or maim to protect property, and you do not have the right to kill or maim at random.

An *alarm* is something that triggers a warning signal when a door or window or room has been entered by an unauthorized intruder.

Under American law you can only hurt the burglar if he threatens the life and limb of innocent persons inside. A booby trap, something that physically harms an intruder, can maim or kill a fire fighter breaking in to rescue your home and possessions from a blaze. It can spring shut on your spouse or child, or even on *you* if you come home preoccupied with something else and forget to circumvent your own trap. Improperly set up, it can go off accidentally and injure or kill you or a member of your family, or your household pet.

One journalist who wrote a book on home security in 1975 understood that, but then went on to say that it would be all right to set up a booby trap on the order of that classic child's prank, a bucket of water set precari-

*Katko v. Briney, 183 N2nd 657 (Iowa 1971).

ously on the top edge of a door. He recommended a bucket of paint, molasses, or glue.

He did admit however, that a person nailed with such a trap might get angry enough to tear your house up a bit. I think he was being conservative. The person would be more likely to light a match and burn your home to the ground; remember, criminals think they have a God-given right to prey on you, and they develop intense and self-righteous anger when you even try to thwart them.

That journalist also didn't realize that a 2½-gallon pail of any liquid weighs 20 pounds or more. Falling, it could crush a burglar's skull or break his neck, leaving you in the same position as the farmer whose shotgun booby trap cost him his livelihood.

One firm is making a lot of money selling a burglar alarm-cum-booby trap that sprays the offender with tear gas. They boast that they've never had anything stolen from a space their unit was protecting. I'll buy that as far as it goes. But what happens if the person who was sprayed staggers out of your apartment, tumbles down the stairs, and breaks his neck? Or what if he staggers to his getaway car and in his half-blind agony, runs over a couple of children down the street? You better believe that you're going to be right back in the position of that midwestern farmer who set up the trap shotgun.

If you doubt for a moment that the court is likely to rule in favor of the burglar who is now suing you, you obviously haven't spent too much time in contemporary American courtrooms.

I *have* spent a good bit of time there, and I'm here to tell you that any sort of booby trap *will trap the person who set it, far more painfully and permanently than it will hurt the person who activated it with his illegal entry* if it harms someone who was not immediately and unavoidably threatening innocent human life.

If you want a good booby trap, invest in something like California's Westec Security; they train their men almost to the level of the LAPD, and work assiduously with the department so that their men and the police officers will interact well when your life or property is at stake. When an intruder breaks in, he trips an alarm that is linked to roving patrols of highly trained security guards who will catch him in the act at gunpoint. If he sues for getting hurt, he can only recover from the security service. They have a lot more money to fight court battles with than you do.

Booby traps are for guerrilla soldiers. They do not belong in American homes and businesses. If you try to use them, *you* will be the "booby" who ultimately gets "trapped."

10. THE FAKE ALARM CONCEPT

Since burglary detectives tell me that ninety-some-odd percent of burglars are afraid to hit a place that's protected by burglar alarms, and since it's true that the *rest* of the burglars are sufficiently confident in their housebreaking skills to be convinced that they can get through your alarm system, it occurs to the logical mind that you might not need to invest one to six thousand dollars in an alarm system at all. (Incidentally, if you doubt that ninety percent is a conservative estimate of burglars who don't want to mess with alarmed premises, just ask your friendly neighborhood alarm salesman. He'll quote you a *higher* figure.) It's realistic then to expect that both segments of the burglar population—the nervous amateurs and the confident and technologically expert professionals—would react in exactly the same way to the mere *appearance* of a home being alarmed.

Let's say that it would cost $3,000 to properly install a hard-wired burglar alarm system into a given home. For only $30, if not less, the owner of that home could create an effective illusion of being protected by a sophisticated burglar alarm system.

If you fake having a gun when you face an armed criminal, you're likely to get yourself murdered very quickly. If you fake having locks, a quick kick on the door will prove if you were faking or not, so you may as well not have bothered. But, because "visibly present" alarms have a great deterrent effect on the majority of housebreakers, a fake alarm system does make sense, *especially for those of you who don't have a lot of money to spend on a real one.*

You can buy decals that say Protected by Alarm System by mail order from a number of national magazines but they won't do you much good. They might scare away a few amateur burglars, but anybody who's been doing it for a while knows that the people who make and/or install burglar alarms like to advertise their names. A *really* alarmed house is more likely to have a company-furnished decal reading Protected by Westinghouse/Westec Security, or Protected by Radio Shack Alarm System.

Some experts say, "You shouldn't post a decal that explains the brand of burglar alarm you have. That's almost like giving a seasoned, professional burglar a map of what to look for, and a guide on how to break into your house." They've got a very good point.

If you've got a Sears Roebuck security system, put decals on your door that says Protected by Radio Shack Alarm System. You can get the decals dirt cheap from any Radio Shack retail outlet. If you have the Radio Shack security system in place, use another brand's decals on your doors and windows. They're available for a nominal fee wherever electronic equipment is sold.

Some expensive systems are set up so that once they're

in place, the owner has to deactivate them from the outside with a special tubular key before he even begins to unlock his own door. Those who do a lot of stealing recognize those tubular keyholes as being hooked up to alarms. All you have to do is go to the hardware or locksmith store and buy an outside key housing unit. It would cost you maybe $15 to have a safe professional install the dummy outside each door (I would suggest a bonded locksmith of proven reputation for this assignment). It's going to drive even a top-notch professional burglar absolutely nuts trying to figure out why he can't find a wire going from that "alarm lock" into something he can put his hands and his wirecutters on.

You can study any of the do-it-yourself books on how to install burglar alarms to get an idea how the pattern goes. Check out a couple of these books at your local library; if you don't want to take them home, a dollar's worth of dimes in the library's photocopy machine will show you how to lay it out. Gray "alarm tape" costs maybe $5 per 200 feet, which should be enough to cover all or most of your windows.

Does this mean that I don't recommend real burglar alarms? No! I have them, and if you can afford them, you should have them, too. In some places, just having the alarms can save enough in insurance premiums to make them worthwhile even if no one ever tries to break into your home.

I'm just saying that when you look at the concept of a total protective system that involves locks, alarms, dogs, and the ability to dominate person-to-person contact with violent criminals, the alarm segment is the one part of the spectrum you can "fake" effectively between now and when you can afford a total protection spectrum.

First, you invest in protecting *yourself* with training in the martial arts, and with less-lethal weapons, and if you can handle it, with deadly force mechanisms. Your own powers are always there to protect you, no matter what the danger scenario.

Next, you protect the places where you dwell, permanently or temporarily, with *locks* built into solid firmaments to hold intruding danger out.

After that, if practical for your life-style, you may augment your own senses and physical defensive capabilities with those of a well-trained dog proven faithful and protective to you and yours. Only after you've run through those possibilities does it make sense to expand your protective spectrum to man-made electronic alarm systems.

---

11. THE TRUTH ABOUT FINGERPRINTS AND BURGLARS

When the average citizen's home is burgled, he often becomes indignant if the investigating officers don't take fingerprints. He figures cops have nothing better to do. If he lives in a place like New York City, he doesn't realize that in three of the five boroughs, the investigating officers not only don't have time to take fingerprints, but don't even plan on doing an investigation at all.

It's true. In New York, which is sneaking up on a quarter of a million burglaries per year, the "investigation" usually ends when an officer visits the burgled premises to take a report from the victim; sometimes, even that doesn't happen. It only becomes a full-blown "case," assigned to a detective, after a burglar using a similar MO (modus operandi, or method of operation) has been unlucky enough to be captured in the area.

Taking latent fingerprints is a precise and painstaking

task. As a former police officer, I can tell you frankly that almost everyone in law enforcement considers it a boring hassle. A "latent" fingerprint is a print left on something touched, as opposed to an identification fingerprint in which an expert has helped some obliging citizen to smear his finger with ink and slowly roll the first digit across a suitably marked piece of white cardboard. A latent is often invisible without fingerprint powder, and when found after that special powder "dusts" the area, is normally photographed, then "lifted" with special materials, photographed again, and copied for the records. It is a task that requires the same sure, patient hands that could otherwise be used for building ships in bottles.

In something of the magnitude of a homicide case, you *bet* the cops take fingerprints. They take them from everywhere, including every square inch of walls and ceilings. It can take a day or so for a complete team of police lab technicians to find, and carefully lift, those latent prints. But it becomes a world-shattering calamity when *your* place is ripped off, and no matter how miniscule the arrest rate may be for burglars, and no matter how much smaller the likelihood is of recovering stolen property, *you're* going to sometimes find it worth your while to pull out all the stops, throw caution (and your checkbook) to the wind, and go the fingerprint route.

There are a great many communities where police officers have been instructed to "go through the motions of taking fingerprints at burglary scenes," purely for public relations. The job is done halfheartedly and halfway, and few if any of the prints may ever find their way into the comparison system. But it doesn't necessarily have to be that way. One pioneer in the use of fingerprints to catch modern burglars is Inspector Danny O'Brien, coordinator of the Burglary Prevention Program for the city of New York's police department. O'Brien was a captain in the Queens detective unit when he put together a system of capturing burglars via fingerprints.

A veteran street investigator, O'Brien was well aware of the fact that the great majority of burglaries were committed by junkies and teenagers who weren't smart enough to live one place and "work" somewhere else. He knew that most of them worked the same neighborhoods day in and day out, and probably lived near where they committed their crimes.

O'Brien came up with the idea of training six officers in each precinct to quickly and efficiently go into every place that had been burgled and take some latent prints, and then feed them into an automated Kodak microfilm retrieval system that kept track of everyone arrested in the borough where the crime occurred. Most burglars are too stupid or too cocky to wear gloves, and as a result, his efforts immediately bore fruit. The people he trained were soon using fingerprints to "clear" one out of every ten burglaries, a rate far, far higher than what the New York police enjoyed prior to his innovation. O'Brien's system is now being used, successfully, in two of New York's five boroughs, and will be used citywide as soon as there is money to fund it.

The key to making it effective, O'Brien told me, is not to take prints at a burglary the way you would at a homicide. "There just isn't time to do that thorough a job. My officers will have taken the latents within two hours at most, and usually within half an hour. That doesn't allow total coverage, but it does let our people take prints from entry and egress points, things they might have touched while removing valuables, and so on. It also allows time for them to take comparison prints from people who are always in the house."

The problem with fingerprints, according to O'Brien, is that the system is not set up to efficiently process the latent prints left at crime scenes. He notes that the FBI, America's central clearinghouse for fingerprints, receives some forty thousand sets per day for comparison. Most fingerprint-processing apparatus is set up around the universally uniform "fingerprint cards" designed by the FBI, whereby all ten digits must be imprinted. O'Brien says, obviously, the system is set up to identify people who have already been arrested and fingerprinted by a police officer. That print card will also contain the age, height and weight, race, and other identifying information on the suspect. It is much more difficult to take a single latent fingerprint and put it through the system, hoping for an identifying "hit."

"The system" is also set up primarily to process whole, perfectly imprinted fingerprints, not the partial prints that detectives call minutiae. A cop can try to run those things through and can often be successful, but it takes time and a police supervisor's permission. If you're a private citizen who wants this done you'd better either know someone at police headquarters, or be ready to pay top dollar for a private investigator with police connections to get it run through for you.

The technology exists to soon allow this situation to change. The Federal Bureau of Investigation and the Miami Police Department are two agencies now experimentally using the Finder System; this utilizes space age technology to automatically identify even partial fingerprints. In most existing systems today, human eyes are still required for the final comparisons. The Finder System probably won't come into wide use in this country until the 1990s.

Since it's tough to process fingerprints at all, and an absolute nightmare to process the latents they pick up off your window compared to running the prints they've already taken from someone they've arrested, it's no wonder that most cops won't even bother. Indeed, most street patrol officers haven't had the special training required to "lift" really good "latents."

Still, the New York system pioneered by O'Brien has much to offer, and not just to those of you who live in Queens and Staten Island, the parts of the city where the program is in force. You can pay to have your violated home *privately* dusted for prints, get them photographed and copied, and keep in contact with (notice I didn't say "keep hounding") the detectives who will compare those fingerprints with everyone they arrest in your area in connection with a burglary.

If the local cops tell you, "Sorry, we don't take finger-prints at burglaries," you have a couple of avenues to explore. One is to try and hire an off-duty cop to lift the latents for you. In most communities, a full-or part-time police officer can be hired for about ten dollars an hour. This is normally for guard duty at a dance or fair or something. Almost *none* of them have the requisite print-dusting and -lifting equipment; that normally belongs to the police department and can only be checked out for use on department-assigned cases.

You'll be a lot better off to hire a private investigator (PI). In most states you have to be an ex-cop to get a PI license, and those who make a living at it tend to be retired career detectives or FBI agents. They are very good at what they do and have networks of friends still "on the job." They can afford their own fingerprint equipment, and having been investigators, they're likely to have had the special training required to use that gear properly.

Moreover, a *good* "private eye" has a lot of contacts within the active branches of law enforcement, guys who "owe him a favor" and can "put things through the system." The FBI doesn't run fingerprint checks for any Tom, Dick, or Harry. They only do it when a request comes in via a recognized law enforcement agency. The same is true of state-level bureaus of identification.

There is a lot more that private investigators can do for you in the aftermath of a crime. Let's explore that approach now.

12. HIRED HELP: INVESTIGATIVE

An article by Nicholas Pilaggi in *New York* magazine early in 1981, stated baldly that in most cases, police in that city didn't bother to investigate most burglaries beyond the extend of taking a superfluous report. At the time, I was working with New York's "Finest" magazine and riding with the street cops in the toughest precincts. I asked several of them, "Doesn't that article tick you off?" "Why should it?" they replied. "It's *true*."

About the same time, a Florida homicide detective was shown on TV, saying that in Dade County murder had gotten out of hand. There were so many killings committed by street criminals and by "cocaine cowboys" fighting drug wars with one another, that the shorthanded homicide investigators could do little more than keep tabs on the body count. And we know that fewer than 15 out of 1,000 rapes are "closed" with a successfully prosecuted arrest that sends the rapist to jail.

Many victims of crime and their families, feel a deep sense of frustration if the investigation is not brought to a swift and satisfactory conclusion. America is used to watching its detectives solve the most difficult cases in sixty minutes, minus time for commercials. Most people don't realize just how slowly the wheels of justice really do grind, even when set at full speed and fully lubricated with manpower and budget.

Today, with the "Proposition 13 Mentality" and the economic situation, many police departments are laying off police officers instead of hiring more. The same economic problem has contributed heavily to the significant increase in street crime. The result is that many cases are not being solved simply because the manpower does not exist to fully investigate them.

There are other factors. Most criminals and the street people they associate with, will "give each other up" if they think the betrayal of a fellow criminal will do them the least bit of good. The trouble is that "snitches" who deal with police generally offer the information only when they themselves are in trouble. If it's your daughter who's been raped, you're going to find it difficult to wait until one of the rapist's friends happens to get arrested and offers to testify against the rapist in return for "taking care of him" on whatever his own charges may be.

Except in large-scale narcotics cases, most police very rarely get "buy money". If a big city detective slips a $20-bill to one of his regular "snitches," it's probably coming out of his own pocket because he feels personally committed to solving the case.

But never forget, if you're looking to find the criminal who violated you or yours, the stool pigeons "have the time if you have the money." If you were to go into the sleaziest slum of the metropolis trying to spread money around for information, you would probably wind up shelling out $1,000 in $50-increments for fake information the first day if you managed to finish that first day without being mugged for the whole bundle. This is a job for professionals.

Enter someone like Odell Jones of Cleveland, Ohio. Jones is a licensed private detective but he makes most of his money as a bounty hunter.

He's a much tougher man in real life than your fictional Mike Hammer, right down to his concealed bulletproof vest and the one or two Smith & Wesson .44 Magnums he always carries. But the real tool of Jones's trade is a nationwide network of informants and his ability to "work on the street with street people." A hulking, mean-looking man, Jones can go places cops can't, and he can pass out expense-account bribes like a department store Santa dispensing lollipops.

Nobody's going to try to flimflam *him* when he cruises the ghetto looking for a suspect the way they would you, because Jones knows the score and is not the sort of person street people care to mess with. Nor is he likely to be mugged for his bribe money; he has very little reluctance to draw his .44, and has been known to take human life with it when someone threatened *him*.

Jones says in his precise, soft-spoken diction, I find it extremely rare to get an assignment like that from a private citizen, although a lot of insurance companies will hire me to recover a piece of stolen property or find a certain individual who is likely to be responsible for its theft. Most people couldn't afford me, and those who could, have no idea that someone like me or my service is even available.

Some private investigators specialize in the recovery of certain specific, valuable objects. Henry Latini, a retired FBI agent who now operates the National Bureau of Investigation in Portland, Maine, is a good example. One of the "new breed" of private investigators—ex-FBI agents who, in a scrupulously ethical manner, play upon their connections made in twenty years of cross-country law enforcement and returnable favors owed them by cops around the country—Latini has an excellent track record in recovering stolen antiques. He knows the antique business and has a good handle on who the most active antique thieves are and where they can most effectively be hunted.

Latini's clients tend to be affluent (how many *poor* people have enough antiques worth stealing?) and they would often pay a substantial price to recover the *objets d'art* that they love, with capture and punishment for the thief being a secondary concern. Latini's long-earned knowledge, his ability to ensure the thieves that the owner does not wish to bring charges against them as long as they just return the goods, and his ability to legally pay for such information, all give him great advantages over any police department's detectives in recovering stolen property.

Good private detectives do not come cheap. Some charge $100 to $300 an hour. Odell Jones is a bargain at $100 a day plus expenses and bribes paid for information, and he'll sometimes take on a stolen property recovery case for a flat fee of 15 percent of retail or insured value. "If I recover it, I get the money. If I don't, they pay me nothing," says Jones. "You could say I like the challenge."

Because the mechanism for finding out who stole what and where it is now, sometimes involves bribery, it is not always possible to guarantee a "good arrest" (something reasonably likely to stand up in court) in some private investigations. That's up to the client who is paying the bills. Remember, though, that the great majority of private investigators are ex-cops, and an ex-FBI man, like Latini in Maine or Ted Goble in New Hampshire, knows how to put together in iron-clad criminal case that will not be thrown out of court.

Some years ago, a young New England man was murdered. The case trailed all over the country and the police investigators kept hitting dead ends. Latini—privately paid, not having to worry about another caseload of crimes—was able to travel the country, putting the loose ends together. The murder was solved, and the perpetrators convicted, by his efforts.

Odell Jones, outraged by the rape of a nun in his city, offered his services for free. Street criminals who wouldn't give police detectives the right time of day, *did* spill their guts to the macho man they perceived to be a street person like themselves. When Jones got the information he needed, he turned it over to the police. They made the arrest and saw the remainder of the case through to conviction.

A private investigator is a logical intermediary to choose if you run an advertised reward in a newspaper, after being victimized in a burglary. You certainly don't want to be taking those calls yourself. You'll get all the cranks, flim-flam experts, and rip-off artists after you.

If you're lucky, you can occasionally get the police to handle this task. You might also be able to find a professional organization to do it, though that is only likely to work if you belong to an association for jewelers or pharmacists or other similar groups.

A holdup in 1979 in Indianapolis left a pharmacist dead on the floor of his drugstore, summarily executed by a vicious killer who apparently just wanted to watch someone die. The druggist had complied with the robber's demands, yet he was shot in the back of the head as he was prostrate. When the case had been concluded, I flew to that city and talked with Dave Clark, executive director of the Indiana Pharmacists Association (IPA), which had solicited and accumulated enough money to post a substantial reward for information leading to the arrest and conviction of those responsible.

It worked superbly. Clark quickly learned, as so many of the rest of us who deal with this dark side of the world knew already, that most criminals will readily sell each other out either for money or for revenge. The reward money in this case went to the key informant after all those who were responsible for the killing had been sentenced to prison. Dave Clark doesn't know who that informant was, and he doesn't want to know. He turned over a cashier's check to a police official, who, through a double-blind safeguarded method, transferred the money to the person who talked and broke the murder case.

Since that highly publicized incident, no pharmacist has been murdered in Indiana. Armed robbers arrested and debriefed by police in that state have made the comment,

> You'd be crazy to shoot somebody in a drugstore today. Everybody on the street knows that that drug store association will pay ten grand for anybody who does. My own wife would give me up for that kind of money, and so would any partner I ever worked a holdup with.

Clark is convinced that the Indiana Pharmacists Association is on the right track with its reward program. So am I. Those Hoosier druggists have taken a hard line against violent crime: Clark has also arranged for several classes in combat pistol shooting for member pharmacists throughout the state, conducted by police firearms instructors and including lectures on the use of deadly force from Indiana judges. Since that program began, there have already been cases of IPA members who had to use guns to protect themselves against robbers.

For eight years, I was a municipal patrol officer, a foot soldier in the half-million strong army of American law enforcement. For nine years, I traveled the country as a researcher for police professional journals studying the most effective approaches to keeping the public safe. I am convinced that America's police are far and away the finest in the world. In the great majority of cases where a private citizen suffers violence at the hands of the street criminal, the police agency that has jurisdiction is by far the best-suited party to handle the investigation. If the time comes when castrating budget cuts and overwhelming increases in crime make the given police department somewhat impotent in its ability to bring certain investigations to a climax, however, there may be some justification in hiring private professionals to pursue the case.

Those private investigators should be chosen wisely. Not all states have rigid requirements as to experience, competence, training, and character, for those who are licensed to offer such services. If you want to find a good private investigator, ask a good lawyer for a referral: Most attorneys use private investigators frequently, and they know who are the aces and who are the charlatans.

The hiring of a private investigator, in the wake of a burglary or a crime of violence, is not a step to be taken lightly. The great majority of investigating officers who are officially handling the case will take it as a slap in the face if you hire someone from the outside. You are, after all, tacitly saying, "You cops are too stupid and incompetent to solve what victimized me, so I'm going over your heads!" You do not want to *ever* alienate and insult the police officers who are investigating a crime that victimized you, unless you are totally convinced that they are incapable of pursuing it anymore. Usually, they'll be honest enough to tell you that to your face.

The purchase of outside services to investigate a crime that vicitimizes you is extremely costly, and usually undertaken with no guarantee of success. But *if* you are well-off financially, and *if* the police have gone as far as they can and have come up empty-handed, and *if* you are ready to handle it responsibly—as an exercise in "property retrieval" and "justice restoration" as opposed to blind vengeance— then the expertise exists out there for you to hire some of the top manhunters and stolen property recovery experts in the world.

13. THE TRUTH ABOUT ATTACK DOGS

The public has many dangerous misconceptions about using dogs for protection. They think an attack dog is more vicious than a guard dog, and that they can just go to some randomly selected "protection kennel" and come home with a Doberman that, on their command, will tear an attacker limb from limb. It's simply not true.

There are four kinds of protective dogs, each with a different purpose:

Watchdogs are the most common, and require the least training. Almost any breed or size will do as long as the animal is a mobile, four-footed burglar alarm. It barks insistently and steadily when an entry is attempted, and goes to the entry point to pinpoint it for you as it yaps. Whatever pet dog you have now, unless it's blind or crippled, can almost certainly be trained to be a functional watchdog, and it's the one form of canine training you can do yourself, at home.

Protection dogs are animals with advanced obedience training. On your command, they will bark and lunge at an aggressor, snapping at him without actually biting him. Also upon your command, they will immediately sit or lie and fall silent. Their training is oriented strictly toward a deterrent show of force; if your attacker persists, the animal will have to fall back on its natural protective instinct and bite him. A properly trained protection dog will also perform all the functions of a watchdog.

Attack dogs have been trained to sink their teeth into

people on their master's command, or when they observe their master under assault. Once resistance from the suspect ceases, a true attack dog will let go of him. It will do the same on the master's command, no matter how excitement-charged the atmosphere, if it has been properly trained and selected. Normally, the dog will only bite if given the proper command, or if the animal sees its owner or a family member under attack.

The attack dog is at the maximum level of obedience training. After the master has ordered it to put a suspect on point, the dog can be called back, and even ordered to "make friends." It feels no personal animosity toward the person it is ordered to attack; it is a canine technician, doing a job on the orders of its human boss.

Guard dogs represent the deadliest level of canine training. These animals either walk with a sentry, or patrol alone in an enclosed space. Their function is to apprehend and neutralize any human intruder. They do not stop biting when the suspect stops resisting; they stop only when the human stops *moving*. They are likely to be trained to go for the throat or the genitals. Guard dogs are trained to kill and maim.

A guard dog is so vicious that it will usually obey only a single handler. While an attack dog can usually function quite well as a family pet when "off duty," the guard dog is capable of destroying any human other than its master, and must be kept securely kenneled. If the master dies or retires, it will often be impossible to retrain the animal, in which case it will have to be destroyed.

The only legitimate use of a guard dog is in wartime, or when guarding an area so sensitive that human intrusion could result in awesome public danger, such as a nuclear weapons facility. Few judges will rule in the department store's favor if the manager leaves guard dogs on patrol and comes in one morning to find a dead burglar.

Such a dog may also turn on its master since you can't bring an animal to that level of indiscriminate antagonism against humans by any means other than by tormenting the animal in training.

Think back to your military days. Remember how rigidly firearms and ammunition were secured at peacetime posts? The sentries *might* have rifles loaded, though at many low-security facilities the M–16s are empty and just for show. Military police might wear loaded pistols. But there was one other group in camp that *always* had loaded pistols on: the K–9 men handling killer-trained guard dogs.

Part of the rationale for the pistol was that such a soldier, with a leash on one arm, couldn't effectively operate a two-handed rifle or carbine. But there was another reason: the dog itself. The services arm guard dog handlers so as to protect them from their own animals.

Some dog trainers, and many veterinarians, question the practice of keeping even attack dogs. Even a gun can be locked up or modified so that it can't endanger children or other innocents, not so an animal that has been trained to sink its teeth into human flesh.

First off, you'll never be able to let the animal run free. It would be like leaving a cocked and loaded pistol on your doorstep. The animal has the power and training to kill humans. It must never be given the opportunity to do so on its own volition.

An essential attribute in a successful attack dog is confidence in itself. This can lead, especially in Doberman pinschers, to an occasional need to "test the master." We are talking here of an obedience problem of much graver import than chewing up your slippers.

To own an attack dog, *you* must have a strong, dominant personality, and you must have not one whit of fear of that animal. It is absolutely true that dogs instantly sense fear in humans and play upon it.

Sadly, many of the people who rush out to buy ready-trained attack dogs are the very people who aren't capable of fully controlling them. They see the dog as salvation for their fear and reinforcement for their weakness. The dog, being much more elemental in the way it interprets people, sees only the fear and the weakness. The result can be tragic.

First Amendment or not, I can't repress the feeling that all books on how to train your own attack dog should be banned. If you must have an attack dog, that's a job for a stone professional with lots of experience. Consider this not atypical case, related to me by a professional dog trainer:

When this old guy bought the Doberman I kept telling him it was more dog than he could handle. When he said he was going to attack train it himself, I told him and told him that he was out of his mind. Awhile later, he boarded the dog at my kennel while he went on vacation, and I've never seen a more vicious, bad-tempered animal. God knows what he did to it. When he came back to pick it up, he said, "Here, Prince." The dog lunged at him, and grabbed him by the genitals. I had to beat the dog off him.

A veterinarian relates,

A friend of mine bought a Doberman and tried to attack train it. I could have warned him. I'm strongly against attack dogs. Anyway, I got a panicky phone call from him one day: He was locked in his bedroom with his wife, and the dog was at the door. I could hear it snarling in the background.

I went to the house with my long-handled noose, hoping to capture the dog and maybe salvage it. But when I let myself in, it launched himself at me, and I had to shoot it in the head with my Colt twenty-two.

An attack dog is likely to use its teeth on whoever it perceives to be an intruder. It doesn't know that the paperboy has come up on the porch you left unlocked to collect his money; all it sees is, *intruder*. If there's a fire in your home while you're out, the dog will already be in a situation approaching panic when the fire fighters force their way in. Guess who's going to get a throat full of teeth?

The most loquacious of dog-lovers credit the smartest dogs with roughly the native intelligence and judgment of a five-year-old child, and many think that's a gross overestimate. Just for argument, let's accept it: An attack dog by itself is a lethal weapon, operating on the commands of a mind comparable to a tot. Would you give a five-year-old a loaded gun, knowing that you would be legally responsible for anyone injured as a result? If you wouldn't, why leave an attack dog to its own devices, with the lethal weapon lying in its jaws?

Some people buy attack dogs who shouldn't have any dog at all; they see the animal only as a burglar alarm, not as a living entity that needs warmth, love, and attention. Without those things you're going to have a mean, misanthropic animal, one increasingly disposed toward turning on you, and on anything human that gets in reach of its fangs. Owning an attack dog, or any large dog for that matter, is much like the commitment to having a child: It requires a certain amount of time and devotion from *you*. Dogs give a lot more of this than they usually get back, but it's not a one-way street.

Elsewhere in this book, I explain why people who say anyone but cops is incompetent to keep guns, are hypocrites. Am I now being two-faced when I say that attack dogs are not for everyone?

Not really. You can lock up a gun where it can't hurt anyone, but not a dog. A gun will never decide of its own volition to kill you. A gun won't jump out the window and shoot the postal worker.

The dog is a separate intelligence, never neutralized by your mere absence. When you're gone, it performs actively, on its own command, with an intelligence far dimmer than that of a human. *And you are legally responsible for everything it does.*

The responsibilities of owning such a killing machine are awesome. So is the owner's culpability for the dog's mistakes in a court of civil law. In my own state of New Hampshire there is a statute whereby automatic double-damages in civil suits involving animals are awarded. If my dog bites the wrong person and the jury awards the victim $50,000, I am automatically liable for $100,000 in damages. The jury won't have been told of this beforehand, in the interest of objectivity. I may be criminally as well as civilly liable. Under the law, siccing an attack dog on someone is the same as assault with a deadly weapon. An attack dog *is* a deadly weapon.

Yet, there is no denying that there are some people who in fact need such animals. Consider the owner of a high-risk retail establishment, like a liquor store in a ghetto. Consider the rape victim whose attacker still roams free, quite capable of attacking her again, perhaps even after he has been processed through the courts. Consider the estranged wife whose husband's threats against her "are not serious enough to lead to his arrest."

Ideally, the dog should be but one component in a total system of self-protection that includes locks, alarms, self-defense training with and without makeshift weapons, and for some, the responsible keeping of deadly weapons. There are some situations where, for moral or other reasons, the citizen chooses not to keep deadly weapons for self-defense. In this case, against a high-threat level of attack, nothing else will protect so well as an attack-trained dog.

For the great majority of private citizens, however, a *protection-trained* dog is quite adequate. The presence of an intimidating dog is usually enough by itself to make rapists and muggers change their minds. Studies indicate that homes with dogs are considerably less likely to be burglarized than homes without them. None of these protective functions requires an attack-trained animal.

The protection-trained dog will be a superb watchdog when someone approaches your door or window, alerting you immediately so you can take the proper action in time. Plus on your command it will snarl, bark, or lunge at the aggressor.

"Wait a minute," you say. "What if the person attacking me isn't bluffed by the dog's show of force? Where does that leave me then, with a dog that isn't attack trained?"

It leaves you precisely where you'd be if the dog *was* attack trained. Your protection dog's response when you yell, "Prince! Protect!" is exactly the same as an attack dog's would be upon the same command. It'll growl and jump at the guy as you pull back on the leash to restrain it.

If your aggressor is going to try to get past that show of force, it's for one reason only: *He isn't afraid of the dog.* Psychosis or monumental stupidity might explain his lack of fear, but more likely, he has a gun to kill your dog with anyway. If that happens, an attack dog will be just as dead as a protection dog. The only difference is that, being somewhat more inured to pain in its training, the former might take more lead before it goes down. (Both protection and attack dogs should be accustomed to gunfire in their training, as all hunting dogs are, so that they won't cringe from any sudden loud sound.)

The attack dog's greater immunity to pain makes it better able to cope with a gunman or knifewielder. If you have reason to anticipate such an assault—you've been threatened seriously or work in a high-risk business—then you belong to that limited category of people who may have a valid reason for owning attack dogs, even though the dog could turn on you and even with the many potential civil liability hassles.

When any confident, obedience trained dog observes its master in trouble, it responds. You can't count on anything a hundred percent, but it's a very good bet that your obedience-trained canine is going to take a bite or two out of whoever has jumped you.

If you're satisfied with only a furry burglar alarm, the watchdog is at a level where you, as opposed to a professional, can train it. You want basic obedience, that is, response to the commands "Heel," "Sit," "Down," "Lie down," "Stay," and "No." It'll naturally bark when someone comes to the door; reward it and pet it lavishly saying, "*Good* dog!"

Conversely, it's "Bad dog! Bad dog," if it barks at anyone walking by on the street. You don't want to be up all night listening to its woofing, either.

Many of the experts tell you that the dog's size doesn't matter. If all you want is a roaming burglar alarm that goes beyond any man-made intrusion detection system, they're absolutely right. The barking will alert you in time to investigate, call the police, or hit an electronic panic button, and arm yourself if you're so inclined.

Do not, however, expect an itty-bitty dog to scare *all* the burglars away with its barking although many of the popular self-protection manuals imply that the woofing of any dog will do this.

True, they don't *like* noise. But burglars also understand a lot more than you do about the human dynamics involved. You may think that the neighbors are going to call the police as soon as they hear Fluffy barking.

They won't. They'll ignore Fluffy the way they ignore every other barking dog in the neighborhood. When was the last time *you* called the Burglary Squad because you heard a dog barking? If anything, neighbors will only call the police if they get irritated enough; by that time the burglar will either have left, or stomped your beloved little Fluffy to death.

Besides, cops don't take barking dog calls nearly as seriously as they take man-made burglar alarms. When the harried patrol officer gets that radio call in his squad car, it goes on his list of priorities: He'll respond to it in half an hour or in two hours or tomorrow for that matter; he's probably got a lot more pressing business to handle than barking dogs.

Little dogs utter little, high-pitched barks. Big dogs issue big, intimidating barks. Giant dogs send deep roaring ga-*roofs* out of their huge lungs, a liability when you own one in the city, but a definite chill-up-the-spine producer to the guy with the celluloid strip who's getting ready to work on your front door.

Some so-called experts even say that a little dog walking with you in the park is all the protection you need, because the barking will scare an attacker away, and because "no criminal wants to get bitten by a dog, even by a little dog." That's ridiculous. To be brutally frank, criminals are afraid of medium to large dogs because they can picture those big, sharp, white teeth biting out their Adam's apple or tearing off their testicles or chomping their wrists down to the bone.

Any hardened criminal, whether a burglar or a rapist, knows that he can make very short work of a small dog. He can kick the poor little thing thirty feet or crush it to death with a single stomp of his heel. Ironically, the only sound little Fluffy can make that might alert witnesses when you're attacked in the park, is the brief and pathetic little *ki-yi* it'll utter as the rapist steps on its neck and kills it.

You want a dog that weighs at *least* fifty pounds. That's an animal long-legged and long-bodied enough to be able to jump and take a man by the throat. That's an animal with big enough jaws and long enough teeth to really intimidate when he growls at someone who threatens you.

For some of you, a mongrel is the answer. You're talking about several thousand dollars for a guard dog, before you even start paying the added insurance premiums. Figure $1,000 to $3,000 for a good attack-trained dog. You start at $100 to $250 for a quality German shepherd,

Doberman, or Great Dane puppy, prior to training, which doesn't come cheap, either.

Mongrel dogs don't lend themselves to advanced obedience protection, and attack training, due to the uncertainties of their intelligence and bred-in traits. Still, it is nonetheless possible to find highly intelligent, deeply loyal mutts who may be ready to protect you unto death. The trouble is, you don't know the animal's qualities until you have it home: a reputable shep or Dobe or other pedigree breeder can almost guarantee certain qualities before the litter is born. That's one reason purebreds are so sought after, and why they're worth their hefty prices.

But a lot of you who live where the crime threat is the worst can't afford to put $1,000 into a trained shepherd, any more than you can afford to move. The ASPCA charges about $15 per dog, and usually a $35 neutering fee that can be split with them, or sometimes underwritten entirely by the Friends of Animals. (Some of my readers in the firearms world will be appalled that I have anything good to say about the Friends of Animals, an organization that advances some incredibly stupid reasons why people shouldn't own handguns or hunt animals. I only wish the group would concentrate on what they do well, which is reducing the proliferation of abandoned and suffering offspring of domestic pets.)

On a lot of budgets, even buying and sterilizing the ASPCA dog is unaffordable. In this case, check the ads in your local newspaper for free puppies and dogs being given away. The trouble is, you won't be able to have an honest opinion like you would have with the ASPCA people who get a lot of abandoned dogs that have been maltreated and that are hopelessly averse to human contact. Private citizens however, are certainly not going to tell the person who is about to take the problem dog off their hands why they want to unload their dog.

At the ASPCA, concerned attendants have learned a long time ago that some dogs are fit to live with people, while others aren't. The ASPCA people will tell you the truth and help you select a compatible dog, because they want you and your friends to come back as satisfied customers so that more canines will be adopted that otherwise would have to be put to sleep.

Examine your cheapie or freebie dog carefully before you take it home. Does it come to you and other humans readily? If not, it may have been mistreated, leaving a deep-seated misanthropy that could one day make it turn on you. Is it free of mange, with a generally healthy appearance, or has it been so maltreated by others that you'll have to nurse it back to health? Despite your loving care, it may never be able to forget the ingrained hatred of the humans who starved and maltreated it.

There are dozens of books in stores and in libraries that detail the basics of housebreaking and basic obedience training. Read them and use them. If you're not willing to housebreak and spend a whole lot of ten-or fifteen-minute intervals saying "Si-i-it," then you should make a point of buying a young dog that has already been housebroken, basically trained, and hopefully, spayed.

We repeat: Never attempt to attack train a dog yourself! You want to take it only through obedience and advanced obedience. It is absolutely imperative that the dog sit and stay on your command, and most helpful if it barks on a code word. As the basic dog-training books will show you, it's no big deal to teach a dog to "speak."

However, don't use "speak" as the command, either for your homemade protection dog or for the finest German shepherd you can buy. To bark when you say "speak" is just a trick for children to do with their pets. What you want is a dog that barks vociferously—and hopefully, also bares its fangs—when you say "Prince! *Protect!* or "King! On *guard!*"

Dog's don't understand English. They learn to respond to certain short syllables. For some time, professional attack dog trainers have been teaching their dogs (and their clients) to use German commands. This lends a certain cachet that seems to please clients who have paid thousands of dollars for purebred, highly trained Teutonic dogs.

The use of this or a similarly obscure language for attack-type commands has a lot of advantages. You don't have to worry about a smart criminal confusing your dog with countering commands, and you don't have to worry about what will happen if your ten-year-old gets into a show-off mood with his playmates and yells, "Prince! *Attack!*"

Obviously, only you, your spouse, and children old enough and responsible enough to be entrusted with the ability to command an animal to harm a human being, should be taught the key commands, whether your dog is trained to attack *or* protect you. You'll need to totally commit the commands to your own memory. You don't want to find yourself trying to remember your code when face-to-face with an attacker. If you have a second language, use that for your protective canine's commands, including "Heel" and "Stay." You don't want a big rapist with a dominant personality and a deep voice to order your dog to sit while he pounces on you.

Those who do have reason to responsibly keep attack-trained dogs have come up with some remarkably effective language and command codes. One woman I trained in self-defense told me the code she had worked out for the attack dog she was going to buy, in the wake of a rape attempt.

She said matter-of-factly,

Look, I know how it feels to look down a gun barrel. I know if I yell "kill," I'm going to get my head blown off. I figure if an armed rapist can threaten me with death, he can kill my dog before my dog can stop him, so I've got to catch him off guard. I'm just going to tell my next rapist,

"Hey, the dog *had* to go for a walk, you know? Let me get it out of the way." Then I'm going to turn to the dog and say sweetly, "Puppy, go someplace and *go potty!*"

The words she emphasized, the words which stood out above the other mundane words in that harmless sentence that would put her rapist off guard, were the attack command. When she said *"Go potty,"* the dog wasn't going to empty its bowels. The dog was going to empty the rapist's *throat,* suddenly and silently and without warning, leaving no voicebox, no windpipe, no jugular veins behind.

You have to be careful with these tricky-slicky commands. What's going to happen if this young woman goes on vacation and leaves her dog at a kennel, and a tired dog handler innocently takes the beast for a walk and tells it, "Hey, dog, *go potty*"? Still, she did have another kind of understanding that escapes a lot of trainers who aren't self-defense instructors and who don't understand the dynamics of the potentially violent human confrontations that people buy dogs to protect themselves from.

An obvious shout to the dog is something the attacker expects, something he's prepared to respond to with savage violence. At the same time, he's used to his victims talking in low, frightened, urgent tones or whispers. If you shout, "Dog! *Now!*" the attacker is going to know what you're up to, and if you or I play devil's advocate and take the rapist's role, we both know we're going to kill the dog first, and then maybe the person who commanded it. But if you mutter a long sentence the dog doesn't understand, punctuated with the clearly enunciated and insistent whisper, *"Now,"* the rapist is a lot more likely to be caught off guard and not realize that the dog has been sicced on him until the fangs are already inside his body.

As someone whose specialty is guns, you can believe me when I tell you that dogs can be as frightening to a criminal as firearms, and sometimes even more effective. A knife in the ribs gives your attacker only sudden pain, and he has six to twelve seconds to a minute or more in which he's still alive and highly motivated to murder you in revenge. In one shooting I studied in Cook County, Illinois, an armed junkie soaked up more than twenty soft-nosed 9-mm pistol bullets while trying to kill some cops until he was finally sledged down by a couple of shotgun blasts.

With dogs, you're not talking about the pain and the slow hemorrhagic shock of the knife, nor are you talking about the relatively puny shock power of a 230-grain .45 slug, a legendary manstopper less than half an inch in diameter, and traveling about 830 feet per second. You are talking about the bone-and-muscle mass of an eighty-pound dog that gets a running start and launches itself into the upper body of a man, tilting him back off the frail bipod axis of his human feet.

A good-size dog can, on most occasions and if it's been trained, put a man more than twice its size right onto his back. Jeremiah Puppybeast, my 210-pound protection-trained Great Dane, can do that from a standing position.

You gain a lot when your attacker is blasted off his feet in the first moments of the encounter, and it doesn't matter whether you do it with a punch or a kick or a bullet, or with your lunging dog. The man who endangered you is now disoriented, much more helpless, and probably much more scared.

If the dog is a part of your total protection system, a system that includes panic buttons and defensive weaponry up to, and including, firearms, your snarling dog is likely to draw the criminal's attention away from you. Fine. It gives you an opening.

If you're a liquor store owner or other high-risk retailer, I advise elsewhere in this book to keep your gun out of sight, because surprise is the only thing that will make it work against criminals who come in on you with their own guns already drawn. If, however, they turn away from you to concentrate on your dog, you may now have the opening you need. In that situation, don't yell, "Drop your guns." Come up shooting, and drop your attackers instead. You'll have to fight with the same tenacity as your dog until the encounter is over, and both of you will possibly be hurt.

Just as you know that you can die in a gunfight, you have to understand that the dog can die, too. Your dog is a line of defense for you, just like your alarms and your locks and the burglar grilles on your windows. Like them, I'm sorry to say, it's expendable.

There's time enough to grieve for your fallen canine comrade later. Instead, make your protector's death mean something: Use that moment in time, when the attacker's mind is focused on the dog, to terminate the threat. Maybe you'll do that by running out the back door, or maybe you'll do it by grabbing your hidden shotgun and terminating the attacker.

Whatever you do, don't stand there and wait for the criminal to kill you, too. The dog didn't die for that, anymore than your Army buddy died so that you could stand like a zombie and put your hands up and yell "Kamerad" to the enemy.

These loyal protectors and friends laid down their lives, so that *you* might live. Fall to your knees and shed your tears later. *Now*, validate their deaths with meaning and save your own life: Escape, or fight back and neutralize the enemy who took your comrade's life in sacrifice for yours.

If your dog is blown away by a criminal's gunfire, it might even survive. Four out of five *people* who get shot survive when they get medical treatment, and it's not that much less a ratio for dogs, even though vets don't always take the heroic measures with *them* that surgeons take with *us* on the operating table. The lesser mammals are more vital and more tenacious to life than we are, they don't smoke or drink or overdose on saturated fats, and they take both punishment and surgery much better than we do.

The difference is in emergency medical transport. If the authorities learn that you or I are down with gunshot wounds, they'll send EMTs or paramedics to rush us to the hospital with state of the art life-support systems going on the way, and with a surgical team alerted to receive us the moment the attendants race our gurney through the doors of the Emergency Room. Dogs tend to get left by the wayside.

If I go to bed after writing this, and wake up in three hours with a home invasion on my hands, my dog will be there before I am when the lethal intruders come in the door. There would be casualties, and the way I have my reaction plan set up, there's going to be some humans with gunshot wounds from Number One buckshot and/or hollowpoint pistol bullets, and some with serious lacerations and/or avulsions from dog teeth, and probably, a big dog with one or more bullets in it.

The authorities will send the ambulances for those human intruders who still live. If it happens out in the boondocks during a windstorm when the phone lines are down, my wife and child and I are going to take my dog to the veterinary hospital, and when I get there I'll call an ambulance for the remaining humans.

At least, that's the way my emotions run. Logic and knowledge dictate otherwise: In the eyes of the court, the Church, and every other authority, any human life is vastly more important than any animal's life. If you were to give first aid to your dog before giving it to a human criminal who had been injured trying to attack you, you could be held liable.

Morally, in that situation, I would owe a lot more to my dog than I would to the predatory humans who had threatened the lives of my family. Realistically, I'd be a fool to take care of my dog instead of the wounded criminals who had tried to murder me and mine.

If your dog ever gets hurt, remember two things: You owe it to it to take care of it, and you can get hurt badly if you respond to it the way you would to a human who was *in extremis* ("at the point of death"). Hurt people won't bite you, but injured dogs will; the pain puts them into a frenzy, and they lash out even at the masters they love the most, out of sheer reflex.

Move in carefully. Use your belt to lash the dog's jaws shut. It may seem cruel, but you're doing both of you a favor. If the dog's back appears broken, put a door or a wide board under it, and secure it. Talk to your vet: He can tell you what you should do in such a situation and he probably has handouts on "first aid for injured dogs" that he can give you for free.

14. SHEPS AND DOBES

The archetypal protection dogs are the German shepherd and the Doberman pinscher. With the exception of occasional dope-sniffing Labradors, Dobes and sheps are almost universal choices of police departments, and both have been used in wartime as well not because of any innate viciousness, so much as for their extremely high intelligence and "trainability."

People back off instinctively from shepherds as a rule, partly because of their wolflike visages and partly because of their reputation. This is even more true with the muscular Doberman. The average burglar, like the average citizen, tends to see the shep as a "police dog," the Dobe as an "attack dog."

In the midst of the so-called fear boom, demand for these two types of dogs has reached unprecedented proportions. Unscrupulous—and sometimes even well-meaning—dog owners have found a ready market for all the shep and Dobe puppies their bitches can produce.

Herein lies the problem. The reason the American Kennel Club and their ilk seem so snobbishly picky about the breeding of dogs is because it takes a breeder, armed with generations worth of papers of both animals' forebears, plus an intimate knowledge of the parent animals and their temperament, to make a match that will create good puppies.

The unknowing or uncaring "backyard dog breeder" could midwife some inferior animals. They may have a profoundly greater tendency toward hip displasia, the crippling curse of all large canine strains. Worse, they may be neurotic, paranoid, and vicious.

Don't buy your shepherd or Doberman puppy from your brother-in-law whose dog just had a litter. Don't haunt the ASPCA waiting for one, either. *Go to the most reputable, longest-established breeder you can find.*

For a pet, go to a pet store. But you're not looking for a pet if you've got a defensive dog in mind: You're looking for a working animal to perform relatively sensitive tasks, and ideally, that's going to require the intelligence, eventemperedness, and natural obedience that only a professional breeder can reliably instill.

Your local veterinarian can recommand a qualified breeder. So can the head of the K–9 patrol at your local, county, or state police headquarters. Don't be put off by part-timers. Unlike the lock and alarm businesses, it's awfully hard to make a living raising dogs, and most of the top breeders do it as a sideline. What you *do* want is someone who has been in the business for many years and who has produced a number of champion dogs. True, you don't care about entering your new animal in dog shows, but a history of winners shows you that this is a breeder who knows his business.

Shepherd or Doberman? Each breed has its staunch defenders. The Dobe tends to fight more readily and tenaciously, bite harder, and sheds less fur. The shepherd withstands cold temperatures better and is often friendlier with children.

You've all heard the rumor, "Dobermans are treacherous and turn on their masters." Dobe fanciers counter, "That's just an old wives' tale!"

When you sit down for a long talk with someone who has been into Dobermans for years, you'll find out that where there's smoke, there's some fire. The Doberman is an extremely intelligent animal, and a rather high-strung one in comparison to the shep. It is, therefore, less likely to accept your dominance over it unquestioningly and forever. "They're not turning on you," claims one Doberman fancier; "they just like to test you every now and then."

That can get a little spooky. If you have any doubts at all about your mastery over the animal, it'll sense it. It's one thing to have a Chihuahua who doesn't think it has to take any guff from its master; it's quite another thing to be locked in the same house with a Doberman who might feel that way. Veterinarians and dog control officers I talk with confirm that Dobes are more likely than any other breed to become uncontrollable, and therefore violent.

This is not to say that shepherds can't get out of control, either. But there are certain things which increase the likelihood of being injured by your dog.

One is buying an adult dog instead of a puppy. The puppy learns from the beginning who's in charge and who feeds him and keeps it warm. Its adulation of you begins at birth and is strengthened as you go through its earliest training with it, side by side.

But you probably don't want to wait a year to be protected by something more formidable than puppy teeth.

You may well have decided that you want your canine guardian *now*. That means the purchase of an adult or adolescent dog that has probably already been through at least its basic obedience training and may already have been "attack trained."

Adult dogs, like adult people, have formed their opinions and their personalities. If you want to win the affection and obedience of such an animal, you better select one raised by a master breeder for good temperament and trainability.

A lot of people place advertisements for attack-trained dogs. I would never buy one. I consider that practice hellaciously dangerous for a couple of reasons. First off, even the gentlest and most loving teacher can't attack train a basically gentle animal without traumatizing it in some way. The dog has to be provoked into attack: prodded, poked, taunted, teased, and even hit. In return, it learns to sink its teeth into a human's arm without fear, and, under certain circumstances, to be rewarded for its aggressive acts against humans.

If you put yourself in the dog's position, you can understand how the creature might become a little mean and a little neurotic and a bit of a misanthrope. Now, enter *you*, the Johnny-come-lately to this dog's life, the person who is going to uproot it from everything it knows and take it to live in a *strange* place with *strange* humans.

Doesn't sound too promising, does it? The trainer may guarantee that, in three lessons, the dog will accept you as its master. Maybe it will *if* it has a lot of innate love for humankind that hasn't all been trained out of it, and *if* you are wise in the ways of dogs, totally unafraid of it, and capable of exerting mastery. If you're not, you may be buying yourself some serious problems. All your money purchases is the dog's body: You can't buy its love or its loyalty, and after what it's been put through and trained to do, it may be a bit late for you to try.

If you insist on owning an attack-trained animal, the

safest way is for you to buy a promising young animal from a reputable breeder, accompany the dog through its secondary obedience training, and *then* turn it over to a trainer of proven reputation. Many such trainers prefer not to have you there during training—partly because they think you'll "misinterpret" some of the things they do to the dog to get it to perform—but toward the end of training they'll encourage you to come in and participate.

You now have, at least, an animal that already loves and obeys you, and associates you with happiness and security instead of taunts and aggression.

Consider, too, that for many people—especially women—a female Dobe or shep might be preferable to a male. They're smaller and easier to control, and as a general rule, less aggressive. They can, however, be trained sufficiently to be more than adequately protective. In training I have been on the sharp end of both male and female Dobermans and I can assure you that there is absolutely no difference in the deterrent effect when the lips retract from the fangs. "Don't criminals know that female dogs are less aggressive?" That's a common question. A rapist might notice that your Doberman has nipples but his main concern is going to be that your Doberman has *teeth*.

With the possible exception of the giant breeds, no dog is so intimidating as the Doberman pinscher. Be sure to buy one within the recommended size of the breed: seventy to ninety pounds at adulthood. Bigness in a Dobe, most breeders agree, is a sign of sloppy breeding that might indicate poor temperament as well. For the average person a female Dobe will probably be a better choice due to the greater controllability.

Many who have studied both breeds believe that the shepherd is the more tractable from the novice owner's standpoint, while giving away very little if anything in its protective capability. I concur. But remember, the world is full of badly bred shepherds—the "backyard-breeding" phenomenon occurred with that breed even before it did among Dobes—and it is absolutely essential to purchase a quality dog from a reputable, established breeder.

It's tough to select between the two. Living in a cold climate is enough to sway me toward the shep, and I also like the fact that while it can intimidate aggressors just as effectively as a Doberman when its teeth are showing, it appears less menacing to neighbors—and to jurors. In the state where I live any civil judgment against an owner for his dog's acts is automatically doubled. I want those jurors thinking, "Rin-Tin-Tin," not "killer Nazi attack dog" when they re-create in their minds what happened between my dog and the man it had to bite.

15. EXOTIC DEFENSIVE DOGS

Let's say you don't think a collie or a Great Dane would be taken any more seriously by a rapist than by a civil court jury, and you want a beast that will strike fear into criminal hearts on sight. At the same time you're deeply concerned about the widespread, haphazard breeding of sheps and Dobes, and you're scared of pit bulls *yourself*. Three excellent alternatives come to mind.

One is the Akita, a chunky, powerful animal two feet high at the shoulders and with a massive neck appropriate to its biting power. They were bred centuries ago in Japan to hunt bear on Hokkaido and wild boar on Honshu, and the animal today typifies strength, endurance, and companionability with man. Aficionados often refer to the Akita as a canine *sumo* wrestler.

A disadvantage is that the Akita is unusually aggressive toward other dogs. I have heard stories of them wasting Shepherds in dogfights. Even so, the dog looks more "powerful" than "vicious."

Only in the very recent past has the Akita become popular stateside. They command top dollar, often in the four-figure range for a promising puppy, and in some circles are regarded as status dogs. The good news is that the breeders tend to be serious Akita devotees, and jealously guard the bloodlines. Your chances of winding up with a puppy that will suit you for the length of its existence are excellent, and the Akita stacks up with the best breeds for protective qualities.

The Rhodesian Ridgeback is another "sleeper." It was bred to hunt lions in Africa and to the untrained eye it resembles a big, ungainly mongrel hound. Fans of the breed see something deeper: an extremely high intelligence, a degree of natural aggression that can readily be controlled with proper training, and an almost indomitable combination of ferocity and fearlessness. Considering the many years of terrorism in the Rhodesian outback—where most of the isolated farms kept machine guns *and* Ridgebacks on hand—this uncommon dog has had an unusual opportunity to demonstrate its violent nature against hostile humans under observation. The results tend to be chilling. You rarely meet a Rhodesian émigré or an American who has spent much time in Rhodesia/Zimbabwe, who does not speak of this animal in a tone of awe.

There are numerous accounts of how this breed easily kills Dobermans and Great Danes in dogfights; for protection against vicious dogs the Ridgeback is probably tied with the pit bull. Its prowess against human aggressors while defending its master's family is well-known. It is an independent creature, however, and not necessarily the most tractable of dogs.

Like the Akita, the Rhodesian Ridgeback is a product of serious breeding, and the likelihood of being sold a sloppily bred puppy is relatively small. Hard to find but worth looking for, Rhodesian Ridgebacks at this time are not outrageously expensive. Decent Ridgeback puppies can be had for about $400. Prices for the even rarer Akita vary more widely, with $400 per puppy a bargain.

16. DOGS: THE GIANT BREEDS

Very few of you are ready to handle a dog that weighs more than you do, and no one in his right mind would recommend a giant breed dog for the average citizen. For those of you who have no physical impairment I favor medium to large dogs—good-size but controllable mongrels, German shepherds, or even in some cases Doberman pinschers. For me, the giant dog is strictly a personal choice. Let me tell you the pros and cons.

The giant breeds—Saint Bernard, Great Dane, New-foundland, and English Mastiff, to name a few—are monstrously intimidating by their size alone. Most of them are also bred to be (a) extremely tolerant of children, and (b) fiercely protective of children in their household. The larger the dog, as a rule, the higher its pain tolerance; it can take a high degree of fur- and tail-pulling, responding at worst by simply standing up.

Those who make a living breeding and promoting these humongous canines call them gentle giants. But you have to own one to realize the problems that ensue when you keep these enormous creatures as a part of your household.

The good news is, they're not that expensive to feed.

It takes only about 24 cups of dry dogfood a day to feed a 200-pound dog. It isn't all that much more than it takes to feed a shep or a Dobe. If you want still more good news, be advised that people who don't think anything of facing a shep or Dobe with a knife in their hands will blanch at the thought of doing that to a dog that matches their weight and height.

The average shep or Dobe has its face at your chest level, uncomfortably close to your neck, when it stands up against you with its forelegs on your body. My Dane has its head there when it's on all fours, and has put shepherd owners on point in stark fear. If it puts its paws on your shoulders and stands up, it reaches 6 feet 4 inches in height.

The canine ferocity remains. The Great Dane, for instance, was bred as a battle dog; so was the giant English Mastiff. Other dogs were bred to hunt other animals, and only lately have learned to kill humans at the command of a human master. The Dane and the Mastiff have centuries of that already in their bloodlines.

When you come to the bottom line of pure combat, after you've already realized that pound for pound an attack-trained, 70-pound shepherd or Doberman, can go against any human enemy with only a 25 percent chance of the human's survival even if the human has the best and most intensive training against dogs, you realize just how awesome a creature you're dealing with.

The giant breed dog is to canine protection what the .44 Magnum revolver is to armed self-defense: There aren't many men who can control that sort of power and even they will recommend something smaller and more controllable.

I pretty much know my way around big dogs. I'm an average-size man and I've still been dragged 20 feet on my belly on one occasion, 15 yards on another with my heels digging furrows in the dirt, and knocked on my backside a couple of times playing "frisky puppy" with my 200-plus pound dog. A 100-pound dog can at least be controlled on a leash by the average adult.

The Doberman's awesome biting power is a function of its jaw design and masseter muscle construction. A giant breed dog equals that crushing power by the sheer size and mass of its jaws. My Dane's jaws and teeth are comparable to those of a small adult black bear. It can crunch through a leg-of-lamb bone with one bite, leaving little question as to what it could do to a human arm.

To attack train an animal of that size would be sheer folly. Saint Bernards especially have a reputation among their owners for crashing through doors and windows when in a high emotional state. The potential for the canine's destructive power getting out of control would simply be overwhelming. Yet such an animal trained *to the maximum levels of obedience only* is ample home protection. It will hold trespassers at the door or window with sheer mass, generally biting only if it or the master is attacked or if the intruder lunges past it. A strong, fast thug can pick up even a shepherd and fling it against the wall, but not a 250-pound Saint Bernard.

There is a very small market for giant breed dogs. As a result, there has been little of the haphazard breeding that proliferates among Dobes and sheps, so you have a much better chance of getting a well-bred animal. For the person who can handle it, the giant breed dog may be the ideal compromise: massive intimidation, sufficient power to protect the master or mistress against any intruder, and the dog is practically "child proof." According to owners of Mastiffs and Danes, those breeds are ideal for the home. They very seldom knock anything over and because of their cumbersome bone structure, too much outdoor exercise is actually bad for them, so they adapt to the indoors with about an hour or two of outdoor exercise a day.

For temperament, especially toward children, I favor the Dane first, with the English Mastiff a close second.

Saint Bernards are somewhat more likely to get high-strung. If you live near a lake or river and have children, consider the giant Newfoundland, a gentle-tempered out-door dog with an outstanding reputation for rescuing children from the water.

My Dane has, for me, another significant advantage. It is easier to defend in court. I know that whenever my dog bites anyone, even a child molester who may have been attacking my daughter, he or his survivors are going to sue me. Remember, any time you're thinking about hurt-ing criminals you have to survive the incident first and court later.

In *voir dire* (the process of selecting jurors in a criminal or civil trial where the lawyers from each side cross-examine the prospective jurors to see how they feel about the issues involved in the case), the plaintiff's lawyers will make sure that no one into "big, vicious dogs" makes it onto the jury. I'll be lucky if I get two who even own cocker spaniels. If that lawyer is smart he'll want to bring the dog into court to scare the jury.

If I had a Doberman I'd be finished right there. To those who don't own them, Dobes connote storm troopers and outlaw bikers. Just *looking* at the Dobe scares a lot of people: Even at rest, it epitomizes the picture of a "vicious, killer dog." If they look at my dog, though, one word will flash through their minds: *Marmaduke*. The big, clumsy, creature of the comic strips that loves children, the dog whose cumbersome size is laughable instead of intimidating.

The man unfortunate enough to menace the house-hold protected by my Great Dane will see horror incarnate when the dog closes on him; the jury will see a big lovable clown of a pooch. Maybe you have to handle violence on the street *and* in the courtroom aftermath, to appreciate that.

I have, and I do.

17. IF YOU ARE ATTACKED BY A DOG

In some places, you may be more likely to be attacked by a dog than a human, though you're a lot less likely to die from it. According to the Disease Control Center in Atlanta, only about a dozen people a year die from dog attacks, and only two people a year die from rabies. Significantly, purebed dogs are far more likely to be involved in these attacks than mongrels; experts feel that's due to the purebred's high-strung nature.

You may find yourself in the position of having to destroy a dog that has bitten someone. Resist the urge to blow its brains out. *The doctors need the whole brain of the animal in question to test and determine if it was rabid.* If a dog were to bite my child I'd capture it alive if I could. ("Fat chance," you say? You're probably right.) If not, I'd kill it without putting a bullet *or* a rock near its brain, because I wouldn't want to put my child through the agony of having big needles inserted in his stomach, and the risk of succumbing to the rabies innoculation, if I didn't have to.

Should you ever face someone who threatens you with a snarling beast that is within easy chomping distance of you, remember up front that this person is threatening your life and limb with the equivalent of a deadly weapon. Eight-pound pugs don't count; we're talking about an animal the size and ferocity that a judge and twelve of your neighbors on jury duty would agree was sufficient to kill or maim you if commanded to do so.

If someone does set a dog on you, you are now facing

122

an unarmed man and a vicious dog. Logic insists that you deal first with the dog, since it presents the immediate danger to your life and limb. You can no longer harm the owner unless he personally tries to kill or maim you, by the same principle that courts have held, "Once a man has already thrown his knife at you, he no longer has the means to place you at jeopardy, and it is wrongful to shoot him."

You're even giving the other guy an avenue to skate in court, and maybe even to turn the tables on you. He'll point to you in your wheelchair and say, "Your Honor, this man threatened to shoot me. I was in fear of my life, and that's why I commanded my dog to protect me." He may even claim that your threatening gestures and words prompted the dog to react without his command. Besides which, you probably don't have a gun on you anyway.

Your best bet is to step back and get away from the animal, which will typically be on a leash. *Don't run;* most dogs will take that as a signal to pursue. If circumstances permit, say loudly, "Don't set that dog on me! I don't want any trouble with you!"

If someone is threatening to sic a dog on you, compliance with his wishes is the commonsense response, just as if he were menacing you with a shotgun. Cooperate now, and seek legal redress later. If the dog attacks you anyway, use the methods we're about to show you for general dog attacks, and use them quickly because the owner is likely to join in the fight.

If the dog is just mean-natured, it's probably because it was mistreated by a human being at some point in its life. At this moment, under attack, you have no time to sympathize, and it's altogether too late to think that kind words and gentleness are suddenly going to change this miserable creature's personality.

Yell at the beast sharply. Say *no,* a word used even by amateurs in dog training. Even if the animal doesn't recognize it, it's a sharp syllable that commands attention.

Speak firmly; that stuff about dogs being able to "smell fear" is *not* an old wives' tale.

Some suggest pointing your finger at it sternly, as its early masters might have done as punishment. That might work, or it might also cost you your finger. The dog may have been trained to bite the nearest part of a human aggressor, or it might just do it instinctively.

There are more effective gestures. Cock your fist as if you were going to swing it down over its nose and snap your foot out in a mock kick. Whether the animal was vicious before or after some human mistreatment, it has probably learned by now that getting hit or kicked by a human *hurts,* and it's likely to cringe back. One gesture I've seen work very effectively is to raise your arm as if you were about to hurl a stone. Your basic junkyard dog has probably hassled some humans before and probably been nailed by a thrown missle in response; if so, it'll back off suddenly rather than repeat the experience.

If the dog is getting serious about putting its teeth into you, feel no compunction about kicking its jaw out of the socket. A kick in the ribs will be extremely painful and possibly even fatal, so don't do it unless you really think you're about to get torn up. Besides, unless you've jumped sideways and the dog is running past you, a kick at its ribs will open your groin to its teeth. If the dog is coming at you, kick straight toward its face; that way if you miss, your leg will at least be up to protect your crotch.

If the dog grabs your leg and hangs on, shaking it off may not be the wisest thing to do; the action can (a) make the dog hold harder, or (b) produce a sawing effect that will greatly increase your laceration. It might be better to fight the instinct to kick it away and reach down (now that it's in a static position) and scratch its eyes.

Remember that any of these techniques work only with an animal that is of small to medium size, and has not been "hard trained" to guard or attack!

The day may come when you're attacked by an animal that was trained to do it right. Ten years ago I never would have written a book on how to defeat or destroy an attack-trained dog, because ten years ago only cops and Good Guys had them. Today, it's different. The attack-trained dog is a prestige possession among gang members, dope dealers, and others on the outlaw fringe.

If a feral dog attacks you while you're in the woods bird-watching, or maybe just walking past a junkyard, one thing that will disorient it completely is to pick it up. Without its paws on the ground it has no balance, no leverage, no power. Grab it tightly by the flesh on the sides of its neck under its jaws (*not* by the loose skin or fur!) and lift it as far off the ground as you can. Shake it hard to emphasize that you're in control, and yell *No!* as loudly and as gutturally as you can. Holding it that way keeps you clear of the creature's jaws. Then, throw it away from you as far and as hard as you can. If you really feel you're in danger, bashing its head against a hard surface makes sense, as long as you don't have to take more than one step to do it.

I know a lot of people who have successfully used that technique, turning a slavering mongrel (or, in two cases, untrained German shepherds) into whimpering critters that scuttled away with their tails between their legs. However, if you try that with a trained attack dog, or even an untrained but intelligent Doberman, you're quite likely to lose a hand. A Dobe will instinctively twist and find balance from your own hands in midair, and a trained attack dog will have been taught to do so as well.

Against an attack-trained canine, you can grab it on the side of the neck, *but you've got to get it exactly right the first time!* It needs hands-on training that I can't give you in a book. However, the next time you take your own pet to the veterinarian ask *him*: Vets are attacked by vicious, pain-crazed dogs all the time, and are the world's leading experts on how to control them. Your vet can show you the "neck hold" in a couple of minutes.

Once you have that hold on the dog, kick it in the scrotum and in the ribs, just as you would a man. If it's a hard-trained attack dog, though, it will be inured to pain. You might have to kill it outright. You can't put a big dog away with a "sleeper hold" the way you can a man; the carotid arteries are buried too deeply in heavy, protective muscle. (see Chapter 28) To strangle one, you have to crush the larynx or block off the windpipe. Trainers do the latter with choke collars, and vets and dogcatchers do it with specially made nooses. You're not going to be carrying either. If you try to pinch off the dog's trachea with your fingers, it's probably powerful enough to twist away. That means you need to deliver a powerful blow to the beast's Adam's apple. "Bear-paw" and extended knuckle karate strikes are usually recommended, but as we state elsewhere, most people don't usually execute them that well without extensive training. Instead, just punch the attacking dog in the throat, with your fist, as hard as you can.

Dogs instinctively go for your throat, your genitals, the nearmost part of you they can reach (usually an extended limb), or lastly, your eyes. Put your chin down to protect your throat, and put your weak arm out in front of you in the Basic Block Position (see Chapter 28), and you've got your best shot: Whether the dog goes for the extended hand *or* for your throat or scrotum, it'll wind up with the former, which is the most expendable. *Then do something immediately to neutralize the dog!*

Among experts, the most common advice is usually, "Move to one side and evade the dog's lunge." That's great if you've got terrific coordination and, like these experts, work out constantly with big, vicious dogs. Even if you can do it, the dog is going to come back at you, and you'd better have another plan to fall back on.

Remember, we're talking about desperate odds here: A fifty percent chance of unarmed survival against an attack-trained dog is an optimistic exaggeration. When a dog is going for your throat or your arm, its forelegs will be at your chest or midriff level. A dog's paw can very easily be bent inward and backward, popping the tendons and breaking the joint. The pain alone will often be enough to put an untrained dog out of the fight. Against a "hard" dog, if you can get clear of it and run, it'll have a harder time following you.

Running from an attack-minded dog is futile unless you have some form of sanctuary close by. The average man can sprint at 24 MPH, the average woman at 20 MPH. By contrast, even a clumsy-looking Great Dane can do over 35 MPH, and a Doberman can do over 40 MPH for short distances. Because of its body structure, the dog gains top speed much quicker than the human.

So, if you don't have a close sanctuary, running is out. For you, a lot of the "attack dog misunderstandings" are going to involve driving up to a friend's house unexpectedly and being set upon before your friend can call off his animal. Use common sense. If the person you're visiting is known to have dogs, let him know you're coming, and ask that the dog be suitably taken care of prior to your arrival. Failing that, when you pull into the yard, don't get out of the car if you hear barking or see a potentially dangerous animal. Roll up your windows and beep your horn instead.

If you must get out of the car, leave the windows all the way up, and the doors *closed but not locked*. Bears move almost as fast as dogs, sometimes faster because of their extremely powerful legs, and game wardens approaching "bear problem scenes" are taught to leave their car or truck doors slightly ajar. I found this out during my days as an outdoor writer when I accompanied a New Hampshire conservation officer to a scene where a family of black bears was terrorizing a cabin full of tourists. The bears were driven away with no bloodshed on either side.

Later the warden explained the rationale of the car doors:

When a bear moves, it covers ground quick. A bullet won't always stop it, but a car will if you're inside, at least long enough for us to get our issue three-fifty-seven Magnum revolver out of our holster and shoot it. If we have to run for the car, we don't want to fumble with a lock or door handle.

In a situation where you're getting out of a car and fear being attacked by a dog, I make one change in that bear formula and close the car door, without locking it. Bears don't climb into cars. Dogs *do* (so do people, and you'll want to hear the door's warning noise); running away from one slavering Rottweiler only to lock yourself in your car with another, is not exactly my idea of a clean escape.

You'll notice that all those experts—dog trainers, veterinarians, and martial artists who are into attack dogs— who say that their chances of survival against an attack dog's assault are only twenty-five percent, *are talking about situations when they're unarmed.* Man is the weapon-bearing mammal; this gave us our planetary dominance over those fanged creatures to begin with, and intelligent deployment of various weapons brings those odds somewhat back in man's favor.

Use anything that can serve as a club and smash that dog with it. Aim for the nose if the dog is a cur, for the jaw or the skull if it's a "serious" dog with a predictably high pain tolerance. To kill animals in a slaughterhouse, vets and professional animal-killers agree, you draw imaginary lines from the right ear to the left eye and from the left ear to the right eye. This forms an X in the center of the forehead. Some people tell you to strike there, but it won't always work. *Professionals say to go an inch or two above that line, and deliver the killing stroke there.*

This may not result in the death of an attack dog as many pet owners will be happy to learn. A friend of mine, a police chief in a rural community, had to serve an arrest warrant on a drug dealer known to keep a savage Doberman for protection. As he approached the suspect's farmhouse, the drug pusher made the dog attack him. My friend struck the dog once on the top of its head with a heavy Kel-Lite flashlight. The animal yelped and ran into the woods. A blow that should have killed it had been absorbed, presumably through a "roll-with-the-blow effect," into the massive neck muscles. Its owner, the chagrined dope pusher, surrendered without further ado.

If you don't have a clubbed flashlight or other blunt instrument at hand when a dog attacks you, improvise. You have no choice. Many dogs can be fended off—at least temporarily, as you sprint for cover—with that ghetto streetfighter's standby, the trash-can lid. It's not as fancy or as sturdy as a battle shield from King Arthur's era, but the shape, handle, and principle are the same, and the outer lips on its edge tend to catch a dog's teeth. Follow up with a slash that brings its edge down on the animal's face or neck; while it probably won't put it down, it may buy you time to backpedal and reach a door, the ideal "human cover" that dogs can't penetrate unless it's made of flimsy glass.

What do you do when you're up against a serious attack dog? Curs and junkyard dogs? You can kick them into submission or, if you have to, kick them to death. Little dogs? You can stomp them into the ground, one good reason why you should not depend on them to take care of *you*. You can even pick them up and throw them away, or scare them by remembering that you're the dominant species and that they're scared of humans who look like they want to hurt them.

But a "hard dog" is a whole different story. You're talking about a predatory mammal programmed to destroy the human it perceives as its quarry, a motivated and thinking death machine that is born and bred to kill you when you and it cross paths under the wrong circumstances. Even those of us who carry guns are a long way from a one hundred percent survival rate against a hard-trained killer canine. If a "hard" Dobe attacked one of *us*, we'd fire into its open mouth to blow up the brain pan or sever the spinal cord. And we'd keep shooting until that dog was *dead*.

18. YOU AND YOUR TELEPHONE

Although the telephone is considered a protective device, most people misunderstand it. Either they think the telephone will be their instant salvation, or they figure there won't be time to use it if a criminal breaks in.

The telephone is merely one more component in your total protection system. True, it can easily be neutralized by a criminal, but you can also make it do a lot more for you than you think.

Telephone lines are used in some types of alarm systems, but that's a matter for a separate chapter. Right now we're talking about picking up the receiver and getting help, or using the phone as a diversionary device to foil burglars hunting for a score.

BURGLARY PREVENTION

A standard ploy among burglars is to call your number to see if you're home. Twenty rings or so and they can be fairly sure you aren't just in the bathroom. In fact, some of them will even maintain the connection by leaving *their* phone off the hook; if yours is still ringing when they get there, they know you haven't come home in the interim.

Realizing this, a lot of people take their phone off the hook when they're going out. The phone company doesn't recommend this practice, on the grounds that criminals may catch on eventually. I disagree. So *what* if some of them catch on eventually? Others won't. Few bother to ask the operator to check and if they do, they'll find out that operators rarely break in on a line to check if someone's talking. That's partly because the phone company is extremely sensitive about privacy issues and, quite frankly, because it's also a pain in the neck for the operator.

Therefore, the burglar who is calling to check and see if you've left the phone off the hook is most likely to be told, "That line is out of order. We'll report it." He's back to square one: For all he knows, you're still at home.

Successful criminals tend to be good students of human nature. They know that most phones are left off the hook, not because the owner is out, but because the owner is *in*, and doesn't want to be disturbed. Maybe you're out, or maybe you're dozing in the bedroom a few feet from the shotgun in the closet and with your faithful Doberman asleep at your feet. Professional burglars don't stay in the business long enough to earn that title by taking such chances. Taking the phone off the hook doesn't cost you a nickel. If you can afford it, though, there are much better ways to make your phone fake out burglars.

On the new Bell systems there is an option known as call-forwarding. Ed Langsam, A.T.&T's manager of media relations, explains

If you're out of your home call-forwarding allows any incoming call to your number to automatically be sent to a relative or neighbor you have selected. When they answer the burglar will have no way of knowing that he hasn't reached someone in your home. If you have told the person receiving calls for you to say, "He or she can't come to the phone right now; can you leave a number?" It creates the illusion that you are home with other people present.

Langsam is right. He claims that there isn't even a telltale click of relays switching when the call is transferred. You can go a step further and have the call forwarded to wherever you're going to be, and come on the line yourself. A slick item, handy for busy people's everyday living, and worth the reasonable cost for the burglary deterrent value alone. Call-forwarding does not require the Touchamatic system (at this writing), and can be installed on your existing phone for $11.00 plus $2.90 per month service charge.

If you use an automatic answering device you can try creating a misleading message, but it won't always work. A friend of mine in the martial arts uses a recorded phone message that says ominously, "We are training right now, but if you leave your name and number . . ."

It's clever and will fool a lot of burglars, but a smart thief will simply cruise by the house and see if it looks like someone is working out in the basement. I'm not so sure that this system is any better than leaving your phone off the hook. I recommend a simple message to the effect, "I can't come to the phone right now."

AGAINST INTRUDERS

Very few burglars will actually cut your phone lines. For one thing, most of them don't know where your phone lines *are*. An exception is the country house, where the phone lines are quite apparent. If your remote home has been targeted for an invasion, the first thing your antagonists will do is sever your lines of communication.

But it is cold comfort that most burglars don't cut the wires. You see, any burglar who has been around for a while will make a beeline straight for the nearest telephone as soon as he's inside your home. Then he'll pick it up and listen to see if you're already calling the police. If he doesn't get that cue to run, he'll leave the phone off the hook which disables every other extension in the house, and if you do hear him downstairs, you'll be unable to call the police from the one at your bedside. If you don't believe this works, put this book down and try it right now.

I strongly recommend that you have a *separate line* installed for your bedroom telephone. Burglars know that relatively few people do this, and once they've popped the downstairs extension, they'll go merrily on their way burglarizing you, not realizing that police are already responding to the call you made from the separate line upstairs.

This is a good place to remind you that, while few officers rush to investigate a burglary after the fact—it may take them hours or even days to get around to it— they treat a *burglary in progress* as a life-threatening emergency. They know very well what that burglar is capable of doing to you, and they'll race to your aid as quickly as if he was strangling you, because for all they know, he *is*.

Cops also love to catch burglars. Because they get away so much of the time, cops take it as a personal insult, and it's the thrill of his week when he bags one red-handed. But never, *never* call the police and tell them something more serious is going on than what's really happening, just to get them there. It's a very transparent lie (one the insurance company's investigators might pounce on as evidence of your character when they come to assess your loss), and it brings with it graver problems.

Those of you who live in remote or secluded locations, or who have reason to fear a home invasion, might seriously consider buried telephone lines. Available in many locales, they aren't cheap, but they sure are cut-proof. Prepare to ask for a supervisor, because this seldom-requested option isn't widely known even within the phone company.*

---

*Prices vary. You provide your own trench, at a price dependent on the topography and the demands of your local ditchdigger's union. The maximum the phone company can charge for the inside hookup itself is $66.00, but the outside hookups vary so widely that Ma Bell will have to send over an engineer to give you an estimate.

Police have done studies indicating that it takes five to six minutes or more before the average citizen who has discovered a crime, reports it. This is largely because it takes them a few moments to orient themselves after the shock of discovering the aftermath of the crime.

You also have problems with people trying to make emergency phone calls while under stress. When the human organism feels threatened the first thing that goes is fine-motor coordination, that is, your fingers tremble and get clumsy. After an accident or anything mentally or emotionally shocking, you are very likely to misdial the phone.

Many people, when they hear an intruder downstairs, are afraid to dial their phone, fearing that the whirring noise as the dial spins back will alert the invaders. This syndrome gets worse in single-floor homes. If you stick with a dial phone, learn to dial it by feel so that you can make it work in total darkness; do the same with a streetcorner payphone where the inside light may no longer work. You should also practice easing the dial back into position after each number, instead of letting go of it, in order to mute that telltale sound.

Another good reason to be able to dial the phone by feel is that you might be holding an intruder at gunpoint, and if you take your eyes off him for an instant, he'll very likely jump you and turn your own weapon on you. We discuss that more in the armed defense segment of this book.

The TouchTone and other push-button designs can be operated fairly rapidly with three fingers; it just takes some practice. I can dial the police number, using three fingers by touch, in 2 to 2½ seconds, and stabbing all the numbers with a single, hunting and pecking finger takes only three or four seconds, while offering slightly greater accuracy. But since you'll probably be doing this in the dark, having developed "touch-dialing" skills will save you considerably more time, and reduce the likelihood of accidentally reaching the wrong number when you're trying to reach the police, and only have the time or the dime for the one call.

Langsam of A.T.&T. recommends the Touchamatic "S" phone, and I agree with him. He explains,

This phone has a green button and a red button, both self-illuminating so you can use them at night without turning on a light. The green is for the police department, the red for your fire department. Simply pressing the properly colored button connects you to the proper authorities, with the speed of electricity.

Touchamatic–"S" service costs $40.00 for the installation, and an additional $4.50 per month.

This is especially important to those of you who have poor eyesight. You can learn to touch-dial a push-button phone in as little as two seconds; a conventional dial will take you more like seven seconds even when most of the seven digits are low numbers with quicker dial return. The Touchamatic? A fraction of a second.

Seven to ten seconds spent dialing a phone is a lot of wasted time when you get into the compressed time frames of a dangerous situation involving predatory humans. Role-playing the part of a burglar in my own living room, if I were to hear a phone dial return in the master bedroom, I could be up the stairs, down the twenty-foot hallway, and through that bedroom door in seven seconds, and I'm not as fast as a young burglar.

If my wife were trying to make that call, she'd probably be stopped before it rang more than once at police headquarters. By the time the dispatcher picked up at the police end, she'd have a dead line: On our end, the phone would already have been ripped from the wall, and the cord would probably be around my wife's neck.

With a Touchamatic, there would have been no sound to begin with to trigger such a savage response: If she lifted the receiver gently, no sound would be made until she began to talk, and a soft whisper won't carry across rooms as will the harsher, mechanical sound of a telephone dial returning. Try it yourself.

Even if the intruder did hear her whisper, she wouldn't have started talking until she was already speaking to police dispatch. In those seven seconds he would hear her say, "I'm at Eighty Smith Road! A man has broken into my house! He's coming after me! It's Eighty Smith Road!"

Don't believe it? Give yourself seven seconds on your own watch and see if you can't get that much out. You'll have less time if you're in a one-story home and the guy is closer, but still time enough for your address and the alarming message.

Put yourself in the intruder's shoes. When he heard the conventional phone being dialed, he knew he had time to run upstairs, kick down the door, and silence whoever was calling the cops on him. Now with the Touchamatic or Touchamatic "S," before he reaches the bedroom door, he has overheard her summoning the police already. He knows they will arrive in minutes if not seconds. He has every reason *not* to harm her at this point, but to concentrate instead on a hasty flight from the house.

Few people have ever thought about what they would actually *say* if they called the police under stress. Use just the phrase we have outlined: Give the address twice, including the apartment number, and that someone has broken into your home, and that you're in immediate danger, and repeat the address. It's crucial that you do it this way. The person fielding your call at Dispatch Center is surrounded by an electronic babble of voices from scanners and multiple emergency channels. He or she may "catch" over a hundred calls a night.

Sad to say, most police dispatchers do not have the same training or undergo the same tough selection process as police officers. They can jot down a wrong address like anyone else, or get confused and interrupt, asking you for your name or some other such time-wasting irrelevance.

Get the address across first! If your voice gets drowned out, or if the intruder is faster than you thought and has already grabbed you, *the one thing you want the cops to have is the complete address.*

In that scenario, the dispatcher can say, "Car six, unknown disturbance at Eighty Smith Road, apartment number twelve, the phone call was interrupted, but it sounded as if it could be an emergency." That will bring you an extremely swift response. What good will it do if you say, "This is Mrs. Jones! There's a rapist here—arrgh"? They'll know that a criminal act is going on somewhere, but where? After they've run down a directory list of Joneses they might eventually get to you, but your body could be cold by then.

The second imperative is to quickly explain the nature and gravity of your problem. Although the investigation of a burglary perpetrated at an unknown previous time is low on the police officer's list of immediate priorities, nothing will bring him faster than knowing that someone is in danger. It makes all the difference: *Let the dispatcher know if an intruder is in your home!*

Then, repeat the address. They won't need your name until later, though you should give it if there's time. The address is what's important.

Among New York cops, the most chilling radio signal is the "10–13." It means simply, "Officer needs assistance," but they don't use it when one just has to borrow another's summons book. In the real-life streets of New York, "10–13" means that somewhere out there, a brother officer is fighting for his life.

The response is electrifying. The first backup car is often there within ten seconds, usually several within a minute, and in two minutes, you could see twenty cops there with drawn guns. This isn't just police elitism, and taking care of their own; they know that anyone dangerous enough to menace a cop is a threat to everyone.

The sad thing is that so often, the stricken officer cries, "Ten-thirteen, I've been shot." Before he can catch his breath to continue, the airwaves are choked off with urgent cries of, "What car is in trouble? What's his location?" The endangered officer's own desperate message is blocked out by the babble of those in such haste to assist him. The result is often tragic.

New York cops are now taught to broadcast a 10–13 just the way I told you to call the police—"Sixth Street and Arthur Avenue; shots fired, officer down, address, message, address repeated. Sixth Street and Arthur Avenue." There's no doubt where it's happening, nothing to slow down the rescuers. If it's good enough for New York cops, who participated in six thousand armed encounters with criminals from 1970 to 1980, it's a system that'll work for *you* when you call the police on *your* telephone.

In some parts of the country, calls from multi-state areas are fielded through operators in a single, centralized location. A hasty call with just the street address and city might not be enough. One phone company offical told us, "We had a call come in to a northern New England operator to send fire fighters to an address in Lee. They were dispatched to that address in Lee, Maine. Unfortunately, the fire was in Lee, New Hampshire." *Call your phone company today and find out how much of an address is "enough" to get emergency personnel to your home, with your phone system!*

There is some question as to whether you should call the police or the operator when criminal danger threatens. In most places, the operator won't answer as quickly as the police. Though he or she has been trained to handle emergencies, it happens to them rarely and they can get flustered; by contrast, the police dispatchers cope with a dozen emergencies a night, and they've learned to stay cool and efficient.

The 911 concept—dial those numbers and you get

quickly plugged in to a central, emergency dispatch center—
makes sense, but it's still not always the fastest. I've ridden
in cities where a call comes in to 911 downtown, is then
transmitted to the police district (which may encompass
several precincts), and finally has to be relayed into the
proper precinct, where it may have to be separately dispatched to the individual sector patrol car responsible for
the given neighborhood.

That's three relays to be made after your call comes
in, three time-consuming operations of equipment, three
conversations between police personnel, not to mention
three chances of the information getting garbled and the
address coming out wrong. Even if you have an effective
system that cuts this process to only a couple of relays or
even one, *you'd still be better off to memorize your precinct's
number and call there directly.* At such times seconds count.

There's another good reason to call the authorities
directly, instead of the operator. Nobody ever makes a
cold, calm emergency call in real life. When it actually
happens you'll be excited and breathless, perhaps stam-
mering, certainly not speaking nearly as distinctly as you
normally do. You may only have five or seven or ten
seconds to get your message across, and it may not be
clear. If it isn't, and if the address is lost, *you* may be lost as
well.

Operators don't tape-record incoming calls. Almost
all police dispatch centers *do,* and if you get cut off and
the message wasn't clear the first time, in just a matter of
seconds the dispatcher can rewind the tape, play your
message back a couple of times until it can be deciphered,
and send a patrol car to your aid.

It's my personal opinion that every adult should memorize the phone number of his local police, fire fighters,
and paramedics. It's amazing how few do, though. Next
time you're at an adult gathering, ask the group how
many know those vital numbers. Most of them will cop out
and say, "nine-eleven."

Local numbers, of course, only work if you're in trouble locally. When you're away from your own turf, 911 can be a godsend. If I'm going to be in a strange place for a length of time, the first thing I do is check a local phone booth or directory to see if they have 911. My own community doesn't, unfortunately, which is one reason why I rely so much on the memorized numbers.

Even if you're going to memorize only one number, make it the police department's. Need an ambulance? They can dispatch one from there, in most cases. Got a fire? If it's a little one, there's plenty of time for the operator to make the connection, and if it's a big one, you get out first and *then* call the smoke-eaters. If you're someplace where you aren't sure if they have 911, go with *O* for Operator, and try to speak calmly. Teach your smaller children to trust the operator in any emergency. Dialing *O* also makes sense if you have arthritis or get confused easily.

HANDLING HARASSING PHONE CALLS

The scope of the obscene phone call problem is so great that the phone companies sometimes seem reluctant to even discuss it. In Massachusetts alone, a typical year will see forty to fifty thousand complaints registered, and most people who get such calls don't even make complaints until the matter begins to get serious.

A.T.&T. has a firm policy on such calls. Ed Langsam explains,

We feel that the best thing you can do, if you receive an obscene or harassing phone call, is to get off the phone immediately. What the caller is really trying to do is get a response that involves you with him over the phone. We recommend that you do nothing which will fulfill these objectives of the caller. Instead, the victim should reduce the amount of contact. Don't threaten, argue, or discuss. Just get off the phone.

Most of the popular literature on this subject takes a different approach. They recommend blowing a whistle into the caller's ear and I've even heard stories where the female victim told the pervert, "Hey, I'd like to meet you so you can do all those things to me." The caller shows up for the *rendezvous* and is arrested by the police.

In real life it doesn't work that well. The old "make a date with the pervert and arrest him" routine may have gone on a few times, but most cops won't go for it. If it had been suggested to me during my police days I would have said, "Look, you made the date; *you* keep it with him." The moment the woman began to encourage the pervert she would have lost her "mantle of innocence" in the eyes of the law; it's entrapment and I know of few prosecutors who would take such a case to court and if a police officer were involved, he could wind up getting sued for false arrest.

If you are receiving harassing calls regularly, or such calls that make you fear for your safety, call the police. The phone company can set up "phone traps" that will enable the authorities to trace the call. The phone company won't discuss it, but they are said to have units that can lock in the trace within seconds after the call is initiated.

Given this limited amount of equipment, it's a safe assumption here in the real world that if threatening phone calls are coming into the Governor's Mansion, they'll be trapped tomorrow, and if they're coming into a lower-middle-class home from an estranged husband or anonymous pervert, they might not get trapped for quite some time.

Before they go to these lengths, the police will ask you to keep a log for a period of weeks, recording the time, date, and length of harassing calls. Also, the police will handle the arrest and the prosecution. "The phone company merely assists the police," says Langsam.

But waiting for weeks is waiting a long time. What the phone company will do depends on what they have available, and there is only a handful of equipment available to trap what some insiders believe is a flood of annoying calls. Langsam won't say what their chances are of tracing your tormentor, but will admit that "with some of our new, sophisticated equipment, we can do it with tremendous accuracy."

As a spokesman for the AT&T, Langsam is unable to say what percent of harassment call complaints end in conviction. However, according to another phone company executive who speaks off the record, only about 20 percent to 30 percent of the people who complain even go so far to ask for phone traps to be installed. Do you fight back or not? By one account, at least 70 percent don't go through the proper channels to do it.

These calls are more than just annoying. They can rob you of sleep even if it's just a "breather," and the real sickies can be absolutely terrifying.

One reason why the phone company insists that you shouldn't do anything but hang up is the possibility that if you blow your whistle in the guy's ear, he can sue you. When I asked him, Ed Langsam admitted that he couldn't think of a single case of that ever happening; he promised to research it and get back to me if he found one, and he never returned the call.

Intrigued, I talked with an electronics entrepreneur who among other interests runs a computer firm serving law offices. We ran it through his Westlaw terminal in September 1981, and came up blank: Nothing in the computer banks of the prestigious West Publishing Company reflected any such case ever having been adjudicated.

When I received a spate of obscene calls a few years ago I was incensed. Never mind blowing whistles in the ear of this man who was trying to terrorize my wife when

I was away from home, I wanted to do something that would blow his eardrum all over his blood-spattered receiver. But only the fictional Fu Manchu had the right tuning fork that, when held to a telephone mouthpiece, would turn the listener's brains to mush.

I have experimented with all manner of destructive sounds and let me tell you something that I learned under controlled experimental conditions: Blowing a whistle into the phone, let alone firing a blank starter's pistol at it, *will hurt you more than it will hurt the pervert on the other end.*

In a small enclosed room (and you aren't going to receive too many obscene calls at the payphone on the corner), any sharp sound you make will be virtually magnified. The sound your caller hears is automatically softened to ninety decibels and it takes him a tenth of a second to pull it away from his ear. *You,* however, get the full impact. It will literally backfire on you.

Besides which, Langsam is right about hanging up on obscene callers. It's a stupid idea to keep the ball rolling; talk to any psychologist and he'll probably agree with Langsam one hundred percent. Don't get the pervert involved with you; don't let him get a rise out of you; don't let him provoke any emotional response from you. Ignore him, like an insect. He'll find some other victim, unless he has a particular reason for wanting to torment *you.* If he does, his phone calls are the least of your concerns; harden the rest of your perimeter and even change your phone number.

The telephone is by no means a constant link to help, but with careful planning, it can do a lot more for you and your family than it's probably doing now.

Do have a separate telephone in your master bedroom, where intruders can't cut you off from help by flipping off the receiver of a downstairs extension phone.

Do consider buried phone lines if you live in a remote area, or if you have real reason to anticipate a home invasion and live in a suburb where the lines to your home are easily identified.

Do work out beforehand a quick, concise sentence to shout or whisper when requesting help, and remember—"address, nature, and danger of problem, address."

Do learn to operate your telephone swiftly and silently in the dark.

Do, at all times, carry coins of the proper denomination for payphones wherever you are for emergency calls. You are more likely to be assaulted outside your home, than to have the assailants invade your domicile. That means you'll probably be calling for help on payphones.

Finally, *do* recognize that a telephone is a lifeline: you have to have it within reach to work, but you must realize that it can be severed, and you must be able to swim to safety if you're in a situation where the lifeline won't reach.

19. HOW SAFE ARE SAFES?

The "fear boom" has enormously increased the private citizen's interest in home safes. A number are available, each with its own advantages and disadvantages.

Wall safes are, for the most part, better left to Agatha Christie novels than to real-life protection work today. Crooks watch old movies on TV, too, and they know enough to check behind portraits and mirrors and in the back of closets or behind loose wall paneling. Once they've found the safe, its contents are *theirs*. Street criminals may not be able to "crack" even the cheapest wall safe where it is, but it's no trick for a thief with even a two-digit IQ to smash the wall, pry the little thing loose with a crowbar, and take it with him to open at his leisure with a sledge-hammer or torch.

The next step up, if you want to call it that, is the small home safe. Some of them even roll on casters, for your convenience *and* the burglar's. To a determined criminal, these are about as theft-proof as a locked file drawer: If either can't be pried open where it is, the whole kit and kaboodle can be moved out to someplace where they can be opened in a more laid-back atmosphere, as the thieves tipple some wine, toke on their joints, and make fun of the clown who thought a wimpy little safe or locked file could mess up their plans.

A safe protects your valuables in three ways: by keeping them invisibly hidden, by presenting an impenetrably locked wall, and/or by being too big and heavy to move. You'll need at least two of those three factors if your safe is to be anything but an expensive joke.

You have to ask yourself first, "What am I going to *keep* in that safe, anyway? Insurance policies and other important papers that have to be flameproof in case of a fire, or expensive jewelry that must be secured from criminal hands?"

If you are dealing professionally in valuables such as coins, jewelry, collectible stamps, or watches, and must keep these in your home, you have a very legitimate reason for a top-quality safe.

But for most people, family jewels and coin collections, not to mention negotiable securities, contracts, and other vital papers, are better off in a bank safe-deposit box. With maybe a million dollar's worth of heavy-duty construction around them, armed guards, and a bank alarm system that probably cost more than your whole house, that's security you can't hope to duplicate. Episodes of criminals actually breaking into safe-deposit boxes are so rare as to be a national news item when they happen even once.

If you don't *have* to have your valuables with you every day, you should let the bank take over worrying about them. If you're going to a soiree and need $100,000 in diamond jewelry for the evening, it's no big deal to pick it up at the bank that afternoon (preferably with a discreet armed guard). The only inconvenience occurs on weekends; for that reason alone, you might want some sort of home safe.

You'd be better off to have some "fake" duplicate jewelry made. Anyone who tells you that they can spot a good-quality artificial gemstone today is either a liar or a senior employee at Tiffany's, and even the latter couldn't tell unless he examined your tiara under a loupe.

When I was in the jewelry business, I had a humongous Mosler safe sunk deep into the concrete flooring of the family jewelry store. I still believe that's the way to go even though it's a hassle to install, and if anything, more of a hassle to remove when you change locations. If you need to store $25,000 or more in jewels or guns or stamps or securities, you probably are living in your "dream home," and are therefore likely to be there for a long time. The installation of a permanent safe will not be a "biggie" for you, and anyone who can afford to buy your home in the next few years isn't going to worry a lot about repairing the broken-up cellar floor where you had your safe removed.

A new, heavy-duty safe costs a fortune. Your best bargain is to look in the classified ads of major newspapers for business auctions and liquidations. You can literally save thousands of dollars with a good used safe. After all, the only "bad" used safes are those that have been in fires or have already been cracked by thieves, and the latter are extremely rare.

Price ranges on new versus used safes are wildly erratic. Used ones run from $200 to $1,000 or more, usually because the business owners or auctioneers disposing of them aren't set up for the hassle of moving them, or maybe replacing their locks. A new safe by Mosler, 36½ inches high by 37 inches wide by 20 inches deep, would cost almost $3,700 if you wanted it truly burglar-resistant instead of merely fire-resistant. That means a full 1-inch thickness of steel in the body of the safe, 1½ inches in the door, and yes, you *will* pay extra to have that 2,288-pound monster delivered and installed.

With a little shopping around, it won't cost you a lot more to hire some heavy-duty movers (make certain that they're insured and bonded since a safe weighing the better part of a ton, if not more than a ton, may be more than the stairway to your basement can handle). Once there, have it sunk in concrete. A lot of people build "safe rooms" (and even fallout shelters) around big safes in a specially reinforced corner of their basement.

Naturally, you'll want to change the combination lock; indeed, you may *have* to, since by the time some liquidation sales are completed, no one is around who knows how to open the safe. *That* requires a bonded professional who will drill out the combo lock and then install a new one. People who have those skills and can be trusted, are few and far between. In fact, it would be a good idea *before* you shop for a used safe to contact the nearest police department or locksmith, and see if they can refer you to such a specialist. If the thing can't be made to work once you've paid to own and move it, you'll have a very expensive white elephant on your hands.

If you have a lot of bulky, expensive items around that you need frequent access to, the answer might be one of the security chests typified by the Treadlok. They are much more affordable than traditional safes, starting at slightly over $400 for Spartan small ones; big, deluxe ones are available for just under $1,000. Originally designed for use inside small dynamite magazines, these are heavy, tough steel chests with combination locks. They can be bolted to your floor or sunk into concrete. Camera buffs and gun collectors love them, and they have a pretty decent track record of thwarting burglars.

The major weakness of the Treadlok-style units is that they are often left freestanding, and some types are secured by padlocks that may or may not resist a seasoned burglar for long. If it isn't flush against a very hard wall, a burglar can just tip it back; then, if it is secured only by a padlock, he can pop it open with a pair of bolt cutters or with a slam-hammer. And if the criminal is sure he's going to get several thousand dollars' worth of valuables, it's worth it to him to hire a couple of colleagues to take that big chest out on a moving dolly, the way it came in. He would be *very* reluctant, however, to spend all day trying to dig it out of hardened cement.

Your steel vault should have the finest, laminated steel padlock with a case-hardened core and shackle (the latter protected by a hardened cover), fitted just barely above the cement floor so that you just about have to scuff your knuckles to get the key in. That setup defeats both slam-hammers and bolt cutters. Some units have combo dial locks that will resist a sledgehammer or drill for a while; and some have combo locks that will resist a sledgehammer for about one blow. You want an auxiliary padlock capability. You *don't* want to buy a $1,500-security chest that is held shut with a $7-padlock.

Treadlok and others make units designed to fit in your living room or playroom, camouflaged with seat cushions and wood paneling that make them look like built-in furniture. This is my personal choice, although I would further disguise it with a fake heating duct in a conspicuous place installed in just an hour, and locate it near a window.

That way, the thief won't think you have any valuables hidden in that piece of furniture. It looks, instead, like a heating outlet with padding on top to provide extra seating when you give parties, and is more likely to be overlooked. You can install a fake heating duct on your "Treadlok loveseat's" wooden veneer with an hour's labor.

Still, a patient professional burglar who knows what he's doing—and knows what he's going after—can get through a Treadlok. It's the same as with locks: You have to bet on how long he's willing to risk staying in that vulnerable position of being a "burglar who can be caught in the act at any moment."

A recent national magazine used as an example of good security sense, a retired grocer who had his business safe moved into his apartment. He (and the magazine, apparently), felt that he was totally protected by his 500-pound safe.

Wrong. Burglars can get that 500-pound safe out as easily as the grocer got it *in:* Two strong men and a dolly is all it takes. I know burglars who would plan on spending the better part of a morning moving out the furniture, stereos, carpets, maybe even deluxe paneling from homes they've targeted for a heavy hit. They come prepared, right down to the rented moving van and moving equipment. They're going to take about as long to get that particular safe out as it took Sears Roebuck to deliver and install the refrigerator in your kitchen.

Safes should be hidden deep, deep, deep, or constructed heavy, heavy, heavy, and should have the toughest door, lock, bolt, and hinge construction that you can afford. For most homes, concealment instead of bulk is the way to go when you select a safe for personal valuables.

For some years now, smart rich people have been using floor safes instead of wall safes. It is lesser known to street criminals, though by no means a secret from professional burglars. You have a lot more room to hide a flush-fitted safe in your floor than in your walls, while still having reasonable access to it yourself. It won't occur to 14-year-old delinquent burglars, nor to nervous 23-year-old drug addicts, to roll up every inch of your carpeting or rip up your tiles to find which could be the fake one, but that *will* occur to professionals.

The best precaution is to do something we've been doing throughout this book: Take cues from professional criminals as to what *they* use to protect *their* valuables. A cocaine dealer making an illicit $250,000 a year is a lot more prone to having his place torn apart by fellow underworld people ripping him off, *or* by a squad of narcotics officers armed with search warrants and dope-sniffing dogs. Do you doubt that these people are a little more ingenious than the guy at the hardware store when it comes to methods of protecting your valuables?

One such piece of equipment was actually developed by some of the more paranoid law-abiding citizens in Middle America. It's known by a number of trade names. I call it an earth tube.

From as little as 2″ X 12″ ($18.50) to as large as 6″ X 48″ ($89.95), these plastic pipelike earth tubes were originally marketed by "survivalists" for the purposes of "hiding your gold and your guns so that you can be part of the underground patriotic movement after the Communists take over America." The original reasoning may not be totally sound, but the engineering is, and so is the practical application.

Using a posthole digger on a dirt basement floor if you own your own home, or with a little ingenuity applied to the walls and woodwork and plumbing, you can find numerous places where you can hide your valuables where no one is going to find it without just about leveling the building to the ground, scooping up all the earth around the foundation ten feet deep, and then sifting it.

I get a little antsy about burying something outside my actual four walls, since then it becomes sort of a "finders-keepers" situation. Remember, you want your burglar to have to really work for what he takes from you—noisily, sweatily, tediously, and fruitlessly.

Remember too that the only reason why burglars *are*

burglars is that they like nice, easy, quick, quiet scores that fatten their pockets. Digging for an earth tube requires the equipment of a construction crew (and nearly the staff), coupled with the patience and selflessness of an archaeologist. Burglars are not into patience, selflessness, and sharing with partners when they don't absolutely have to, *or* working long and loud on a "score."

Earth tubes are cheap. Suppliers to write to for prices and catalogs include: Survival Sports, P.O. Box 18206, Irvine, CA 92713 and S. I. Equipment, Ltd., 17019 Kingsview Avenue, Carson, CA 90746.

Incidentally, another thing to learn from the hiding techniques in vogue among drug dealers is *not* to follow some of the old standard advice on burglarproofing. I've lost count of the number of books and articles where citizens are advised to keep their household cash and jewels in a fake mayonnaise jar in the back of the refrigerator. Most burglars are drug users; most burglars therefore make a point of scoring the household's "stash" of recreational marijuana or whatever; *and most of them know that the old mayo jar in the back of the fridge is the standard place to keep it.*

The earth tube is almost unknown to the law-abiding civilian populace (except for the survivalists), yet it is the cheapest—and probably also the safest and most cost-effective—of "safes." In fact, it's the one such piece of equipment that most burglars haven't caught onto yet: In the criminal world, only big-time drug dealers and gunrunners are using them right now.

If all you need is fireproofing for valuable papers, the cheapest way out may be a simple freezer. Even if you get an old broken-down one at a yard sale, the thing was designed for total insulation against heat; whether or not the freezer coils are still working, it will keep your precious papers about as incineration-proof as a moderately priced fire-safe. If there's a lock on it, you might even want to gamble on leaving some of your "hard valuables" in there, too, though you should only do so if you have nothing else to bet on.

For a lot of words now, you may have been wondering why we simply don't tell you what type of safe you should have. It could be done on a graded chart; the problem is, it would be meaningless.

Obviously, a wealthy man who stores his diamonds and Krugerrands at home should have the biggest and strongest safe available. Yet, such a rich man is more likely to be targeted by high-precision, professional thieves who have the technology to defeat his high-precision, professional safe. If necessary, they'll come with "burning bars," the superpower cutting torches that require multiple fuel and oxygen-mix tanks to get through such an obstacle. These are the "weapons of choice" for the handful of superprofessional burglars who hit banks. Burning bars will make short work of any safe this side of the vaults designed for banks . . . and, given time, the bar has been known to make *long* work of even *those*.

Even a tinny little safe, so long as it weighs at least a few hundred pounds and is bolted to the floor, will stymie teenage delinquents and burglars who come in for a quick score.

Indeed, you can even make use of a totally unworkable safe. If you can find a fire-damaged one at a salvage auction that someone will let go for $25 or so, and you and some buddies have a truck and the moving gear to take it home, you might just want to do so.

No, it wouldn't be cost-effective to try to restore the thing. Just sand the outside and paint it to look like new, put it someplace conspicuous, and leave it empty or filled with valueless dead weight. It'll drive the burglars nuts. If you have silent alarms, this decoy safe might just keep them there, greed flashing in their eyes as they try to figure out how to crack it open or get it out, long enough for the police or security guards to respond to the silent alert.

This sounds farfetched to people who have not been burgled. To those who *have* come face-to-face with losses of $25,000 to $100,000+ in burglaries, it's just one more practical obstacle to distract a burglar, cost him time, and make him stumble in his plan to rip them off again.

Some years ago, as a reporter for a professional police journal, I did a story on how some Indiana State Police (I.S.P.) detectives wrapped up a major burglary, and put its perpetrators out of business for good. They had received a tip that a gang of professional burglars was going to hit the home of a wealthy man who made a point of ostentatiously displaying his priceless gun and coin collections in his sumptuous home. (Would you believe antique rifles lining the walls of his living room, visible from the street through the picture window, and precious coins .embedded in Lucite on his toilet seats?)

A point man who had done some handywork around the house learned that the family was going on vacation soon, and sold the info to the burglary gang. The I.S.P. got wind of the same info, including the fact that the hit was already scheduled. When they talked to the homeowner and requested his cooperation in a stakeout, the man was so incensed that he offered to wire his quarter-million-dollar house with strategically placed dynamite.

As it turned out, the officers persuaded him to go on his scheduled vacation, leaving heavily armed police officers instead of explosives. When they sprung the trap, the three burglars came up shooting. Two were killed by return fire, and the third gravely wounded. No officers were injured. The homeowner was not displeased.

A multimillionnaire friend of mine has a big Mosler safe, *within* a massive vault under his Colonial home. My friend, not having much faith in the future of paper money, has gold and silver ingots lining his shelves. He also has lead ingots lining his shelves, molded and painted to exactly duplicate the gold ones, so that few people can visually tell the difference. "Why?" I asked him.

"Simple," he snarled. "I know that real professionals could get in here and rip me off, if they really want to. They'll leave here with *all* of this, and if I'm not mistaken, they'll fence it quickly instead of trying to melt it down themselves. I've discussed this business with a lot of cops, and the guys who steal this stuff all have buyers. They'll sell it as is to *somebody*."

I asked him, "So? . . ."

"So," he replied, "a fence, or anybody else who buys gold ingots from private parties instead of through brokers, will do an immediate test and find out that they're being sold lead instead of gold. Fences aren't like cops. People who deal in stolen merchandise can get very ugly with people who try to sell them fake gold. You know what that means?"

"What?" I asked.

"It means," he said, "that the lead ingots buy me some remote control justice. The fences will murder the bastards who stole from me!"

Very few of us would go as far as my friend, but very few of us have as much to protect. The point is, if you *do* have a lot to protect, the "decoy concept" can work for you. I would recommend that you do it with a fake safe and keep them from stealing anything.

The thing you have to remember with any concept of a "safe" is that you have to assume the worst and buy something imposing enough and/or well hidden enough to escape the most skillful of criminals. After all, most people willing to invest in safes already have put considerable money into locks and alarms to protect their possessions. By definition, then, the safe is a "third circle of defense" against hardened criminals who have already penetrated your locks and your alarms, and perhaps also neutralized your defensive dog.

Analyze your needs and make your choice. If you feel you really need a safe or a Treadlok cabinet, either sink it in concrete or bolt it to the floor. The bolt holes can be filled with plastic wood when you move out, but I'll tell you something: Leaving your Treadlok right there can often more than pay for itself in an increased selling price to the new owners of your home. If you manage it properly, you can use the proceeds to buy the newest model Treadlok and have money left over. This is because it is readily apparent to anyone that if you cared that much about your belongings, you're the sort of person who took terrific care of *everything* you owned, including your home. Translation: quick sale at *your* price. Security features hold their value in more ways than one.

No one component of the home security system means total protection unto itself, and that includes valuables hidden in *any* sort of safe. I personally believe that the more of your valuables that are socked away in safe-deposit boxes, the better, both for protection and for cost-effectiveness. Yet I can understand why many people feel they must keep their valuables immediately accessible to them and to them alone.

20. THE TRUTH ABOUT CARS

Most of the contemporary advice on self-protection that has to do with cars implies that they are either traps or sanctuaries. If you know how things work on the street, you'll realize that they're neither. You're always instructed to check the backseat because attackers will lurk there and pounce on you when you're all alone and helpless in that steel cocoon. You're told, if your car stalls, to keep your windows rolled up and lower them only a crack if someone offers to help, and above all, *never* get out of the car for a male stranger if you're a woman. OK, I'll admit, *that's* good advice.

But when someone threatens your life, your car is two things: It is an escape and it is a weapon. It can get you away from danger fast and if worse comes to worse, it's a multithousand-pound guided bludgeon that strikes with an impact force that makes a Magnum bullet seem like a hiccup. The .357 slug delivers about 350 foot-pounds of energy. A 4,000-pound car at 30 miles an hour delivers 120,000 foot-pounds of energy, and almost half a million foot-pounds of energy at 60 miles an hour.

Let's look first at what kind of car you should be driving. You probably don't have $80,000 to convert your already-purchased $60,000 Mercedes 450 SEL into an "executive protection car." I've been inside facilities where such vehicles are modified for sheikhs, Dallas oil execs, and government-funded diplomats.

Now you are talking about a vehicle that can take practically any explosive and drive away at 80 miles an hour; a vehicle that will absorb a machine gun full of NATO ball ammunition, broadside, whether it hits the doors *or* the windows; a vehicle in which, after the VIP in the backseat has triggered the fail-safe lever, the bodyguards can actuate hidden ports that will open and spew out clouds of choking gas, in case the limousine is surrounded by street rioters; or if a car rams from behind, another panic button can trigger a charge of high explosives that will be directed straight backward, blowing the entire front end off the "chase car" while your car is sufficiently intact to drive through a steel roadblock and send a blockading pickup truck end over end.

If you can afford a car like that, you can afford bodyguards. Give them this book and save yourself the time reading it, or better yet, sign them up for my Executive Protection course.

Back here in real life, we're talking about the car you

drive to work every day. We're talking about someone attacking you in a parking lot, or trying to force you off the road. A large number of people have been killed and maimed when they became unwitting participants in that sort of game.

Women in particular are vulnerable to being victimized when driving alone. This chapter is directed primarily toward them. What works for them is also highly functional for males in similar situations.

First, consider your automobile. I realize you have more immediate concerns than self-defense when you choose your personal car, but you should still understand that the bigger and more rugged your vehicle, the safer you're going to be. A larger, heavier car is better for resisting or countering a ramming attempt, while the smaller vehicle has an edge in evasive tactics because of its superior maneuverability. Since a ramming or force-over attempt may come without warning—evasive action capability is meaningless if you don't have time to make use of it—the larger car is probably "safer," given the choice. Just as muggers don't go after professional wrestlers, rapists in VW Rabbits don't try to force International Travelalls off the road. That's because they realize up front that if push comes to shove, they're going to get creamed.

Just as an aside, you're vastly more likely to be killed in a car crash than in a criminal act, and you should consider that, too, when you talk about self-protection. The bigger and heavier your car, the less likely you are to be seriously hurt or killed in a collision. Good gas mileage from a subcompact is great, but after two totals in which I would have been dead if I were driving a mini-car, I find it very cost-effective to amortize my big Pontiac vis-à-vis being alive and supporting my family for another ten years.

It's most unlikely that you'll ever be caught up in a riot, like the race riot that cost a few people their lives in Miami in 1980. If that were to happen though, you want a car that's hard to pick up and turn over, and a car that nobody's going to want to stand in front of when you lay on the horn, put the pedal to the floor, and try to drive clear. Whatever size car you have, let's look at some accessories that you might or might not want to order.

Air conditioning. You should have air conditioning so that you won't be leaving your windows open. It's only an extra mile or two per gallon in its power consumption, and then only when you're driving under 40 or so miles an hour. Faster than that, and the superior aerodynamics of a car with closed windows actually save you money on gas mileage. *What's more important is that you won't be leaving the windows rolled down where purse snatchers, muggers, and rapists can pounce you at stoplights.*

Power versus roller windows. Some self-defense experts recommend power windows as a defense for women who get grabbed while their car is stopped. In real life, people who can afford power windows can also afford air conditioning, and don't need to leave their windows open in the first place.

If somebody reaches in for you, you want to discourage them quickly. You want to catch their arm in that window, very quickly and *very* hard. If this is not a sufficient deterrent, give panic its reign and start driving toward the nearest police station. Once the dragged rapist starts screaming, it's an indication that he probably won't try to rape you if you lower the window enough so that he can fall to the asphalt behind you while you continue on *without* slowing down. I did an impromptu test at my Pontiac dealership using my new Grand Prix and one of theirs. Mine had roller windows, theirs power windows.

We found that if the window was all the way open, the person with power windows could close it tightly in 2.3 to 2.7 seconds. With the conventional roll-up window, that took 1.0-1.2 seconds respectively.

Since there was considerable and valid concern that toddlers could get choked to death in power windows when they were first introduced, the power needed to operate these windows was reduced by the automakers. Power windows now, as a rule, close with considerably less power.

Remember however, that when you look at your car as your sanctuary, it may be in a moment when you're stranded somewhere in harm's way. *If the motor isn't running, the power windows won't work.* If your car dies with the windows down, you haven't got much of a sanctuary. If it dies with the windows up, then you may have to open your car door to talk with the stranger who could be your rapist or your rescuer. Once you crack that door open, you're going to find out very quickly which he is, and there won't be much you can do to shut him out if he's the wrong guy. As you may have gathered by now, I prefer roller windows for safety.

Automatic locks. Definitely. They're an absolute must, and all on present-day cars have manual overrides in case the power goes out, so that you can escape if your car goes into the river or rolls over and burns. Human nature being what it is, we don't keep our windows up and our doors locked all the time. It makes sense for the woman who's driving to be able to touch one button and lock all four doors instantly.

Your car should have rearview mirrors on both sides, *both movable from the driver's seat* so that you can always see behind you at various angles. If it's dark, a touch of your brake pedal will give you some reddish light for seeing behind you; if that's not enough, *keep your foot on the brake* and ease the gearshift into REVERSE. The bright whiteness of your backup lights will illuminate a lurking attacker. (If he's wearing a nylon stocking over his head and holding a pistol, you have the option of stepping on the accelerator.)

For some time now, major automakers have placed the hood release locks inside the passenger compartment. It used to be that any street criminal could walk up to a woman whose car broke down, flip open her hood from the front, and disorient her long enough so that he could drag her out.

One of my female students, driving such a car, was forced to hurt one of her three would-be rapists; she ran over him instead of sitting there like his last victim and thinking, "Oh, gosh, I can't drive away because I can't see where I'm going." The attacker's first victim was viciously slashed. His second intended victim, my student, put a car fender through his pelvis. She's *nobody's* victim.

What the three would-be rapists did was hide their car on a country hilltop where there was little traffic so that they could scan the area with their binoculars in order to spot a lone female motorist. By the time she reached their hilltop, there was a motorcycle down on the road with a man sprawled next to it and another waving his arms for help. When the woman stopped, the first would jump forward and flip her hood up as his "injured" partner leaped back to life. Their accomplices would simultaneously spring from cover and rip the car door open and grab her.

Even though my student knew of the first attack, she stopped anyway. But when she saw the "injured" partner jump up, and the other fling up her hood, she knew she was in trouble. Three of her doors were locked, and as she hastily locked the fourth, she looked in her rearview mirror and saw a third man—naked—approaching from the rear. She slammed the car into REVERSE and floored the accelerator. The naked rapist was flung into a ditch by the impact. My student stopped after she had traveled fifty yards in reverse. Then she got out, slammed down her hood, locked herself in the car, and threw the transmission into DRIVE/LOW.

She went straight for the first two. They stood there numb, still bewildered by the fact that their broken friend was now lying in the ditch. The headlights and roaring engine loomed closer upon them. At the last moment they scrambled into the ditch themselves as their intended victim's Dodge roared over the place they had been standing.

It is standard advice to lock yourself in your car if you're stranded alone. Do not, however, presume that you are ensconced in a Sherman tank. A man with a rock or heavy boots can kick out your windows in a matter of seconds. If he opens the door before he grabs you, you may be lucky. Ever see anyone who was dragged through a broken car window?

By all means, stay in the car. Opening the hood is a universal signal of distress, but it also blocks your view. Instead, flash your lights and wave to attract help.

The CB radio is extremely useful in such moments. It's more likely that you'll get a helpful trucker on Channel 19, which has more traffic and is more widely monitored than Channel 9, the emergency channel police officers and service stations keep tuned to. True, there is a chance that cruising criminals might hear your message for help and come to rip you off first. It has happened, but rarely. Most criminals know that someone else may have monitored your call, and they don't care to be found attacking a woman by a couple of burly truckers with monkey wrenches. The greatest fear among street people is "street justice."

Once you're there in your dead car, alone in the boondocks at midnight, you'll find the presence of defensive weaponry most comforting. Unlimber your dashboard fire extinguisher and have it next to you on the seat, ready to use. Naturally, your doors will be locked and the windows just cracked for ventilation. Also on hand should be your police-style flashlight; it's not a good idea to waste the batteries reading the newspaper in the backseat. On a cold night, keep the light under your coat for body heat so that the chill won't weaken the batteries.

Never use Mace-type sprays in a car! As you spray it at an attacker, some of it is liable to stay inside your car. *He's* out in the fresh air, and *you're* trapped inside, blind and choking. Two useful devices to have with you in the car, however, are a can of touch-up spray paint and a small fire extinguisher. Apart from their obvious uses, both have been employed successfully as self-defense weapons.

Sprayed in the eyes, the paint can disorient an attacker and does a fine job of marking him for the police. Depending on the paint formula, the eyes might not be seriously irritated or even damaged. Probably a good deal less reliable than Mace, the spray paint at least won't dose *you* in close quarters, and requires no license. Make sure it matches your car so that you would have a good reason for having something in your possession that you wound up using as a weapon.

Carbon dioxide fire extinguishers cause temporary blindness and disorientation, not because of anything caustic in the formula, but simply by the force and volume of the spray in the attacker's face. The key with this *or* the paint is tactics: Once the suspect is disoriented, *run*, because the disabling effect is only temporary. On one talk show I did a caller told of his experience with a fire extinguisher: Attacked by a much larger man, he sprayed him in the face and knocked him down. Not knowing what else to do, he stood there spraying him until the extinguisher was empty. At that point, the attacker rose and beat him savagely.

If you have an unloaded and/or disassembled firearm in your trunk, you might think about putting it together and either loading it, or putting the ammo next to it. It may be against the law, but if you have reason to expect danger consider your own sense of priorities. Many police officers will be very understanding under the circumstances, so long as the gun is not in a position where it would be threatening to them when they approach your car.

If circumstances are such that you want a firearm at hand, don't have it in obvious view, or in the glove compartment with your license and registration. A police officer who does stop to help, and routinely checks you out, could get the wrong impression. During my police days, I came within about a second of killing a trucker when, as I approached in uniform, picked up a .30/.30 rifle. It turned out that he kept it to protect himself from hijackers. He had stopped for a nap, and seeing me get out of my patrol car (I had stopped to see if he was OK), he was afraid I might see the illegally loaded gun and arrest him. As he fumbled to get it under the seat, I spotted it, and drew and aimed my .45 service automatic. He had the presence of mind to drop the rifle with great alacrity.

Avoid such potentially tragic misunderstandings with common sense. If you're stranded on the road you're far more likely to eventually have a police officer come up to your car than the Hillside Strangler. So long as the gun is where you can reach it and you stay alert, you'll normally have plenty of time to get at it if you're faced with a serious robbery or rape attempt.

The automobile, then, is not an inviolable sanctuary. Being inside it merely buys you time to grab a defensive weapon and surprise your attacker with a counterassault.

It is not uncommon for rapists and other criminals to force the innocent off the road to get at them. Some will even fake a fender-bender collision with you and grab you when you get out of the car to exchange information. In Illinois in 1973, the infamous "I–57 Murders" were perpetrated just this way. A group of young street criminals, motivated by racial hatred, faked accidents with three people, assaulting and murdering them all with a shotgun. One woman died from a shotgun blast with the gun muzzle inside her vagina.

Every year there are sporadic cases of psychotic snipers who fire randomly at passing cars. The isolated, anonymous highway is also a favorite ambush ground for those who have real or imagined grievances against you. Alex Keritsas staged the infamous Indianapolis hostage siege because he felt he had been cheated on a financial deal: a young man in the South had his penis cut off by his girlfriend's husband and brother-in-law. Are you *sure* there's nobody out there who thinks they have a reason to hurt you?

Even if you're a randomly selected victim who offended a psycho only by being in the wrong place at the wrong time, you want to be able to drive out of a highway ambush, whether you're being attacked with bullets or with a couple of tons of hurtling automotive steel. The first rule is, *don't stand and fight.* Even police officers are taught that if they're ambushed by gunfire, they should first attempt to drive out of the "kill zone." Sure, the cop and his partner have pistols and maybe a shotgun and enough ammunition to annihilate a Soviet infantry patrol, but they also know that the ambusher is probably behind cover, someplace where he can see them but where they can't see him. Fighting against odds like that is suicidal.

If any psychopath ever opens fire on your car, react like a police officer: Hit the gas pedal and *move.* Drive in a zigzag motion if the shots are coming from behind or in front of you; when fired on from the side, about the only evasive action you can take is a speedy straight run out of range. Get down as low as possible on the seat, for maximum protection by the engine up front, the doors on the sides, and the sheet metal and upholstery behind you. Look up through the windshield and use the tree line and buildings to orient yourself as you drive from this dangerous position. Cut a corner and get behind a tall building as soon as you can, if you can.

What if someone is trying to force you off the road? First, be sure that it's a genuine assault attempt, and not a drunk driver or a short-tempered motorist who thinks you're driving too slowly or blocking his passing lane. Slow down, pull to the side, and give the other car a chance to pass. Watch the other car through your rearview mirrors carefully, and pay particular attention to the facial expressions of the occupants. Be wary of flying bottles or rocks as the car passes you.

There are a lot of drunks and street criminals out

there who just get off on harassing motorists. Harassment, you can handle, until it puts you and the innocent passengers in your car in deadly danger. *Don't* escalate a situation by yelling back at someone who screams obscenities at you.

Let's assume that you're in serious danger. If somebody is going to be driven off the road, decide now that it isn't going to be *you*. No one is ever going to know how many fatal one-car crashes have occurred because a terrified driver lost control while trying to escape a criminal in another car.

If your pursuer has a big, bulky vehicle and you've got a little, nimble one, evasion is the strategy that will work for you. Accelerate, and when you come to a turn, take it quickly without warning or turn signals, as fast as you can do it without losing control. The guy behind you will take at least a fifth of a second to react, probably more like half a second to a second before he starts turning his steering wheel to follow. At 55 miles an hour he'll cover 16 feet in that fifth of a second, 40½ feet before that half second, and there's a good chance he'll either overshoot the turn or lose control trying to follow you.

Pickups and vans are highly prone to rolling over when the driver attempts a sudden, sharp turn at any kind of speed—something to remember if *you* drive one. A passenger car with a low center of gravity is almost rollover-proof. When I went through the Emergency/Pursuit course at the Illinois State Police Academy, instructor Dan Mascaro had me spin the wheel as hard as I could at 35 miles an hour to kill my fear that the car would roll over if turned rapidly; every police student is taught this. The Pontiac sedans we used suffered traumatized suspensions but never rolled. The rollovers you see on TV and in the movies during that sort of maneuver are staged by stunt technicians who place ramps at strategic points in order to flip the cars. Your low-slung passenger car won't roll in a hard turn unless the wheel "trips" on a curbing or something else that duplicates that Hollywood stuntman's ramp. A high-bodied pickup or van, however, *will* turn over very easily during such a panic maneuver.

Whenever you take evasive action on the highway remember your responsibility to all the other innocent motorists on the road. This is why, in recent years, police are no longer engaging in high-speed pursuits: Too many family cars full of children were getting in the way of the people who were playing cops and robbers and dying grotesquely in the inevitable head-on collisions.

Few of you have the thousands of dollars it takes to go to a driving course like Tony Scotti's in Massachusetts, or Bob Bondurant's in California, where chauffeurs of executives are taught how to take evasive action during kidnap attempts. I've had considerable training in this discipline—the Liberty Mutual Insurance Company's advanced course developed for the Massachusetts State Police, the New Hampshire State Police "chase course" run on the famous Bryar Motorsports road race track, the Illinois State Police course, and the Indiana State Police pursuit program—plus time with other professionals ranging from the NYPD's Tactics unit to the U.S. Secret Service Executive Protection Service, which trains the President's chauffeurs in some nasty car-killing techniques developed by the CIA and test proven on mountain roads in certain Third World nations.

With that training I can tell you up front that *nobody* can teach you that stuff any way but hands-on. It's expensive since it destroys the cars: Tires go fast, then power steering systems, then suspensions, not to mention the attrition in autobodies that "kiss the wall" of the racetrack when students panic. Without pretending to teach you how to do it (Bantam Books and I have no intention of being civilly liable if you try this stuff on your own and get killed), let's give you an idea of some of the techniques you *could* learn from master instructors that would enable you to escape the most determined criminal trying to drive you off the road.

The J-turn. You brake to the fastest possible stop, turn your wheel all the way left, and kick into REVERSE with your accelerator to the floor. As your car's rear end whips into the other lane, you put the lever into DRIVE without taking your foot off the accelerator (let AAMCO worry about what it does to the transmission) and in about two seconds you're heading in the opposite direction while the person who was trying to force you off the road is still wondering where you went.

The bootlegger turn. You're driving 35 miles an hour and suddenly up ahead looms a pickup truck that's blocking the road, behind which stand your wife's psycho ex-husband and a couple of his buddies with sawed off shotguns.

You want to be going the other way as quickly and as promptly as possible. OK: You turn the wheel very slightly to the left and swiftly hit the EMERGENCY brake. You use that instead of the conventional brakes because it locks up the front wheels only, allowing the rear end to fishtail around, an unnatural and dangerous but extremely effective way of pointing your car in the opposite direction (no telltale brakelights for pursuers, either. The bootleggers who developed this technique in the 1920s didn't put as much value on their lives as you do yours).

Before you're turned 180° around, you release the EMERGENCY brake. This instantly gives you back your rolling traction, a principle we'll explain shortly. You now countersteer (turn the wheel in the direction you want to be going), and hold your accelerator to the floor if it isn't there already. You'll burn enough rubber to make you gag, but if you've practiced with a good instructor, you'll be speeding away from the danger before your surprised antagonists have time to wince at the piercing squeal of your tires.

To carry this off you'll have to alter your emergency brakes. It works well only with pedal-type brakes that are released with a pull-lever under the dashboard; you *could* do it with the sticklever emergency brake control used on some compact cars, but you'd really rather have both hands on the wheel to handle the very tricky timing. If you have a pedal-type emergency brake, you *must* block the release handle into a permanently released position. That way, as soon as you take your foot off the emergency brake pedal, the system disengages and you have rolling traction again without having to take your two vitally needed hands off the steering wheel.

I use a simple clothespin; it holds the handbrake release in a permanently released position. If I want to engage the EMERGENCY brake for routine parking, I simply snap the clothespin off and put it on my sunvisor or on the key in my ignition. In fact, I do the latter anyway when I put my headlights on at dawn or dusk, so that I won't forget to shut them off and find my car with a dead battery at a moment when I may sorely need live transportation. It's no trick to put it back on the handbrake by feel if I need it, which is much less likely to happen than forgetting to shut my headlights off, anyway.

The 180. This is a technique developed by the master drivers at the General Motors Proving Grounds in Detroit and is slowly becoming standard among cops and others who have to drive emergency vehicles at dangerous speeds in the interest of protecting lives.

What the 180 does is give you an instant lane-change without having to really think about it. Once you've found an advanced driving school that can teach it to you hands-on, there's one chance in a thousand that you'll ever have to use it to escape a criminal, but it's more likely that at some point in your life you'll use the technique to escape a collision with a car or pedestrian.

The 180 is a 180° turn of the steering wheel (*not* the car). You start with your hands at 9 o'clock and at 3 o'clock on the steering wheel, instead of the "10- and 2-o'clock-" position most driving schools teach. To execute the 180, you simply turn both hands until your elbows slap each other. Once you've cleared the obstacle, you then repeat the 180 in the opposite direction so that you don't go flying off the road, and then you return to your 9- and 3-o'clock-position and stay straight.

To appreciate it, you have to learn it as I did, driving through "serpentine maneuvers" between plastic pylons a short distance apart at 25 miles an hour. That is literally impossible with conventional wheel-spinning techniques. With the 180, it can be done. Use this technique only at speeds between 20 and 35 miles an hour; try it at greater speeds and you'll skid across the median strip, and if you try it at slower speeds, you won't move the car's nose enough to evade close danger.

Let's talk now about something you're unlikely to have to do: ramming another car off the road to keep it from doing the same unto you. If a rapist in a big vehicle has chosen you for his target, or if you're an executive with Coca-Cola in a South American country and your number has just come up on the local terrorist group's list, the topography of the roadways may not be such that you can evade this danger with a quick turnoff or a bootlegger spin. All you've probably learned about running cars off the road was what you saw on TV and in the movies. The stuff is faked and choreographed, and nothing like real life. We've already told you about the ramps the stunt directors use to make cars flip over. Well, you can also forget about rammed cars veering gently off sideways from you (once the other car changes direction, your speed carries you past, and it looks as if the offending automobile was just sucked backward away from you) or little cars knocking big cars off the road; it can happen, but in real life it happens at about the same frequency that Woody Allen would win arm-wrestling contests with Arnold Schwarzenegger. Catch the big guy completely off balance and you can do it, but the odds are horribly against it.

On the highway, wait until the opposition is off

balance; then strike hard to throw him completely out of the way. Then you run and leave him behind.

To force you off the road, the rapist has several things *he* can do, and you can counter all of them and turn the tables.

Most attackers will try to drive ahead of you and push you sideways with their car nose ahead of yours. They may have mechanical leverage, but the CIA and the Secret Service have come up with an interesting counter for this that supposedly was proven in South America: You unexpectedly turn left and ram the attack car just behind the front right wheel with the left edge of your front bumper. This jams twisted sheet steel against the tire, causing an unexpected (and, for the rapist, uncontrollable) braking action; in an instant he'll be behind you and unable to turn his wheels. Just remember to hold your own wheel tightly, because if he's coming at you at the moment of impact, your car is going to have to hang tightly (perhaps accelerating) to shrug his car off.

I never had to do it on the police job, but I learned in training that if I had to take a fugitive vehicle off the road, driving up next to it was *crazy*. As soon as the nose of the chase car gets about a third of the way up alongside the fleeing car, the driver of the fleeing car has only to turn lightly and quickly left to slam the chase car into the trees. If I were chasing a car I wanted to run off the road I'd ram it from behind, *from a sharp angle to one side or the other, on the side of the rear bumper instead of center to center.*

The most effective technique for bringing a car to a sudden stop is "bulldogging" (getting in front of it and keeping yourself in front of it, slowing down all the while, until you come to a stop in a tight space where it can't pass you). This is almost useless for self-defense; it is done by cops to stop drunk drivers, and by Good Samaritans in the Rocky Mountains when somebody behind them loses their brakes.

If somebody is smart enough to do this to *you* to make

you stop so that they can attack you, it's no problem to put them off the road and keep going merrily on your way. Wait until you're coming up on a curve. Then brake suddenly to put some distance between you as their car continues forward. Now, accelerate, and *ram* that car with the left edge of your front bumper against the right rear of his if you're going into a left-hand turn, vice versa in a right turn. At that point, his wheels are almost at the maximum limit of their adhesion to the roadway, and your impact in that specific direction is going to break them loose and send his car off the road. Be prepared to countersteer after the impact to your own car, and be sure to keep off the brakes so that you have rolling traction.

Rolling traction is perhaps the most vital principle in handling a car under emergency conditions. So long as the wheels are rolling, the car will go in the direction you turn the steering wheel. But if you lock the wheels via your brakes, the only contact surface with the roadway is four little bits of static rubber and you have no control at all; your car will skid like a hockey puck on ice, and you'll be totally out of control. Keep the rubber rolling, and your car will go where you point it via the steering wheel. It is that simple. Thousands of people have lost their lives because, when things got ugly on the road, all they could think of was stopping their car, so they stepped on their brakes and lost their rolling traction, and their lives as well.

If you're not going to attend a Scotti- or Bondurant-type training school, that should be about enough to hold you when fighting with cars in runoff attempts. But suppose you are being attacked by people on foot, and you manage to gain the very temporary sanctuary of your automobile?

It may not be a fortress, but your car is still an escape avenue and a mobile battering ram, a weapon deadlier than any gun. Innocent people have died when they were surrounded by fanatical rioters and panicked—look at the horror of the Miami riots.

The Miami riots occurred while I was with several hundred cops at the National Law Enforcement Parade in Rhode Island. We watched it on our hotel TVs in the evening, we discussed it, and we agreed that none of *us* would be pulled out of our cars and stomped to death.

We would have driven clear, using our cars as mobile, guided bludgeons. Even if they tried to pick our sedan up with ten sets of arms, we would have accelerated when the first hands touched the vehicle, and would have driven through the mass of people who wanted to kill us and our innocent passengers with absolutely no compunction.

If you ever have to do that, order your passengers to lie down sideways on their seats and be ready to duck down yourself; an automobile will hit a standing man in the legs, and he could be catapulted right through your windshield with enough force that his corpse could kill you by its sheer impact.

Most of you have never seen what happens to a pedestrian hit by a fast-moving car. You are talking—no exaggeration—about literal dismemberment and decapitation and internal human organs that burst out of the body from the pressure of a 3,000-pound vehicle's wheel rolling over them for a fraction of a second.

You won't see that, though. If your life and the lives of your children in the backseat are on the line, you'll just drive, feeling the bumps through the steering wheel (it feels a lot harder than you'd think) and you'll keep driving. "Steer for the open sea," and head for the biggest, nearest open roadway where you can put on some speed and get away from the nightmare.

If you ever get caught up in the bloody frenzy of a riot, drive over the rioters. Sound your horn first, the universally understood warning signal, if you have time. If they still stand there ready to die for the chance to kill you, that's their decision, not yours. It's nothing you need to feel guilty about.

It is most unlikely that you'll ever be in a riot situation. It is somewhat more probable that you'll be getting into your car and a rapist or mugger will pounce on you at that moment, because you have your hands full and are in a parking lot between two automobiles where there probably wouldn't be too many witnesses.

If I were a woman, I would first parallel park wherever I could, with my front wheels already heading out. If I had to park head-in, I'd stop the car and then turn the front wheels all the way to the right. If I were attacked in my parallel space by someone who was grabbing at my door or at my arm, I'd hang onto the wheel tightly and brace my legs, start the engine, and drive away. The hapless individual trying to pull me out would be dragged on the asphalt. If he lives, he'll suffer what motorcyclists call road rash—an acute case of getting your skin and muscle tissue scraped off on the rough highway surface.

If I were parked head-in and someone twice my size was trying to drag me out I would still be able to start the ignition if I would be able to get my feet inside the car. (You should *always* carry your keys in your hand when you go to and from the parking area.) Why should I try to claw at my attacker's face with the car keys when I can bring my car to life, hit the accelerator pedal, and—since the wheels are already turned to the right—use a few thousand pounds of mechanical energy to crush his body between my car and the one next to me?

Even if there isn't a car next to me, the turning front of the car will take the assailant off balance and put him on his back, and in a fraction of a second, the left front wheel will roll over his body. He may or may not still be alive, but he isn't going to rape anyone, ever again.

In parking lots, try to leave the car where it will be most visible. This isn't always possible in parking garages, unfortunately, but I find it worth the extra time to cruise up and down the ramps until I've found a location where the car will be safe while I'm gone, and where *I'll* be reasonably safe walking to and from it. That means I avoid dark corners. I've had one mugging attempt in a darkened corner of a parking lot, thank you, and that was quite enough.

I want an open, well-lit area, near the busiest section where there will be lots of witnesses. I also want to avoid the car being buried amid rows of autos, where a thief could work undetected.

In an attendant-operated parking lot, always lock the glove compartment and trunk, taking the key with you. Note the odometer reading, so that you'll know if anyone was joyriding in your car while you were gone, or if the car was moved to some point where it would be more convenient to ransack it. Parking lot attendants are not usually well paid or well screened, and have been known to augment their income by working with thieves.

When the attendant asks me how long I'm going to be, I reply, "I won't know until I get to my appointment. It could be ten minutes or four hours."

That does a couple of good things. First, the attendant knows I could return at any moment, so if he *is* a little shady, he'll know that my car is a very bad bet for ripping off. Second, if he knows I could be back for it soon, he's not going to bury it on a back lot where it could take him seven or eight minutes to move other cars to let me out if I came back early. This means that my car will be parked near the front of the lot, visible to honest attendants and passersby alike. It's much less likely to be broken into when parked in that position.

Incidentally, don't get too finicky about the odometer reading. In a large, fully packed city parking garage, it's entirely possible for the attendant to put a mile on the thing, between driving all through the place to find a slot for you, and then retrieving your car. In any garage you use regularly, tip the lot attendant a little extra so that he won't flag your car to his buddies if he's into doing rip-offs. Your tips in a year as a regular customer may add up to more than his share of a ransacking.

Even though you've left your ignition key with the attendant, you should have a spare within easy access for reasons that relate primarily to convenience. There's also a safety concern: If someone tries to pounce on you in the parking lot and you manage to run to your car and lock yourself in, you want to be able to start that car and get moving *immediately*, without having to rummage under the seat and floormats to find where the attendant left the ignition key if, indeed, it isn't hanging up in his office. Even if you're traveling, most Rentacar agencies have no problem giving you a spare set of keys.

21. SHOULD YOU INVEST IN AUTO ALARMS?

Virtually every burglary detective would recommend the installation of an electronic alarm in your home. Yet surprisingly, few auto theft detectives recommend similar technology for your car.

The reason is that there are more places in a house to hide alarm switches than there are in a car, and with the various combinations of locks and doors and windows, it's tough to learn everything a superprofessional burglar knows. Thus, a very high percent of home burglars are amateurs easily intimidated by electronic alarms.

Cars are much simpler to hit. There are only a few places to look for alarms, and by and large, they're easier for a thief to bypass. Says Joe Fitch of the Indiana State Police auto theft detail in a 1980 interview I had with him for *Indiana Trooper Magazine,*

If you own a twenty-two-thousand-dollar Cadillac Eldorado, it's probably worth the expense [to install an alarm], because it may deter about fifty percent of the amateur car thieves. If the thief is a professional, though, it'll only slow him down by two or three minutes.

Shortly before I interviewed Fitch he had completed another of his several successful "Sting" operations against organized car thieves. Posing as a middleman, he was able to trap many on both ends of the racket. In the process, he learned a great deal about the "face of the enemy," including the fact that most professional thieves considered auto alarms a joke. "When I was posing as a fence buying stolen autos, I had them delivered to me with all sorts of antitheft devices on them, including the types that bypass the ignition."

A colleague who shares Fitch's opinion of alarms is Trooper Fred Moore of the Indiana State Police. I sought out Moore just after he won his department's Eagle Award for the highest stolen car recovery rate in the state, some half a million dollar's worth in a year. Says Moore of alarms, in light of the stolen vehicles he has recovered, in a 1980 interview I had with him for *Indiana Trooper Magazine,*

If you have a superexpensive luxury car, you might want to equip it with the most sophisticated antitheft devices on the market. The problem is, if you have a car like that, which is highly desirable to auto thieves, they'll get it if they want it . . . and they most certainly *will* want it.

In my opinion the professional car thieves of today are sufficiently skilled and equipped to circumvent the most sophisticated antitheft devices. I wouldn't say, "Don't go out and buy an antitheft device," because you obviously want to make it as hard as possible for them to steal your vehicle, but I certainly wouldn't recommend sinking five hundred dollars into such an item. I don't install special antitheft devices on my own cars.

Moore's advice for keeping your car in your possession is much more simple:

From what I've seen and learned since I've been concentrating more intently on auto theft, I will probably never buy another new car as long as I live. They're simply too desirable to thieves, and therefore too vulnerable to theft.

Fitch believes the best bet is to purchase one of the automobiles that car thieves find less desirable. Luxury and sports cars, and top-selling economy vehicles, lead the shopping lists of car thieves, he notes. His solution: Buy a Chrysler or American Motors product, which is statistically much less likely to be stolen.

Auto alarms are not necessarily a waste of money. They *do* intimidate a limited number of amateurs who might otherwise try to steal your car. More to the point, they can do a lot to lighten the burden of your auto insurance premium.

Shop around with your local insurance brokers and ask two questions. First, how substantial a premium discount will they offer if your car has an antitheft device? Second, does the company specify a certain type of device, for instance, something approved by Underwriters' Laboratory?

With that information in hand, it's time to contact your car dealer or alarm installation shop. Get a *complete* written estimate of the total cost of alarm installation. Now, in a very short time, you and your pocket calculator can determine whether installing an alarm can save you premium money over the expected time you'll be keeping that car, even if no one ever tries to rip it off.

22. REAL PROTECTION AGAINST PICKPOCKETS AND PURSE SNATCHERS

Most of the contemporary literature on self-protection offers pretty good advice about protecting your wallet from pickpockets and purse snatchers, but if you believe *everything* they tell you, you could wind up in the hospital instead of at the police station reporting the theft.

Everybody tells you that the hip pocket is the worst place for a man to carry his wallet, and that the side trouser pocket is a close second. They ignore the fact that most men find this the most comfortable and instinctive place to reach for their cash or ID. Look, if everyone has always told you that you're asking to lose it if you carry your wallet in your hip pocket and you're still carrying it there, it's not going to do either of us any good for me to repeat the same old advice, is it? *I* still carry my wallet in my hip pocket. Let's look instead, for a moment, at ways to carry it there safely.

I agree with the prevailing advice offered by experts who claim that the inside breast pocket is much more "pickpocket-proof" (they have to take it literally from right under your nose), but your wallet is by no means totally safe there.

For a great many men, the inside coat pocket is not

the answer. A lot of us don't happen to wear sportcoats or suits every day, and if we do, we frequently hang the garment up someplace or carry it folded over our arms on a hot afternoon. The wallet is thus either left completely unattended or quite vulnerable to falling unnoticed onto the sidewalk. In any case, professional "dips" have long since learned how to double-team you in a crowd situation; one bumps into you on one side, and as you instinctively turn to look at him, his partner on the opposite side takes advantage of your distraction and snakes his hand inside your jacket.

The preventative measures I prefer are seldom mentioned elsewhere, but offer you and your valuables a great deal more security.

It's cheap and easy to sew strips of Velcro inside the openings of the pockets where you carry theft-prone items. This is double insurance: It keeps your wallet or money clip from slipping out when you sit awkwardly or drop your pants in a public toilet, and it stymies pickpockets. Even if the Bad Guy does manage to get his hand inside that pocket, you will be alerted by the distinctive ripping sound the Velcro panels make when they're parted. It's sort of a burglar alarm lock for your wallet.

Money belts are an excellent way to store most of your folding money. There are several styles available. Leather dress belts with hidden pouches are sold in many good-quality men's wear or luggage stores. Cheaper units are available by mail order (advertised in *TV Guide*, assorted men's magazines, and other publications for ten dollars or less). These often have zippers; you literally have to undo your belt to get your money out. So long as you have enough pocket cash for your immediate needs, though, you needn't worry about having to look like you're disrobing.

Some of the better leather money belts allow you to dig out the folding green without having to unbuckle, but if the belt is snugly fastened for conventional wear, you're going to look like a contortionist. Clawing into your belt and coming up with money can draw the attention of unsavory types who tend to assume that money belts are only worn by people carrying very large sums of cash.

A much better approach is the soft elastic money belt, as typified by the Bianchi unit produced by the holster company. Four inches wide and very soft and supple, it's worn over the underclothes at about navel height or a little lower and is equally suitable for men or women. It can be worn all day in complete comfort—I often forget to take mine off until I undress for bed—and money can be removed from it very discreetly. You simply undo one shirt or blouse button and discreetly slip your hand in, perhaps covering it from view with a parcel or purse held in your other hand. Your fingers can quickly "do the walking" through the elastic pouch and come up with the bills. To even a noncasual observer it looks as if you've had the cash clamped in your fist the whole time.

For those of you who take a harder line on personal protection, the Bianchi unit comes with a small pouch that holds a hidden short-barrel .38 revolver or a flat .380 automatic next to your belly button. I often wear mine in "shirt-sleeve weather." I pack the gun inside a tucked-in shirt with the butt forward and just to the left of my navel. The second button above the belt is left undone, a breach of fashion taste that is discreetly concealed by my necktie.

I find that I can reach the gun lightning quick from this location, and can hold my right hand ready without *looking* as if I'm about to reach for a gun. It won't even be found during a cursory frisk, and the gun is so well hidden it's virtually invisible. I used such a holster one day when a couple of big-city muggers chose me for their next victim. The .38 appeared from it instantly, giving my knife-wielding assailant and his accomplice the surprise of their professional lives.

Naturally, the gun is optional. The $26-Bianchi belly band holster-cum-money belt is not sold in men's shops, but can be ordered through any gunshop, sports store, or police equipment dealer that stocks firearm accessories. You can also order from the Bianchi factory at 100 Calle Cortez, Temecula, CA. Send $3 for their current catalog, price list, and ordering instructions.

Another little unit, sold primarily by mail order to those who read the magazine *High Times* and the biker magazine *Easyriders,* is the "Stash Pouch." This little item is made of elastic with a Velcro closure. It wraps around your upper calf, just below your knee, and is unobtrusive under almost any trousers, slacks, or midi-length dress.

The ads, which don't exactly appeal to the *Better Homes and Gardens* crowd, imply that it's a good place to hide your marijuana or your .25 automatic. I prefer to use it for cash and credit cards.

The same product is available for $8 from the American Federation of Police, 1100 N.E. 125th Street, North Miami, FL 33161.

A theft protection device long since proven on the street is the "trucker's wallet." This stoutly made leather folder slips into a trouser pocket and is secured to the belt by a rugged little chain. Pickpockets, after all, don't carry bolt-cutters. Payroll couriers, truckers, and others, swear by them. So, as it happens, do drug dealers and outlaw motorcyclists. It suffices for me that drug dealers and Hell's Angels don't get their pockets picked any more often than truckers, which is to say, not very often.

Trucker's wallets are $20 and smaller biker wallets are $12 and are available from IRS Limited, P.O. Box 109, San Fernando, CA 91341.

The trucker's wallet works. The problem is that to many people the item has a blue-collar or macho connotation and they would sooner die than chain one to their Gucci belt and slip it into the pocket of their Hart, Schaffner, and Marx trousers. It's a pity, but I have yet to see a name-brand maker of fashion wallets design a "socially acceptable" trucker's wallet for the guy who considers

Gentlemen's Quarterly a fashion Bible. Since the average businessman is less likely to be a target than a long-haul trucker, courier, or someone else who predictably carries large amounts of cash, he could get by with a much smaller unit with a lighter chain. After all, the chain only has to resist the pull of a human hand.

If someone does try to grab your trucker's wallet and run with it, just turn toward him with your right side if that's the side where you keep your wallet, stamp your right foot down, and if you can remember to, lower your buttocks a little. He has hold of the wallet at the end of his arm at waist level, which doesn't give him a lot of leverage, but it's attached to *you* at the *belt:* A lower center of gravity is working on your behalf, and when he reaches the end of the chain, the wallet will probably slip right out of his fingers.

Most pickpockets will take their hand out of your pocket the minute they feel a chain, anyway. Don't, for goodness' sake, even think about booby-trapping your pockets. I remember the story of my grandfather, the last Ayoob to be successfully victimized by a pickpocket.

My dad remembers the snowy Boston Sunday when Gramps returned home, livid with rage. His expensive overcoat (which, in the fashion of that year, 1920, draped down to about mid-calf), had been slashed wide open from shoulder blade to hem. A razor-wielding pickpocket on the trolley car had then sliced open his trouser pocket as well, stealing his cash.

Gramps immediately went out and bought small-size rats traps, which he strategically placed in almost every pocket. He quit the practice after a year or so, during which he snapped the traps shut on his own fingers uncounted times.

Purse snatchers are a different breed. It's an extremely rare pickpocket who ever harms his victim; the hallmark of his trade is to get away completely undetected, with no wasted motion and nothing that calls attention to himself. The purse snatcher is a much more violent species.

It is not at all uncommon for purse snatchers to savagely beat women who resist them; some prefer to take a preventative step and punch the woman in the face *before* they seize her pocketbook.

It is for this reason that I take strong issue with those "experts" who recommend that women wear shoulder bags and hold onto their purses with both hands. That's good advice only for women who place a higher value on their money than on their lives. *Fact:* When a running man "hits" and grabs the strap of your shoulder bag, he is going to catch you by surprise, take you immediately off balance, and probably throw you to the ground even if he doesn't mean to. *Fact:* A significantly high percentage of women who are killed or seriously injured in muggings and purse snatchings are hurt primarily by the impact of their fall when they are hurled to the pavement.

Holding the purse against your body is fine. But it's a very good bet that your attacker won't be averse to harming you to make you let go of it. A favorite trick of street criminals is to grab a woman's breast, dig their fingers in as deeply as they can, and twist savagely.

Carry your cash in a Bianchi elastic money belt under your blouse or dress. Ninety-nine percent of robbers don't even realize this technology exists, and they won't be looking for it. If they get a (hopefully inexpensive) purse, some cosmetics, and $10 or $20 in cash, you can live with that loss. So long as your keys are on your waistband, and your ID with your home address is in your money belt, you don't have to worry that they'll come to your house later, either.

Some firms offer breakaway straps for shoulder bags. These prevent the purse snatcher from using the strap like a lever and flinging you head over heels into the gutter. If he grabs the purse, he runs away with a loose strap and you've still got your bag. Of course he *could* just run back, break your jaw, and loosen your teeth with a left hook, and take the purse anyway. One such firm manufactures a breakaway strap that also contains a canister of incapacitating aerosol. I don't like it. The purse snatcher is likely to get your spray can and now turn around and use it on you. Even if that doesn't happen, the violent tugging on the strap is going to inhibit your ability to get the canister out and use it.

Besides, how many women are going to slash away the permanently sewn and precisely matching straps that came with their shoulder bags! Personally, I think the whole concept of breakaway shoulder bags is something of a joke. Carry your regular shoulder bag slung on your right shoulder if the purse is on your right side (*not* slung around your neck!) and be prepared to shrug it loose.

Pickpockets are easy to foil because they're nonviolent for the most part, and have to operate surreptitiously; they're vulnerable to any obstacle you can put between their fingertips and your valuables. Resistance to purse snatchers however, often triggers them to violence. The good news is that once they've got the purse, they're usually gone. Let them go, with a cheap purse, some lipstick, and a few dollars. It's easier in the long run. Even if he just clips you lightly with a punch, you'll be lucky to get out of the emergency room for less than twenty dollars a stitch.

If you do choose to fight for your valuables, consider several things. First, don't fight with, or chase, a suspect unless you are *certain* that you will have the upper hand in a battle, especially if he pulls a deadly weapon on you. Sure, you could be like the elderly woman in one city who got a heroism award because she used her umbrella to pummel a purse snatcher to his knees, but you're more likely to wind up like the young woman in another city: She chased the man who grabbed her handbag into a deserted park where he brutally beat and raped her.

If you carry a gun or other weapon, *never* carry it in

your purse. The thing is going to be torn away from you in the opening moments of the encounter, before you even have a chance to reach for it. Consider also that you may not have the legal right in your state to use physical violence in such a situation. Every store detective in America has been counseled to let a shoplifter go if he resists arrest, because he probably hasn't stolen enough to warrant more than a misdemeanor charge, and if the thief is injured in the struggle, the store could be held liable in civil court for enormous damages.

If I were in downtown Boston tonight and someone lifted my wallet or snatched my briefcase, I would probably shout up a storm and let him go. My .45 would stay right in its holster. The wallet contains credit cards and probably less than $50 in cash; counting my $50-deductible insurance on the credit cards, I would stand to lose no more than a hundred dollars.

I am licensed to carry a loaded and concealed gun in Boston, and while the permit is stamped For Protection of Life and Property, I've been around long enough to know that it doesn't really work that way. I normally have a gun on in Boston, but if you think I'm going to pull it out and chase that guy, you're *nuts*.

If there were something so valuable in that attaché case that I might risk my life to get it back, I still wouldn't draw the gun. A man running with a gun down a city street does a very convincing imitation of a psycho criminal, and there are several thousand on- and off-duty cops in that city who, observing, might take action with their own guns. If the cop assumed I was a Bad Guy, or if his actions in plainclothes convinced me that I was about to be shot by the bag snatcher's accomplice, one of us could kill the other by mistake.

If I *were* to pursue, I would be shouting at the top of my lungs, "*Thief!* Stop that man! Police! Stop that man! Thief!" This would reduce the chances of my being mistaken for a Bad Guy, and there might also be a hero in the crowd who would trip that street criminal and make him fall on his face. My hand would be on my holstered gun where I could react in an instant if *he* turned on *me* with a lethal weapon, but my side arm would not be visibly drawn.

When you feel that you must chase a man down the street, you're wise to run *to his left rear*. If he does turn and fire a shot at you while he's running, chances are five out of six that he's right-handed and will be shooting over his right shoulder. You will be much harder to hit if you're on his left; he'll almost have to twist enough to fall on his face if he tries to bring his pistol to bear on you.

Since this is a very real possibility—a number of Good Samaritans have been shot or stabbed—be ready to take cover. Naturally, you'll instinctively be concentrating on your quarry as you run, but you also want to have a constant mental fix on every car or doorway in front of you that can offer hard cover or an escape route if he pivots on you with a weapon.

Another problem is that when you chase a criminal, you're like a dog chasing a car: You're not altogether certain what to *do* with the target once you've caught up to it. If you grab the guy by the collar or by the arm, either you're both going to lose your balance and fall to the ground, or he is going to turn like a cornered rat and lash out at you. The criminals who meekly surrender are usually the weak ones, and it's safe to assume that the criminal wouldn't have picked you for a victim if he wasn't bigger and stronger than you. Most of the successful apprehensions of criminals by citizens that I've seen, either involved a citizen with a gun in his hand, or a big strong guy who chased and caught a smaller man who had picked on an even smaller victim.

You're going to be so close, and things are going to be happening so fast, that if the guy *does* have a weapon you probably won't even know it until the blade slips into your belly or the first bullet burns into your chest.

Personally, I think it's foolish to run after a criminal

under any circumstances. Wallets and pocketbooks are cheap. Life is precious. Act accordingly. The inexpensive money belts like Bianchi's, the cheap "Stash Pouch," and the not-that-expensive truckers' wallets, are safe from the vast majority of pickpockets and purse snatchers. Carry a "throwaway purse" or a "throwaway wallet." And don't fight unless that's your only escape from physical injury. Money and throwaway money carriers aren't worth killing for, let alone dying for.

23. SPECIAL ADVICE FOR THE ELDERLY AND DISABLED

The physically disabled and elderly tend to be victimized much more frequently by criminals than the rest of us. Less capable of fleeing or fighting, they are natural targets. Because most forms of effective defense require some degree of physical ability—and because medical bills and fixed incomes make people in these categories somewhat less able to purchase expensive and sophisticated protective systems—a great deal more thought must be given to modes of defense.

With *dogs*, a physically frail person should steer clear of the giant breeds, and of extremely aggressive animals like the contemporary Doberman. For someone who is not physically prepared to chase a dog or restrain it, advanced obedience training is imperative.

The good news is that a retired person, or someone so severely disabled that he is unable to work regularly, has more time to spend with his protective canine, reinforcing their relationship and ensuring that the dog *will* as closely as possible, react with a positive response to verbal commands.

Arthritis, strokes, palsy, and numerous other disorders, can impair one's ability to manipulate defensive equipment like a canister of Mace or a firearm. One of my clients was a paraplegic with limited use of his hands and confined to a wheelchair. He had very weak hands; about all he could handle was shaving himself with a Norelco, lighting a cigarette, and working an electric typewriter. He was not strong enough to pick up a heavy handgun, nor to pull the trigger of a double-action revolver, nor to work the spring-loaded slide of a conventional automatic pistol. A powerful gun with any sort of serious recoil would have "kicked" itself right out of his grasp.

The solution we worked out for him was a Beretta Jetfire/Minx system. These tiny autoloading pistols are identical save for the fact that the Jetfire spits nine .25 caliber bullets, while the Minx holds only six .22 Short cartridges. The Minx, like the majority of small automatics firing "rimfire" cartridges, was not totally reliable, but the rimless .25 rounds fed perfectly through the Jetfire. The .25 became his protection weapon; the .22 Minx was the "understudy gun" that he practiced with, because .22 Short ammo costs only about $2 for 50 rounds, compared to $15 for the same number of centerfire .25 cartridges.

The light recoil was easy to handle. The small Berettas have a button that, when pressed, tips the barrel upward so that a round can be inserted into the firing chamber by hand, without pulling back the spring-loaded slide. So long as a friend or relative has loaded the cartridges into his several spare "clips," my client can use his weakened hands to manipulate, fire, and reload his little pistols with deadly accuracy and efficiency. The .25 is decidedly weak on "stopping power," but the accuracy he has developed through constant training with the .22 practice gun has made him quite proficient with both. Two shots from his .25, directed into the head of his attacker, will keep him safer than an able-bodied person who would be spraying .44 Magnum bullets into the attacker's extremities.

With well-thought-out training, a disability can be turned to the victim's advantage. Ted Vollrath, who lost both legs at the hip during the Korean War, soon learned to "walk on his hands," using his arms to drag his bulky torso up-and-down stairs. Before long, his upper body was more powerful than that of many weight lifters.

Vollrath studied karate and developed three approaches for streetfighting from his wheelchair. First, he worked out ways to slam the chair into his standing opponents' knees, knocking them into his lap where his powerful arms could strangle them. Second, he practiced ways to instantly unfasten the hard metal "armrests" of the wheelchair, using them to block punches and to smash able-bodied attackers brutally. Finally, knowing that a smart mugger tips the wheelchair over when he attacks a paraplegic, he studied methods of "fighting from the ground," taking the attacker off his feet and plunging him into the alien environment of "balancing on his back," an environment where Vollrath had long since become comfortable and confident.

Others in the Martial Arts for the Handicapped Federation (MAHF) developed methods of fighting with cane and crutch, often with their backs to a handy wall for balance. One member I talked to left a surprised mugger writhing in the gutter with a shattered kneecap, and then, with great dignity, put his crutch back under his arm and slowly walked away. It's unfortunate that the MAHF is now defunct since I saw an enormous increase in both health and confidence among the practitioners.

Disabled people quickly become bored with the not-immediately-meaningful repetition of conventional physical therapy and exercise. But in a wheelchair, karate is exciting. Each movement is a blow or a defensive block, a lashing out against your persecutor. It's something a physically impaired person can relate to in more ways than one.

Handicapped youngsters and young males especially, seem to thrive on martial arts training. Every boy needs a degree of machismo in his life to conform to his own "peer ideals," and wheelchair karate is a dimension beyond the more benign sports that can be practiced by the handicapped.

For elderly or handicapped persons, *aikido* may be the ideal martial art. Stressing "a light touch" that requires little if any physical strength, *aikido* teaches methods of using the opponent's strength and momentum against him. There are few *aikido* teachers in this country, and none that I know of who work specifically with the aged or the infirm. But all are masters of human engineering who can come up with a dozen techniques that will work for the wheelchair-bound student against an able-bodied attacker.

T'ai Chi Chuan is considered by many to be the martial art best suited for senior citizens. Balletlike, with gentle and flowing movements, T'ai Chi requires very little physical exertion and less "violence in practice." The movements are remarkably similar to what physical therapists use in exercise regimens for arthritis patients. It ensures flexibility in those who need it the most. T'ai Chi is low on the scale of martial arts forms that "prepare you for streetfighting," but it does teach a number of blocks and evasions that could be extremely helpful to a person under physical assault.

For the handicapped, a protective dog can sometimes be more trouble than protection. It's hard enough piloting a wheelchair through doors, without having to get a dog through ahead of you. Still, if you have a compact animal that has been deeply obedience trained, it could work out. Were I to find myself in a wheelchair tomorrow, I would probably invest in a small German shepherd bitch and some intensive obedience training.

The Seeing Eye dogs employed by the blind used to be primarily German shepherds, but now encompass virtually every intelligent breed, and a great many smart mongrels. Were I stricken blind tomorrow, I would make a point of acquiring a shep to function as my eyes. German shepherds might not be that much better than other Seeing Eye dogs (though it *is* the most proven breed for that mission), but a lot of people who wouldn't be afraid of a Labrador retriever *would* seek victims elsewhere if they saw a blind man holding a "police dog."

The bad news is, Seeing Eye dogs are not trained for protection. The good news is that (a) most street people don't know that, and (b) the Seeing Eye dog becomes so devoted to its master that instinct alone will probably prompt it to defensive action if necessary. Should that happen to me if I'm blind, I want the dog protecting me to have the body and instincts that generations of breeding have instilled into it for counterassault against violent human beings.

The very phrase *blind man with a gun* implies reckless danger. I have dealt with three *blind men with guns*. One was my history professor in college. He never carried a gun, but he used them for recreation. Behind his country house, he had installed a firing range with large metal targets that "rang" when hit. He was able to hit his target with an uncanny regularity. Naturally, he wouldn't have been able to "coordinate" that on the street, and never carried a gun in public, but he did keep a weapon loaded in the house. Knowing where his wife was (they were childless), he didn't think he would be on the short end of the stick if people invaded his home. He had one simple secret: In the master bedroom was a single switch that could plunge the entire house into darkness.

I met another blind man at a gun owner's rally. He wanted to enlist my aid in convincing his local police chief to issue him a permit to carry a concealed weapon in public. "Just because I'm blind," he cried, "doesn't mean I'm a second-class citizen!" I told him, "I'm sorry. Having a gun at home may be a right, but carrying one in public is a privilege. I hope you understand why I can't help you."

A friend of mine I'll call Howard is legally blind without his thick spectacles, but with his glasses on, passed his driver's license exam. A small-statured guy who has been a mugging victim, he also carries a snub-nosed .38 revolver. With his glasses on, I've seen him win first place in Sharpshooter and Marksman class at combat pistol tournaments. If the specs were knocked off in a struggle, though, he admits that he would be unable to distinguish muggers from innocent bystanders. His solution?

> If I'm under attack and my glasses are knocked off, I'll either holster the gun if it's drawn or not reach for it at all. I would never pull the trigger after "going blind." If the mugger got my thirty-eight away, fine; it has a Magna-Trigger conversion and can only be fired by someone like me who wears the special magnetic ring. The mugger can pull the trigger all day and not make it go off—I'll be running in the meantime—and if a police officer sees the mugger standing there with a gun and shoots him, that's the mugger's problem!

Were I to lose my sight, a part of me would want to sell all my guns and another part of me would cry, "No, you need protection now more than ever." Like Howard, I would use only a gun like the Smith & Wesson or Ruger *with Magna-Trigger conversion;* I have one already. It would be loaded with high-speed, "explosive" bullets so that I wouldn't have to worry about them exiting a felon I shot, since I could no longer determine if innocent people were standing behind him. I would immediately resume study in *aikido* and get sharp again to the feel of close-contact fighting.

As a sighted man, I prefer to fight physically with karate and Mu Tau ("Greek-boxing") techniques, in which my fists and feet keep the opponent a comfortable distance away from me. Blind, I would want to be able to positively identify the homicidal attacker, pull him in close to me, and jam the revolver barrel into his midriff as I pulled the trigger rapidly, to ensure that no one else would be in the way of the gunfire. Since his dying convulsions could throw him clear of me, I would want to make sure that he was unable to threaten human life after that moment. That would be another reason for pressing the gun against him. The bright flash you see at the muzzle when a gun goes off is a burning cloud of gunpowder and violently expanding gases; when the muzzle is pressed against the body, that fireball is directed inward, creating a terrible "blast effect" that usually kills or disables outright, no matter where the bullet strikes.

I would keep the gun if I were sightless only because I have been using that instrumentation all my life, and am confident that I could handle it responsibly under those limited circumstances. I would never recommend it to anyone else.

But I *would* recommend the *aikido* training to any sight-impaired person. It teaches you to get close to your opponent, to touch him, to control him—something you can do better blind than most sighted people can, since the blind develop a greater awareness of things around them that is almost like radar. Those who have gotten used to the permanent darkness and have learned to keep their balance without the visual indexes most sighted people need, actually have something of an edge in close-range *aikido* techniques.

Especially in the dark.

It is not a screenwriter's fantasy when, in a play or movie like *Wait Until Dark,* the blind victim shuts out the lights on his sighted assailants and then takes over. If you are a sighted person, you know how you stumble even in your own familiar home when the lights are out. You know that in a strange place in total darkness you feel as helpless as a fetus in a womb. But the blind person has already learned to make his way in the dark (especially on his own turf) and can move stealthily, at will. His more finely tuned other senses, and his sharply honed sense of balance, now gives him an advantage over the opponent *when the physical ability to deliver* force is equal . . . and when surprise, planning, and sudden darkness can be used as weapons against the cowardly slime who prey on blind people.

Build around your strengths and weaknesses no matter what physical shortcomings you have. If you suffer from an ailment that makes your bones brittle, you obviously don't want to study a system of defense that will have you punching your opponent in the jaw, because you'll shatter more of your bones than his. If you have a breathing ailment of any kind, steer *very* clear of Mace or other incapacitating sprays, since inhaling these irritant substances can aggravate a respiratory problem and possibly be fatal.

Even if you don't have any respiratory problems, the frail or disabled face two other dangers in the use of Mace. In my experience in teaching weaponry and chemical agents to police officers, class feedback from my cop students indicates that the chemical sprays only work about half the time in fight situations and may only inflame opponents to further violence.

The second danger is that, in real life, Mace tends to permeate the atmosphere and get all over the person spraying it, if they don't step quickly back. An infirm person who cannot immediately vacate the area can be dosed almost as badly as the perpetrator, especially if the latter gets close to him and hangs on.

I don't want to sound like a vigilante by harping on guns and dogs, but the fact remains that in my prison interviews, these are the two things that muggers and rapists tell me scares them more than anything else. The properly selected handgun requires fine motor coordination instead of gross physical strength—I have seen men in their sixties dominate pistol matches—and it is the one easily manipulated device that is all but guaranteed to neutralize a young, violent man.

In the hands of the elderly or infirm, the deadly defensive weapon offers a greater latitude of use than when carried by a healthy young man. The concept in law is "disparity of force." That is, a person who is much more powerful than you is deemed, even if he has no weapon, to have the ability to kill you. If he is acting in a violent manner that places you in grave jeopardy, the law treats him as an armed man, since his great strength is now in effect a deadly weapon with which he demonstrably intends to inflict death or grave bodily harm. Thus, it now becomes legally justifiable for you to defend yourself with the lethal force of a gun.

Aikido, T'ai Chi, and Mace, all have their place, but none by themselves can put a frail or physically disabled person at parity with a powerful, physically violent attacker. Yet a good instructor can train a physically weak or elderly person, even an arthritis sufferer, to employ a handgun with the same close-range skill as the average police officer.

I am sorry to be the one to have to tell you that there is no safe middle ground between submission and shooting your assailant. Indeed, neither of *those* alternatives are totally safe.

We each must examine our capabilities and our souls and our fears before we decide on the measures we shall take to protect ourselves and our loved ones from criminal violence. It is not for me to say what you *should* have, but as a specialist in the field of controlling human violence, I can point out what you *can* have, and if you are elderly, frail, or physically disabled, that includes a spectrum of specialized martial arts training, the use of a dog with an intimidating appearance and extremely advanced obedience training, and a firearm you have been professionally trained to use effectively within your physical and emotional limits.

24. IF YOU ARE KIDNAPPED OR TAKEN HOSTAGE

After the epoch of the Iranian hostage crisis it would be hard to find an American who has not thought, however briefly, of how awful it must be to be held in a strange place, against your will, by dangerous fanatics who could kill you at any moment. Captivity is an alien and terrifying condition. It has been known to drive its victims to extremes of hysterical panic that caused them, and sometimes fellow victims to lose their lives.

The concept of "hostage negotiation" was developed in this country primarily by Dr. Harvey Schlossberg of the New York Police Department (NYPD), founder of that agency's Psychological Services Unit. His protégé Captain Frank Bolz, headed the NYPD Hostage Negotiation Unit, founded in the early seventies. The unit's job is to open lines of communication with the kidnappers, bargain with them, and defuse the situation in a manner that results in the safe release of the hostages, and usually also the bloodless surrender of the perpetrators. Since that time, Bolz's team has worked with hundreds of kidnappers. Most of them are psychos or suddenly cornered holdup men who took hostages, but occasionally they turn out to be militant terrorists. Bolz and his people have never lost a hostage once they were on-the-scene.

Bolz and the hundreds of police experts he has trained around the country, agree that the behavior of the hostages themselves is vital to their survival. Let's look at some of the principles they teach.

Don't argue or resist! The captor is usually either a criminal or a psycho, often both. Holding you at gunpoint and the police at bay is a big deal for him; he never before felt the sense of power that is surging through him at this moment. If you challenge him you're provoking him to exercise that power in the worst possible way. So long as ordering you around makes him feel good he'll want to keep you alive.

Don't try to talk him out of it. He probably has a background of crime and/or mental illness and has already received well-intentioned advice from psychiatrists, parole officers, and other professionals. If you, the victim, presume to give him advice, he's likely to feel that you're implying that you're smarter and wiser and better and stronger than he. He's going to want to cut you down permanently. Keep your advice to yourself. Be docile, obedient, and *quiet.*

Beware of the "Stockholm Syndrome." Several years ago in Stockholm, Sweden, a gang of gunmen held a group of customers hostage in a bank for several days. By the time it was all over, many of the victims sympathized with the captors, and one of the female hostages even married one of her captors in a prison ceremony. Since then, this development of identification with, and sympathy for, the captor has become known as the Stockholm Syndrome. Many consider Patty Hearst to have been a classic case.

The Iranian hostages never showed signs of the syndrome. Cohesive and often left alone among themselves, they developed few ways of tormenting their captors. Some made small talk with their guards and greeted them with a deep bow, knowing that Islamic tradition required the captors to respond with the same. This forced the guards, in a sense, to treat their prisoners as equals. The hostages got away with it. They were lucky. Don't *you* try it. Remember: One reason the Embassy hostages acted with such psychological aggressiveness was that they had at least partially given up hope of coming out alive. *You* don't want to give up hope, so don't antagonize your captors in any way.

Remember the early photos that showed the hostages in Iran being led about blindfolded? This was the first thing the Red Cross strenuously objected to, and it was a major victory when they shamed the revolutionaries into removing the blindfolds. That's because the Stockholm Syndrome works both ways: The captors start identifying with their victims and becoming sympathetic toward them, too! Blindfolded and gagged, you are faceless, a cipher. As soon as your face becomes familiar to your captor, he "knows you," and it is haroer to kill someone you know (so long as he or she hasn't antagonized you) than it is to murder a nonentity.

If you are ever kidnapped or taken hostage promise your captor that you will be totally obedient and cooperative, so that he won't blindfold or gag you. The sooner he comes to know you as a benign person who won't threaten him, the safer you're going to be. Before long, you and he will have become "us." Just make sure that you don't fall victim to the Stockholm Syndrome to the extent that you begin to think of the authorities who are trying to rescue you, as "them."

Remember that time is on your side. While your captor throws threats and ransom demands back and forth with the authorities, try to calm down. Curl up and take a nap, if at all possible, or at least rest. Your captor is running flat out on an adrenalin high, doesn't dare sleep, and is going to be showing exhaustion symptoms within twenty-four hours or so. This makes him edgy and irritable and is another good reason to stay calm and benign and non-threatening. Fatigue also slows his judgment and his reflexes.

So long as you haven't threatened him, he'll be concentrating his hostility on those outside. That means he's likely to drop his guard against you. As time goes on he will get more lax about your captivity and make more mistakes. Before long, escape avenues may become open to you.

Be careful and pragmatic about this, however. An escape attempt that fails will be taken by your captor as a betrayal. With his twisted sense of values this may justify in his mind your summary execution as "a traitor." *Don't make an escape attempt unless you're absolutely sure you can succeed!*

There have been many cases where tired, careless kidnappers left a loaded gun or other weapon where the victim could get at it. In many cases the victims ignored the temptation; some outside observers attribute this to the Stockholm Syndrome, but there's some question about that. It's one thing to imply weakness when you talk from an ivory tower about kidnappings; it's quite another to be an untrained layman in the terrifying clutch of kidnappers and have serious misgivings about picking up a gun and using it. Most people don't have the training or the psycho-emotional preparation to shoot their way out of a deadly danger situation, and such people are wise to leave the gun alone. (They should *never* try to hide the weapon. The kidnapper who discovers such an act is likely to feel betrayed and castrated and respond with savage violence.)

At the proper time, use mild crisis intervention techniques. If you're still being held captive after twenty-four hours, it might be time to meekly open a conversation with your captor. Don't start whining about your wife and children at home. He doesn't really care about *your* problems.

Instead, let him talk about *his* problems. Be a very good listener; ninety or ninety-five percent of the conversation, *at least,* should emanate from him. When you speak, don't chastise him or lecture him. Everything you say should either be noncommital or subtly sympathetic. A good sympathetic remark might be, "Hey, you've had it rough. I'm beginning to see why you did something big to 'make a break.' I'm not saying I understand, because I haven't had it as rough as you have, but after talking about it with you, you don't seem to be such a bad person."

Let him keep talking and keep a sympathetic ear. If you want or need something, a trip to the bathroom even, ask him for it. It won't hurt your position to toady to him somewhat, and once he gets used to having power over you, he's likely to feel a certain sense of paternal responsibility toward you. A comment from you like, "The cops aren't going to start shooting the place up, are they?" might even make him feel a little protective toward you, and that would be good. You don't want him to be thinking, "These are my *hostages*." You want him to be thinking, "These are *my* hostages."

Be ready to leave at a moment's notice. The police negotiators are going to be bargaining with your kidnapper for everything he demands. The only two things they'll never give him are more weapons and more hostages. When he gets hungry and starts sending out for a pizza and a six-pack, the negotiators are going to try their hardest to make him trade one or two hostages for each item he wants. It's going to take him awhile to agree to this, but when he does, it's going to be a sudden decision.

Don't wait for him to change his mind. Go now. Don't say something dumb like, "Let me stay here and send Mrs. Smith out instead. She's older and she's frightened, but I'm not scared." When you do that, you're questioning his judgment and antagonizing him. Even if he does let you stay, he's going to be wary of you, maybe even hostile. Your taking issue with him may so antagonize him that *nobody* gets out. In that situation follow orders, and come to terms with your indignation and your frustrated sense of heroism *later,* when no one else stands to die for the sake of your dignity.

If the you-know-what hits the fan, dive prone and stay there. The only time a *police* team will ever come into a hostage scene shooting is after the criminals have executed one of their victims, *while the negotiations are in progress.*

Understand this difference well. If you're in a liquor store and a couple of holdup men come in, get into a shootout with an off-duty cop and kill him, and then take the customers and clerks hostage in a back room, the cops are *not* going to come in shooting. They're going to "freeze" that scene, throw up a cordon of heavily armed officers around the store, and bring in their hostage negotiators. Anyone killed in the situation that immediately precedes the hostage crisis are, for purposes of the operation at hand, written off.

It gets dangerous when the kidnapper tells the police, "It's noon. I want my chauffeured limousine here with the three million dollars at *exactly* one P.M., and if it isn't, I'm going to kill the first hostage and throw his corpse out the window." At that point, the police Emergency Reaction Team or SWAT unit will mobilize for an immediate assault, but will hold off until one P.M. If the kidnapper lets the hostage live, the SWAT officers will return the favor.

But if, at 1:05, a gunshot rings out and a lifeless hostage is flung from the window, all bets are off. The real negotiation is over. The hostage experts believe, "Once they start killing their captives, they won't stop." The death of the first victim is the signal to attack. You can expect it within seconds or minutes, and certainly before the next "murder deadline" the kidnappers specify comes due.

They will hit hard, like an infantry assault team. Expect clouds of tear gas or perhaps the deafening explosion and blinding flash of a concussion grenade as the heavily armed rescue team makes its entry. For a period of several seconds you are going to be in very grave danger because these "police combat soldiers" *will* charge in shooting, perhaps even throwing out a spray of fully automatic weapon fire. Under the circumstances, their bullets tend to be indiscriminate. At Attica Prison, at the Maalot Commune, even at Entebbe, innocent hostages were struck down in the firestorm of their rescuers' bullets.

When the Israeli commando team hit the Entebbe airport, they yelled out their identity *once,* and ordered the Good Guys to dive for cover. In the din of battle however, you may not hear that warning. At the moment you hear gunfire or an explosion, you are wise to fling yourself to the floor behind the nearest hard cover, and stay there.

You can expect this sort of counterassault, on American soil, only if the kidnappers have already executed at least one victim. Elsewhere, it could happen at any time. Israel, West Germany, Egypt, and other governments, have made it strict policy not to bargain with those they consider to be terrorists. If you are being held prisoner by skyjackers at New York's LaGuardia Airport, it is safe to assume that so long as all the hostages are OK, no SWAT team is going to charge in behind a wall of flying lead.

But if you're in an El Al jetliner commandeered by PLO terrorists in Lod Airport on Israeli soil, an assault team could hit your plane at any moment, without warning, and with their Uzi submachineguns blazing; that nation considers individual hostages relatively expendable, in the name of deterring future attempts at terrorism.

If you are truly convinced that your captor is going to murder you, try to escape at an opportune moment. Let's say that your estranged spouse has walked into your office with a gun and taken you hostage. If you think he's just "making a statement" or "declaring himself," cooperate fully. But if he says, "I'm gonna take you out there in front of the TV cameras on the sidewalk, and then I'm gonna blow your brains out and let 'em kill me in a blaze of glory," *and if you are convinced that he means it,* be ready to make a very desperate move to save your life.

Once you are out on that sidewalk you may be assured that your tormentor is in the cross hairs of more than one high-powered rifle, manned by a SWAT officer fully prepared to blow his brains out at the first necessity. If you should feel his gun barrel stray from your head and feel the hand that's holding you loosen, *rip free and dive to the ground.* If you know there's a SWAT team in place it's safe to assume that you'll hear a loud noise, be splattered with blood, and maybe have a two-hundred-pound corpse fall on you, but the chances are that you'll still be alive to talk with your psychologist about the symptoms of "posthostage trauma."

It is most unlikely, however, that you'll have to go that far. The great majority of hostage cases are resolved without bloodshed by the expert police hostage negotiators. The cops will almost certainly get you out alive. You'll be scared, sweaty, dirty, with your attitude toward your fellowman changed forever for the worse, but you'll be alive.

25. AGGRESSIVE, SUBMISSIVE, OR NONCOMMITTAL IN THE FACE OF DANGER?

It's happening now: You're on the street being stalked by person or persons you believe mean to harm you. Quite apart from your tactical movements, you have one choice to make: Do you come on hard and mean, or meek and mild?

This can mean the difference between getting involved in a violent encounter or not. Yet if a violent encounter is going to happen anyway and you're prepared to deal with it, whether you were aggressive or submissive will mean the difference between being acquitted in court for beating/crippling/killing your attacker, or winding up paying through the nose for it for the rest of your life.

There are no clear-cut rules. You must first decide if you can be so convincingly aggressive that you'll frighten a potential criminal and make him stop picking on you. Or, are you naturally submissive?

Next, consider your training, your equipment, your wherewithal. If I'm accosted on the streets of New York's notorious Forty-first Precinct by six members of a South Bronx street gang, and I turn on them and do a macho act, one of two things will happen. Either I will be un-armed and will be kicked, stomped, or even stabbed and shot to pieces, or I will reach for my customary high-powered handgun and probably escape unscathed.

I've had more than one potentially lethal encounter on metropolitan streets. When I carried a gun legally, I was aggressive and stopped the action without anyone getting hurt. When I didn't have a gun, however, I ran faster than the guy with the knife and still nobody got hurt. You tailor your approach to your ability to back it up.

Finally, you decide whether it's a "maybe" danger situation, or a "definite." If you are prepared and equipped to go all the way in a life-threatening encounter, we as-sume that you're going to wind up wasting somebody. This means time in court and having to prove that you were really the one on the defensive at the moment you broke your attacker's neck or shot him in the chest.

Let us look at the pros and cons of an "aggressive response to danger" versus a "submissive response" or a "noncommittal response."

A show of aggression, either verbally or transmitted in body language, can *sometimes* forestall violence. This is especially true if the aggressor is not totally sure of his own ability to overwhelm you. However, *aggression only works when you can back it up.*

Remember, criminals have twisted values. They con-sider you their natural prey and resent any incursion on what they consider their God-given right to attack you.

When they perceive an *ineffectual* attempt to thwart them, they fly into vengeful rage.

It takes a *very* tough and confident person to work the sort of bluff Al Pacino did as Michael Corleone in *The Godfather*. In the film, an unarmed Corleone and a nonmob friend are leaving the hospital where the Mafia *don* is lying, wounded in a murder attempt. Up pulls a carfull of underworld assassins intent on going in and finishing the job. Corleone and his friend fake threatening, "ready to draw their guns" stances, and after a moment of reconsideration, the attackers drive off.

That is not entirely Hollywood hokum. Jeff Cooper, a master combat pistol instructor, used to do a lot of training of pro-U.S. governments in Latin America. He once stepped off a plane in a Third World nation and before he had a chance to strap on his .38 Superautomatic, he was suddenly confronted by a carload of thugs who pulled to the curb in front of him.

Cooper is a man who might well have lived by King Arthur's standards; to run and hide is not in his blood. Besides, he knew, they would shoot him in the back if they *were* the leftist assassination squad he had been warned against. Instead, Cooper came to a dead stop and facing them squarely, his right hand dropping into a gunfighter's "ready position," he fixed them with a cold-eyed look. Their own faces dropped. This was not the reaction of the typical unarmed political assassination victim. Suddenly, they realized that they were trapped in an automobile, with nowhere to hide, in front of a man whose reputation for fast and accurate gun-handling skills made him perhaps a modern counterpart of Wyatt Earp. They sped away with a squeal of rubber. Cooper made a mental note to henceforth don his gun as soon as he retrieved his baggage.

Though he was unarmed, Cooper's wordless show of aggression was sufficient, because it was backed up by a reputation that would have been known to any guerrilla attempting to whack him out. The question is, could you count on the same tactic working for *you?*

Submissive behavior is even trickier. In the animal world, dogs roll onto their backs and baboons bend over and show their rumps when they are intimidated by a fiercer member of their species. The act is the animal's way of saying, "I acknowledge your superior strength. You don't have to fight me. Please don't hurt me."

Although it would go deeply against my own principles to *be* submissive I would have few compunctions about *acting* in a submissive manner. *This is because once the opponent thinks he has you utterly dominated, he usually gets smug and drops his guard very quickly.*

In the training I give to police officers I talk about the "Onion Field Syndrome," named after Joe Wambaugh's true story of two police officers who were disarmed and kidnapped, while one was murdered. In that case, as in almost every case I know of where an officer was disarmed and kidnapped, the criminals got extremely sloppy and careless the instant they had the officer's gun. The criminals figured they had won, had rendered the officer impotent and helpless, and didn't even bother to manacle their captive with his own handcuffs. Officers who carry hidden "backup guns" have been able to shoot their way out of such nightmares, as would those two cops in the onion field had they been carrying spare weapons.

Doing the human equivalent of the baboon offering his buttocks to the aggressor is quite likely to only make your attacker more sure of himself, and convince him that he's safe to go ahead and violate you. Thus, ironically, I would personally be submissive only if I believed I was about to engage in unavoidable violent combat. Why? Because if it's gone that far I know two things: I'm going to fight back, and if all goes well, this person is probably going to be very seriously injured, which means that I'll have to defend my actions in court. But when I step back, the witnesses will remember seeing me attempt to retreat from a savage criminal attack. For my attacker to reach me as I'm moving back, he has to move forward, usually bending somewhat at the waist. This makes it clearly visible to the witness's eyes that *he* is attacking *me*.

If I'm already under attack I'll yell, "Don't hurt me!" Since it's too late to worry about making him feel confident enough to attack me, I can at least reinforce the witness's impression that I am the frightened victim, lashing out only as I fall back desperately under the assault.

Then, when I lash out at his kneecap with my foot or flashlight, or when the gun clears my holster and there's a loud noise, there will be fewer uncertainties among the witnesses as to whether or not it was a clear-cut act of self-defense.

Often, the best approach is to be noncommittal—no snarling rage and no aggressive body movements, but not an obvious attitude of surrender. Speak coolly and calmly, if you speak at all.

When I was a cop, I was a real "Officer Friendly," to the point where one brother officer confided to a sergeant that he thought I might have a cowardice problem. This was because when someone hurled verbal abuse at me, I didn't snarl back an epithet; I just spoke a little softer than he did and said with a smile, "There's no need to use language like that."

There had been a time when cops could arrest people for "using abusive language to a police officer." That ended before I joined the force. I found that talking to even the loudest and most offensive "subjects" with a soft voice and a smile did me a world of good as a cop. Speaking more quietly and calmly and rationally than the other person is an accepted "crisis intervention" technique. Most of the time, without thinking about it, the other guy would respond by either lowering his voice or even apologizing for using abusive language.

If a criminal yells at you and you respond with abusive language, he now feels committed to keeping the fight going or he'll lose face by backing down. By acting aggressively, you've locked him into a "fighting mode." That's like cornering a rat: Now you and he are probably going to *have* to fight. Also, once you've acted in an aggressive manner, there's no place to go but to start hurting him physically. I found that with the smile on my face as I approached a belligerent disturber of the peace, that in itself made me seem (to the offender and to bystanders) more in control and without fear than if I had come in snarling and yelling. By simply allowing the smile to quickly disappear, I had another warning gesture at my disposal, one that could never have been used against me in court as a threat or an act of aggression, even though *he* would correctly perceive it as such.

As a police officer I often had to be aggressive, more than once barking the command "Police! Don't move!" This was reinforced by the fact that (a) I had the authoritative mantle of the police uniform; (b) I had a gun either visible on my hip or in my hand pointed at the offender; (c) I look a lot tougher in black leather patrol jacket than I do in a three-piece suit; and (d) as a cop, I had more latitude than a civilian. As one street person commented, "Cops are the biggest street gang in the world. There's half a million of 'em, and they all got guns and clubs, and if you hurt one of 'em the rest take it awfully personal."

But none of that is working for you, the private citizen. All things considered, you're better off in most civilian encounters not to act too aggressively. It locks the situation at a high-intensity level of potential violence, and you could be charged with contributing to the fracas with "overaggression" or "excessive force."

On the other hand, a civilian who feigns submissiveness toward his or her violent, criminal attacker gains a lot. First, it puts the Bad Guys off their guard and makes them easier to defeat with lawful, judiciously applied, countervailing violence. Second, it makes it clear to all concerned—witnesses, after-the-fact investigators, *everyone*—that *he* was the attacker, and *you* were clearly the innocent victim who was on the defensive, and who tried every other way out before you injured or killed the criminal who threatened you.

26. IS SURVIVALISM FOR YOU?

"Survivalism" isn't just a new fad. It has been growing steadily among a small number of people since well before the fallout shelter craze of the late 1950s. Its adherents seriously believe that cataclysmic acts are going to shatter American society.

Their scenarios vary. Some perceive a doomsday nuclear exchange; others anticipate a slightly less destructive WW III that will destroy cities and industries, throwing America back to a technological level of the agrarian 1880s. These are the "hard-core survivalists," who expect to return to living off the land without the benefit of government, or any law but the gun.

"Soft-core survivalists" are more concerned that inflation will make the dollar look like something out of the Weimar Republic, where you'll need a wheelbarrow full of greenbacks to buy a loaf of bread. These folks stock up on Krugerrands and freeze-dried foods and plenty of ammo to prevent hordes of crazed, starving city dwellers from ripping them off for their provisions and their gold.

The late Mel Tappan, the financier-turned-doomsday prophet who became the guru of the survivalist movement, once told me that I was a soft-core-survivalist. That was because, in a magazine column, I had predicted nothing worse than a six- to eight-week upset of social services.

Years ago, I thought Tappan was a flaming paranoid. Today, I find that in some respects he may have been an optimist.

In a country like America where riots occur during brownouts, and people stab each other for cutting ahead in service station lines during gasoline shortages, one has to wonder how our society would react to a total disruption of its artificial life-support system. In researching magazine articles I've interviewed urban disaster planning authorities who are more skeptical about saving their citizens from major civil disruption than Mel Tappan ever was.

Modern America has never faced famine. The colder regions of the country have never faced a winter without fuel for their urban and suburban homes. Half of American households contain firearms. *Is* it viable to assume that, a few days after the supermarket shelves were bare, a number of unprepared Americans would take desperate measures to feed their families?

Soft-core survivalists like Howard Ruff don't really see the day coming when you'll have to shoot your neighbor to death for his case of Star Kist tuna. At the same time, a long-term Middle Eastern oil embargo could result in a fuel crunch that would eventually shut down the trucking industry, America's primary food supply line.

Reasons for stockpiling two or three months worth of food and liquids and basic medications go beyond any "doomsday scenarios." A natural disaster on the order of earthquakes, Mount Saint Helens, or the great blizzard of 1978, can isolate you from your grocery store for many days. So mundane a "natural disaster" as losing your job can make a basement full of food a godsend while you're trying to keep up your life-style on $100 a week or so of unemployment insurance while "stalking the elusive career position" in a tight job market.

As Howard Ruff has graphically pointed out, you don't even need a disaster of any sort to make a food stockpile work for you and your family's budget. Take a look at the "market basket index" in any newspaper's consumer pages, and you'll be appalled at the rate of escalating food prices. Several hundred dollars worth of nonperishable foods, bought on sale or in quantity through wholesalers in March, can feed you at March prices right through December, saving you a goodly percentage in your food budget. Canned goods should be regularly cycled onto the dinner table anyway, since they begin to lose their nutritive value after several months.

Overstocking on frozen foods is not the way to go since a major natural or man-made disaster is likely to knock out your electricity for an indeterminate period of time. A small generator and a supply of fuel is not terribly expensive. Indeed, the first time a snowstorm or flood whacks out your powerlines, it will more than pay for itself by preventing hundreds of dollars worth of meat in your freezer from rotting. Home generators run the gamut from $200 for a 12-volt unit, to the Winco 8,000-watt, 120-volt air-cooled diesel model, running at 800 revolutions per minute and costing $6,000.

Home canning is made easier than ever today by kits and well-drafted how-to books available at any hardware store. Home units for drying or smoking food are not terribly expensive and can help out your food budget even if you're not a survivalist, since they allow you to buy your favorite foods in bulk when the price cycle is right.

All survivalists recommend firearms. The hard-core groups recommend military-style assault rifles, both for guerrilla warfare against invading armies and for fighting off gangs of looters. Almost everyone suggests at least one shotgun for close-range home defense against multiple attackers, and .22 rifles for shooting small game.

Hunting for your family's protein is a fallacy. Only a very small handful of hardy country folk are able to feed their families with squirrel rifles and fishhooks. If most of us had to depend on fishing and hunting for food, most of us would starve. Why do you *think* the first thing the pioneers did, in every wave from the Pilgrims to the opening of the far West, was to establish farms and raise livestock? In many states, only about seven percent of even experienced deer hunters actually collect their venison in a given hunting season. With everyone running around in the woods, edible wildlife in a given area would probably be close to extinction in a couple of months. Trout ponds would be permanently barren of edible aquatic flesh after being blown up with dynamite to collect hundreds of stunned fish from the surface.

Those of us who only anticipate a short-term social disruption of the American living machine, are less into firearms than those who plan to fight an underground guerrilla campaign in the wake of WW III. Still, if one envisions any sort of riots or mob violence or mass hunger, one is foolish not to realize that personal danger will be greatly increased. Shotgun time? Probably.

In the riots of the sixties and seventies it was noted that the stores in the central area of the pillaging that were least likely to be looted, were those where managers and employees were waiting conspicuously inside with firearms ready.

Most survivalists suggest that all pets who can't breed edible progeny be put to death "when the balloon goes up." Others argue that protective dogs can be used to help warn against, and fight off, pillagers, but that cats should be put to sleep. I would argue that big dogs eat more than cats, and that in such a world I would be constantly armed anyway, and therefore a more formidable protector of myself than any dog.

Cats, on the other hand, eat very little and would be invaluable in any long-term breakdown of society. That is because, historically, such disasters are followed by epidemic outbreaks of disease, often spread by rats. In such a society there would no longer be sanitation departments to control them. (Stockpile some insecticide, too, if you really anticipate nuclear devastation. Birds have low tolerance to radiation and will die from it en masse, while insects can tolerate an enormously high roentgen count. In a few breeding sessions, without their natural predators to control them, insects would breed out of control like a plague of locusts.)

The most logical pet for someone who doesn't love fluffy things, would be rabbits. A stud buck and a couple of breeding does can furnish you with about 120 pounds of dressed rabbit meat in a year. Easily raised on a small scale in the home, rabbit flesh is highly valued in European cuisine, can be cooked like almost any chicken recipe, and its protein-versus-calorie balance is higher than most other meats, as is its meat yield per pound of live weight. Even without a natural disaster, rabbits are an extremely cost-effective avenue of reducing your annual food bills, if you have the heart to slaughter your own meat. (Don't think of them as cuddly; think of them as delicious.)

Those of you who do have guns should stockpile ammunition. Like guns, ammunition always appreciates in value and can last indefinitely if stored in a cool, dry place. Ruff considers .22 cartridges one of the most stable items of barter.

Most of the survivalist measures (for instance, keeping several months supply of food on hand, owning a generator, and being able to raise your own food) make good sense to any economist, quite apart from any doomsday scenario.

Many survivalists believe they can take their families into the woods and live off the fat of the land. They are doomed to either starvation or to pillage by roving gangs if their worst fears do come to pass. Armed, socially bonded groups would hold great sway in a post-doomsday environment. A couple of hundred Hell's Angels, heavily armed and already having sworn an oath of greater loyalty to their group than to themselves, would be deadlier than an army of Vikings. And what would happen if the United States *did* lose WW III? From the rubble of a crumbled government and shattered food supply chain would arise groups of renegade soldiers and national guardsmen, armed with automatic weapons, portable artillery, tanks, and emergency fuel reserves. What ragtag band of survivalists could resist such a force?

Those who believe they can conquer such an occupying army, *or* one from the Soviet Union, have been watching too many John Wayne movies and have probably never actually *seen* a tank in action. Afghan *mujahdeen* in mountaintops and Vietcong in jungles have proven that seasoned guerrilla fighters can defeat armored vehicles on terrain poorly suited to tank maneuvers, but flatland America, with its millions of miles of paved roads, is the world's most favorable warfare scenario for an enemy tank commander.

The ultimate survivalists, though they don't call themselves that, are members of the Mormon Church. Mormons are not *survivalists* in the gun-toting, camouflage-wearing sense of the word. But their extraordinarily powerful degree of social bonding, their tradition of relying on one another, and their mandate that each family have a year's supply of food in the home, are the strongest bulwarks against a societal collapse. Incidentally, nothing in the Mormon religion would prevent a devout practitioner from using weapons to protect his family and food from human scavengers in the wake of a large-scale disaster.

I do not personally believe that hard-core survivalists will ever see their prophecies become reality. However, *it is* entirely possible that our society could be thrown topsy-turvy for a short period of time by any of several natural disasters, or by equally disastrous machinations of international, geo-financial politics. Thus there is no compelling reason *not* to bring oneself to a level of preparation that includes stockpiling food and medicine and guns and ammunition.

III. COUNTER-VAILING FORCE

27. THE WILL TO RETALIATE

Most people are decent and law-abiding. They have a horror of inflicting harm on fellow humans, and a loathing for those who do so. They may therefore find it difficult to reconcile themselves to the concept of countervailing violence, of hurting a criminal to spare themselves and others from being criminally harmed.

You see more of this in women, though it is by no means confined to them. They just have, as a rule, to be pushed to a higher limit before they will retaliate.

One pregnant woman was kidnapped along with her husband, by an armed rapist with a long criminal record. The couple was understandably intimidated. They obeyed the street criminal's order to get in the car and drive where he told them. As night fell, the rapist ordered the couple to pull into a motel courtyard. He sent the husband inside to register, warning him that if he gave a "help" message to the clerk, his wife's brains would be blown out. The husband obeyed. Once in the room, he trussed the husband securely and locked him, without resistance, in the bathroom. Then he shoved the woman viciously toward the bed. The woman argued that she was near delivery and that intercourse could harm her unborn child. He slapped her in the face. In tears, she offered to fellate him instead. He slapped her once more. A strange calm settled over the woman. She turned away and fumbled with her maternity blouse, as if beginning to undress. Satisfied, the rapist set his pistol aside and looked down as he began to remove his trousers. He never saw her pick up the heavy lamp from the night table, probably didn't even hear its cord rip loose as she swung it with both hands. It caught him on the cheek, shattering half the bones on that side of his face. He screamed and reeled back, clawing for the gun, but his pants were around his ankles and he fell to the floor instead.

The woman reached the gun first. The rapist scuttled toward the door, squealing like a pig. The woman raised the pistol in both hands and fired, methodically, again and again. The police found the rapist outside, bleeding from several gunshot wounds.

This story was told to me by a state trooper who worked near where it happened. "She probably shouldn't have fired at him as he was running away," he remarked, "but no one ever thought of charging her; not here, in a state where the public elects the Attorney General. I admire her for what she did. I've often wondered how her husband coped with it."

The will to resist. This woman suffered physical and psychological abuse, as did her husband. This suffering was noble. It was also practical; they both wanted to be left alive. At the moment when she realized her baby's life was in danger, however, she passed the line. She retaliated, suddenly and decisively, instinctively understanding the vital ingredients of successful counter-assault.

And she and her baby and her husband all survived.

No one who has studied the murders of the eight Chicago nurses ever really understood why they stayed so docile, to be led like lambs to the slaughter, one by one. It is said that the sole survivor Corazon Amurao, had urged the others to gang up on Speck, take him off guard, and to fight back. "It's too big a risk," she was allegedly told. "He's only going to rape us." The indignity of rape seemed far preferable to the certainty of being murdered if they resisted. They couldn't conceive, apparently, that this man was going to kill them anyway. Besides they weren't yet at the point where that pregnant midwestern wife was; they still felt they had options.

I once asked Duke Murtaugh, one of the leaders of the prosecution team that convicted Speck, if any of the eight nurses had a gun in that apartment. He shook his head. "What if there had been one?" I asked him. "What if one of those women could have gotten her hands on a gun? It was never conclusively proven that Speck had anything more than the knife he killed them with."

Murtaugh shrugged. "They could have killed him," he answered simply. "Speck left himself wide open."

Even if you do have a gun where you can reach it, you may be unable to pull the trigger. Isn't it immoral to take the life of another human, for *any* reason? Do two wrongs make a right?

I can't decide that for you: That's a decision for you alone, perhaps with some input from your spiritual advisor. If you do decide that you are capable of dealing death or grave injury in self-defense, be warned that people who feel that it's immoral will constantly be challenging you.

This will be an intensely personal chapter because it's such an intensely personal subject. I won't try to make your mind up for you. I can only give you the arguments I've found successful in defending my own decision to resort to countervailing violence before submitting myself or my loved ones to the hands of criminals. There are, however, certain questions you have to be able to answer with conviction. I have been asked them many times.

Does the Bible not say, Thou shalt not kill? Frankly, no. Biblical scholars tell us that in the original Hebrew, the Sixth Commandment was, "Thou shalt not *murder.*" Like contemporary American law, the Scripture defines murder as the illegal killing of the innocent by criminals, and accepts killing undertaken in defense of certain entities, including innocent life. Discuss it with your religious leader, who will tell you the same.

How can you be so arrogant as to take upon yourself the power over another human life? That power belongs to God.

Any Boy Scout who ever got a merit badge for first aid understands the concept of *triage.* In emergency medicine, triage takes place on a battlefield or disaster scene where there are far more casualties than there are facilities to repair them. In such instances someone has to decide who will get treatment, and who won't. Those most likely to survive are those who will receive attention. Were the doctors and nurses and paramedics to say, "No, we'll try to save them all, no matter how hopeless," their scant resources of manpower and supplies would perhaps be spread too thin to save *anyone.* This selection of which victim has the best chance to be a viable human being again, and will therefore be rescued, is triage.

A situation where you and/or other innocents face death at the hands of criminals is similar. Like the doctors performing triage, you didn't create the situation; you are only exercising your moral responsibility to salvage as much human life from this disaster as possible. Like the doctors, you must try to save those who will be the most viable human beings.

If a burglar in your bedroom is about to crush your spouse's skull with a crowbar, you must again perform triage between two victims. You can do nothing, and let the criminal, a victim of his own society, kill your wife and then kill you. He will survive. Assess the potential of his contributions to society as a viable human being.

Your alternative then is to choose to let him die instead by the active expedient of pulling the trigger of a gun. Do you feel that you and your wife, also victims of a society that lets predators run loose, can contribute more good to society and less destruction than the burglar? If so, the principle of triage (universally accepted in the healing arts) demands that your survival, and not the burglar's, be ensured.

The citizen who uses countervailing violence against a violent criminal is not presuming to be God. Like the doctor at the disaster scene, he is using the disciplines and mechanisms created by man through presumably God-given intelligence and skill, to rescue innocent human beings from a death they have done nothing to warrant. Though the citizen defender, like the doctor, didn't create the situation, he must, like the doctor, face the awesome moral responsibility of what triage means.

If a criminal attacks me homicidally, isn't that God's will? Maybe. But if God allows you to fight back, then is that not also God's will?

Is it not a moral victory to surrender to a homicidal criminal assault, rather than descend to his level of base animal violence? The morality of lethal retaliation versus suicidal submission must be addressed at two levels: practical and spiritual. I never understood why, within a space of eighteen months, American television correctly depicted the Guyana tragedy as a sickening, debasing case of sociopsychological cancer, yet in the TV movie *Masada,* glorified a similar mass suicide-murder as a "moral victory." Mass suicide and killing your children to make a political statement of self-righteous morality is still murdering your children, whether you do it in the name of the People's Church or of Judaism.

One wonders if the Roman Legions, upon entering the corpse-strewn mountaintop fortress of Masada, ever really believed they had lost a moral victory. Suppose American forces had landed on Saipan in 1944, and found that all the Japanese had killed themselves. They wouldn't have looked at each other and said, "Aw, jeez, we've been deprived of a moral victory." They would have said, "Yay! Thank God! None of us are going to be killed! The crazy Japs killed *themselves!* Let's break out the beer and celebrate!"

The generals of the Roman Legions entering Masada

must have felt the same revulsion and hatred for Eleazar Ben Yair as *we* all had for Jim Jones when we saw the bodies of those hundreds of women and children who had been forced, weeping, to swallow poison at the command of a mad fanatic. Both leaders had forced women and children *who didn't want to die,* to surrender their lives in the name of a "moral principle."

The message of Masada was supposedly that, by killing your wives and childred instead of letting them be captured and made slaves, you further your own righteousness and the glory of your God. But suppose instead of slaughtering their wives and children, the defenders of Masada had surrendered.

Perhaps the men *would* have been executed, fulfilling their wish to experience moral superiority. The children *would* have been slaves, but would have been sown like seeds within the bosom of the conqueror's society, each filled with a burning motivation to avenge Masada. A generation later their heritage and righteous hatred might have flowered into a Nat Turner-like rebellion. Such a firestorm could have rocked the oppressor society to its roots. Who is to say that history might not have been changed, that centuries later, wars might not have been averted and six million Jews might not have been spared the horror of the Holocaust?

In 1966, Moshe Dayan did not say,

Gosh, people of Israel, we are surrounded on all sides by superior military forces of another faith, sworn to annihilate us because we are Jews. Therefore, to preserve a moral victory, the government of Israel orders all of you to kill your wives and your children, and then commit suicide.

Hardly. Instead, Dayan's defensive military machine lashed out as soon as the genocidal assault on his national entity was imminent. I have yet to talk to a Jew who considers this a moral defeat, nor an Arab who considers the outcome of the Six-Day War a moral victory.

As it is with nations, so it is with individual men and women. When one lawlessly threatens another's right to exist, one waives one's own; this has been the law of God and of man since the dawn of time. Moral victory is constituted by the defeat of the evil and the survival of the innocent, not by acceptance of, and submission to, an act of wickedness.

This is the practical side of the issue. Many must still grapple with the religious connotations. Within that context is it still moral to use violence, even up to the awesome level of justifiable homicide, to protect the innocent against violent assault?

Discuss it with your spiritual advisor. You may think it more moral to depart your earthly body as a murder victim than to taint your soul by shooting the criminal who is about to punch your transfer ticket into the Hereafter.

I'm betting, though, that your spiritual advisor will tell you that it is worse by far to destroy a man's soul than to destroy his earthly body. By letting him murder you and/or your wife and children, do you not therefore aid and abet him in condemning himself to the everlasting fires of hell? Would it not be more compassionate and self-sacrificing of you to salvage him from eternal damnation by preventing him from committing that abominable act? What would be a nobler and more selfless act than to leap between this poor unbeliever and his hellish fate, taking the onus of homicide upon yourself to save him from selling his soul to the Devil? When you discuss this with your spiritual advisor you will realize that this is an argument theologians have been debating for two thousand years. But you must make the decision for yourself, as I did. I shall turn the other cheek morally, and give my homicidal attacker the moral victory. The most efficient way of doing this is to shoot him until he is no longer able to harm me and mine.

He may not appreciate the fact that I've risked my own soul to preserve his, and "destroyed his village in order to save it." But unlike those who called in the heavy explosives on that Vietnamese village, I won't be responsible for the deaths of innocents. What I *will* be responsible for is the *survival* of innocents, and the destruction of an entity that threatens innocent life, and the responsibility of spending the rest of my own existence proving to the Almighty that my life was worth saving at the expense of the criminal aggressor's.

I shall have a whole, rich, delicious lifetime to do this, to ponder my fate, and to savor the joys of helping others. I shall take my chances with that—morally, practically, and theologically.

Philosophy and religion apart, how can you stomach the thought of taking another human being's life? Quite frankly, I *can't*. Those of us who make our living studying real-life gun battles in America, and training the Good Guys to survive them, know that there is a very real phenomenon called postshooting trauma that afflicts people who have been forced to lawfully kill in defense of innocent life.

The symptoms are many and frightening. Nightmares are universal. Depression and social withdrawal are more likely than not. Impotence and alcoholism are all too frequent among people who have had to "drop the hammer" on a predatory human being to protect the lives of themselves or others.

In war, propaganda and patriotism combine to create an artificial atmosphere where the enemy soldier is considered subhuman, a target that it is good to destroy, an entity you will be rewarded for killing or maiming. In civilian life, however, shooting a fellow citizen is a far different thing.

You must understand that *for a civilized normal human being, the taking of a fellowman's life is an unnatural act.*

I have been faced many times with the hypothetical choice between the death of myself or a loved one by an outlaw human being who is threatening us, and committing what I consider an unnatural act—homicide. I have not yet had to kill a human being. I have been at the edge of it, though, and was saved from having to kill only by the criminals' reaction to their realization that I *was* prepared to shoot them to death if they did not break off their criminal assault.

Even when you don't kill, you have the "postincident trauma" aftermath. When you experience it, you'll realize that killing people is an unnatural act. Persistent nightmares or depression or impotence or alcohol dependency regularly plague those who have killed criminals in self-defense.

I have come to the conclusion that I *will* commit the unnatural act of homicide against a lethally dangerous criminal if it is justified to protect innocent human lives, including my own.

This is because there is only one act more unnatural, more despicable in the eyes of virtually every person and virtually every faith in the whole history of the human epoch. To let innocent human beings die by a criminal's depraved and wanton hand without raising your own hand in their defense—*that*, to me, is the most sickening and unforgivable aberration of all.

This is how I reconciled my willingness to retaliate, with my principles as a human being. No one else did it for me; and no one but you can make that decision for yourself.

If you do make that decision, you'll need to be able to implement it skillfully and efficiently in the unlikely event that your convictions are ever put to the test. The eight nurses in Chicago died, in one sense, because they didn't have a gun to shoot Richard Speck with. Had the defenders of Masada had sufficient firepower to fight back the Roman forces, their mountaintop citadel would have become a true monument to the courage of the free human spirit, and not a charnel house where hollow claims of "moral victory" echoed over the all-too-real corpses of slaughtered women and children.

If you choose to fight back, then so must it be with you. You must command the tactics, the determination, and perhaps above everything else, the physical where-withal to successfully defeat the entity that is about to destroy you.

We shall address the realities of these disciplines in the following chapters.

28. THE TRUTH ABOUT STREETFIGHTING

There are dozens of books that show you how to defend yourself against violent assault using your bare hands and feet. Many are pure hokum but a few teach some good techniques. The best of these is *Mu Tau: The Modern Greek Karate* by Jim Arvanitis ($15 from Police Bookshelf, P.O Box 122, Concord, NH 03301). It teaches, in an easy-to-understand way, *how* to put all your weight behind a punch, or how to slip an opponent's blow.

Streetfighting is not martial arts. Streetfighting is between you and a man who is trying to hurt you. He has probably done it before and enjoys it. He has also probably been hit hard before and has learned to shrug it off if you don't hit him in a way that impairs his bodily function and takes him out of the fight.

Those aspects are what make him *seasoned*. A seasoned streetfighter will probably beat a karate expert who has never been in a real fight before. In exhibition matches where professional boxers, using only their gloved hands,

BFS-1: For the untrained person, this is the best stance: strong side is toward offender (right arm and leg, your longest and strongest "weapons," are better within reach of opponent). Right hand is at high chest level, left hand at low chest level. Forward thigh protects groin. Hands are open so they can instantly grapple or strike, closing into a fist as the blow is launched. Note especially (dotted lines) arcs in which either hand can block to ward off an attack.

go against karate experts who fight with hard, bare hands and feet, the boxer will usually win. Although the karate expert has range going for him with his kicks and possesses a much greater repertoire of striking and grappling techniques, the boxer tends to be better conditioned, inured to pain, and able and willing to ignore blows that strike him while he drives his fists mercilessly through his opponent's defenses. With its emphasis on conditioning, boxing trains you *to be able to take punishment and to love to dish it out.* That's the mentality of the streetfighter.

But boxing is a sport for young, strong men who devote their lives to that type of conditioning. Many of you saw Chuck Wepner fight Muhammad Ali in the mid-1970s. Chuck was the only heavyweight title boxer in recent times who didn't fight and train all the time; he made his living working in the liquor wholesale business. Maybe you didn't think Ali was in trouble when you watched that fight, but I know Wepner; I've seen him work out in the gym, and I guarantee that not one in a hundred of you would last a minute in the ring with him. Wepner was, and is, a streetfighter as well. Chuck was, incidentally, the real-life inspiration for Sylvester Stallone's Rocky.

Can *you* learn to hold your own against a streetfighter? You've got a decent chance *if* you learn to apply those martial arts that fit your personality, physique, and general physical condition. You can learn a lot in training, but the main thing you'll need to develop is the streetfighter mentality, for once you're committed to a physical conflict, you have no choice but to go all the way.

Focus on your offensive. Ignore the pain. Your mind dwells in your fists and feet as you drive through your opponent (you don't aim your blow *at* the attacker; you aim it *through* the attacker to deliver maximum force.) Adrenalin pours into your system, adrenalin being the magical substance that doctors in emergency rooms inject into cardiac arrest patients to bring the dead back to life. It puts your pain tolerance through the roof. Don't worry about the pain, because when you're in a fighting mode, you'll feel very little of it, and if you win, you can get to the hospital and get a shot to make it go away. Besides, it's human nature to forget pain. Think back to the worst, screaming pain you ever experienced—childbirth or something sharp in your eye. Now close your eyes for thirty seconds after you finish reading this sentence, and try to conjure up the exact sensation of that pain.

Ah, your eyes are open. You couldn't do it, could you? No one can. It is impossible for the human mind and body to duplicate in memory the sensation of pain. It is the most forgettable of all earthly experiences.

Another exercise. When you've finished this paragraph, I want you to think back to the most bitter defeat, the most shameful and humiliating put-down, that you ever experienced in your life. Take thirty seconds for that too. Did you notice that the remembered helplessness and shame and humiliation *didn't* seem diminished, even after all these years? Few of you were able to concentrate for thirty seconds on remembering physical pain, but a great many of you lingered longer than thirty seconds remembering the defeat you were ashamed of.

Pain is cheap, easily dealt with and forgotten. Defeat and shame however, stay with you forever and especially, the sense of fearful helplessness they engender. So does crippling injury, another predictable side effect of freezing up in a fight because you were afraid of pain.

Don't be ashamed of fear. As pain is the body's warning system of injury, fear is the mind's warning system to your whole organism.

You don't want to be without fear or without pain. A man who felt no pain would constantly be getting burned when he touched hot things because his warning system would be out of commission. Without fear, you would not sense danger, would not be able to react to it with the full powers of your ingrained human survival instinct and mental resources. Without fear *or* without pain you would be a handicapped person whose lack of danger warning systems would soon lead you to destruction.

Fear is manageable. Even if you feel yourself losing control of your bowels, that's not a sign that you've already lost the fight. Indeed, you should find it comforting. It means that your fight or flight reflex has kicked into gear. In man, the fight or flight reflex is nature's response to the threat of the continued existence of the organism: It prepares the body system to instantly be supercharged to do violent battle, or to run until its heart bursts. Adrenalin pours into the bloodstream. Pulse rate and blood pressure skyrocket. Muscles tighten violently—the reaction that can cause evacuation of the bowels—and you become stronger and faster and meaner and more impervious to pain than you ever thought you could be.

Don't curse your fear. Welcome it. The shortness of breath and the chill up the spine you feel merely signal the onset of this period of literally superhuman strength. It won't last long, but if you've been trained to take care of yourself, that training will lock in automatically. You will literally watch your body perform what it has been trained to do, with your fists and your feet or with your makeshift weapon or with your gun, without really having to think about it that much. And, if you and your body have been properly trained and equipped, the programmed reactions to the danger *will* be carried out.

In the following chapters we'll show you which streetfighting techniques can be learned without intensive martial arts training, and which ones can't; which makeshift defense weapons work on the street, and which ones will get you killed; and how to put together a simple, rational training program that will teach you how to take care of yourself without having to make the martial arts an avocation.

But remember that the control of fear, and the commitment to ignore pain, are the keys to your positive, aggressive response in a street survival situation.

Amboss oder hammer sein. You will be either the anvil or the hammer.

29. THE NECK-TWIST TAKEDOWN

Here we have perhaps the most controversial of the unarmed self-defense techniques you'll see in this book. The carotid restraint choke-out or neck-twist can, very occasionally, prove fatal under unusual circumstances; the neck-twist is often *taught* as a killing technique among the experts in the martial arts.

Here's how the neck-twist takedown works. I'll teach it to you civilians because the cops don't need it anyway: They've got batons, guns, chemical agents, and a lot of other unarmed techniques they can use to restrain someone without killing them. If *you* are savagely attacked by a street criminal, you'll find it easier to defend yourself in court for breaking this person's neck than if you were a cop who just did it because the guy grabbed you by the shirt. *You* probably don't have a nightstick, a gun, or a portable radio to call for patrol officers to back you up.

What you do is, lever the Bad Guy's head backward and then spin it like a steering wheel. You want your right hand (if you're right-handed) under his chin, while your left hand grabs the top rear of his head. Pull his hair if you want, but it works just as well if you grab hold of the skull or ear if the guy is bald.

Your right hand comes up from below, suddenly,

from a point out of his field of vision. He won't know you've got him until he feels your right hand cupping his chin, and your left hand either wrapping around the top back of his skull, or taking a handful of hair back there.

Now, you've got him. Spin his head as if it was a steering wheel and you had to go hard, *hard* left. Lean your right shoulder forward as his head turns.

You will either take him to the ground or break his neck. If he poses so deadly a threat to innocent life that you probably *should* break his neck, this will be facilitated if you (a) have his shoulders already back against a wall where he can't move to "roll with the attack," or if (b) after his neck starts to turn, you step back, pulling his head toward you, and bending him over, so that his neck breaks on the suddenly created fulcrum of his bent torso. You could help that along a little bit by slamming your right knee up into his right chest or front right shoulder as he bends toward you.

Of course, if you break his neck this way, you'll be in trouble if you're both the same sex. That's why I tell you elsewhere in this book loudly and vehemently to decline streetfights. If, however, you're a five-foot woman and you break the neck of a six-foot male rapist, you might want to cover side bets on whether or not you'll win in court.

The neck-twist takedown won't always break necks. That's why John Peters, who has been around the world of the street for a while, put it in his defensive tactics book.

Peters is considered one of the top defensive tactics (DT) instructors in the United States. Police DT is not martial arts; rather, it consists of techniques that allow a person with relatively little training, to fight off an unarmed assault, or to place a violently resisting suspect in a helpless "control position."

An advanced black belt himself, and president of the U.S. Combat Judo Association, Peters has abstracted the simplest and most effective martial arts techniques into forms that the average person can learn to use with great leverage effect in a very short time. The neck-twist takedown is one of these.

Peters and Shihan Takayuki Kubota, one of the world's leading martial arts masters, have produced a book called *Realistic Defensive Tactics*. The 104-page, large-format softcover is replete with easy-to-follow line drawings, and is one of the very few "books on streetfighting" from which you really can learn effective techniques without the hands-on aid of an instructor. It is available for $10.95 postpaid from Police Bookshelf, P.O. Box 122, Concord, NH 03301.

Most people who get twisted around by the takedown just fall on their backs, "going with the flow" of a movement that is agonizing to them.

If the Bad Guy isn't against a wall, he probably will just fall down that way. Due to the strong neck muscles on most men, it's not likely that their cervical vertebrae will break from violent torquing. On the other hand, this is taught as a killing technique in at least one martial arts system, and *I* teach it as a potentially lethal technique.

When you readers examine this technique, your first question is going to be, "what if I'm facing a mugger who outweighs me by a hundred muscular pounds, and who has a neck like a bull? Is this really going to work?"

You bet it will, *if* you understand how to apply it. You're worried about someone resisting the technique. You should be, because I've seen books on self-defense where they only halfway taught the poor readers how to properly execute this technique.

It's hands-on training time again. Reach up and grab your own chin. Lock your neck muscles tight, and try to push your chin sideways with that one hand. It doesn't move, and it's not going to. Your neck, like your attacker's, is surrounded by muscles that hold a twenty-pound head

NECK TWIST TAKEDOWN

NT-1: Defender steps in toward attacker, turning right hip toward him and positioning right leg to block groin attack. Both hands rise up quickly toward attacker's head. Note that both attacker's arms are now blocked from punching defender in face.

NT-2: Left hand grabs back of attacker's head, optionally grabbing hair. Heel of palm strikes under attacker's chin, rocking his head back and to the side (if he resists backward pressure, twist to side; if he resists side pressure, rock back).

NT-3: Using pressure with both hands, twist attacker's head over left shoulder, around, back, and down, like rolling a ball. Your right leg is already in position to increase his loss of balance and trip him. Fling supect to ground.

(As taught by John Peters, Defensive Tactics Institute.)

NT-4: LETHAL VARIATION, TO BE USED ONLY WHEN IN IMMEDIATE AND OTHERWISE UNAVOIDABLE DANGER OF DEATH OR GRAVE BODILY HARM. Execute neck twist takedown as above, EXCEPT: Maintain hold with both hands and continue rotating head as suspect topples back and to the side. Insert right knee beneath his shoulder. With your arm perpendicular to the ground, lean forward heavily utilizing maximum power as you continue rotation. This will break the neck, causing quadriplegia or death.

up all day. Those neck muscles are strong. If you lock them in they aren't going to go sideways.

Continue the exercise. Reach up again, cupping your hand under your chin, and now, slowly push backward, tilting your own head upward. Once your head is as far back as it can comfortably go, try again to turn the chin sideways with that cupped palm. *Now, it's going to move, and move easily.*

It's very simple. Once the human head goes backward, the muscles that keep it from being turned sideways go out of play, and don't do their job anymore.

So, you use the cup of your hand with a palm heel strike to tilt your attacker's head backward. Now, you can twist his head any way you want, and the way you'll want to do it is hard and fast.

Finish the exercise on yourself, *gently,* and you'll feel how effective the neck-twist takedown is. You'll also realize how easy it is to break someone's neck doing this.

I hope police Defensive Tactics instructors will forgive me for this, but I think the neck-twist takedown is inherently too lethal to teach as a technique for subduing unarmed men of equal strength. I *do* think it offers a lot to a small person who has no other way to stop a big person from hurting him gravely.

I fear that the first accidental death with the neck-twist takedown will be of a woman, by a woman. When a female suspect goes bonkers, the male officers will sometimes call for a female cop to subdue her, so that *they* don't get charged with using excessive force. That female officer will have to take out that female suspect using the only defensive tactics techniques she was probably taught, techniques designed to work on men.

But the neck of the average woman is much more fragile than the neck of the average man. That's why they're so easy to strangle, unfortunately. The woman's neck is relatively longer and thinner and weaker, thus relatively easier to break when the totality of her physiology is considered, and the female police officer who fights this tough woman and uses a neck-twist takedown, is quite likely to break her neck and leave her dead or paralyzed, whereas it's more likely that a man she did it to would only fall to the ground, disoriented.

The neck-twist takedown, in my considered opinion, is a potentially lethal technique. It should only be used when the person applying it believes himself to be in immediate and otherwise unavoidable danger of death or grave bodily harm.

When a woman is compelled to do that to protect herself from a much larger male rape suspect, the technique *probably* won't kill him, and will *probably* take him off his feet long enough to resort to whatever she may have selected as "Plan B."

Understand that nothing is one hundred percent effective in real life, though, and also understand that, applied between people of equal strength, it *is* considered a killing technique in the world of the martial arts.

30. EYE ATTACKS

Nothing frightens humans more than being blind. Bring the subject up at a cocktail party, and most people will say that deafness would be a mere inconvenience compared to sightlessness. A good number of them will tell you that they'd sooner lose their life than lose their sight.

From the defensive standpoint, the eyes have always been a "Number One Target." No matter how big and strong your attacker is, and whether or not he has abdominal muscles a jeep could drive over without hurting him,

EYE ATTACK

NT-5: Hand positioning in neck-twist takedown also allows two-finger gouge of attacker's eyes. Hand at back of head prevents him pulling away. Since fingers come up from underneath, attacker's eyeglasses or sunglasses will be no protection. The cupping action of the other fingers create a "claw hold effect" that prevents attacker from twisting away befor his eys are gouged. TO BE USED ONLY WHEN FACING DEADLY DANGER: THIS TECHNIQUE CAN CAUSE TOTAL AND PERMANENT BLINDNESS.

his eyes are still just as soft and sensitive as the weakest person's.

If you blind your opponent, you've won the fight 98 times out of 100. The couple of times you'll lose will be when you're grappling at close range with your opponent; in such a situation he doesn't need sight to find you; he'll tear you apart in the frenzy of his agony and rage.

Novice students of the martial arts are always taught that going for an opponent's eyes will be his or her salvation.

As a long-time observer of the martial arts scene, I'm concerned with teaching such a technique.

First, *the eyes are the hardest part of your opponent's body to strike*. Moving the head sideways to slip a punch, or raising the thigh to block a groin kick, is something you have to learn. Eye protection however, is instinctive and automatic.

If someone unexpectedly tries to kick you between the legs or karate-chop you across the throat, chances are that the blow will land before you can react with a block or evasive movement. If they go for your eyes, though, your head will *automatically* snap away, and your eyelids will automatically close, before you even realize what's happening. This is also going to happen if you try to jab your criminal attacker in the eyes: He'll evade without having to think about it, and he's going to be more psychotically vicious than before.

This is not to say that the eye attack is not effective because even a feint to the opponent's eyes can disorient him and cause an involuntary backward movement of his body. If you do intend to permanently or temporarily blind him, you're going to have to do it in such a way that he doesn't see the attack coming until your fingers are already in his eyes. We'll elaborate on both those strategies shortly.

The second thing you have to remember with eye attacks is that, as with groin attacks, *they're something seasoned street criminals and rapists know about better than you*. They're waiting and watching for it. This means that you must use an unconventional attack that comes out of nowhere.

Thirdly, because you're talking about such a small target, *most people can deflect an eye attack if they see it coming*. The two most common eye attacks are the V-finger jab (used by the Three Stooges) which is taught in martial arts academies worldwide, and the thumb-gouge in which the hands are slapped against the side of the opponent's head while the thumbs go into the eye sockets.

The V-finger jab can be defeated simply by nodding the head forward; nature has protected your eyes with the bony brow of your forehead; inclining the skull sharply forward causes the attacking fingers to slip off and do little more than scratch the skin on your face. You can also break *your* extended fingers against *his* forehead.

Your rapist or mugger will instinctively pull his head back if you try a thumb-gouge, and your palms on the side of his head will slip harmlessly away before your thumbs even touch his eyes.

Finally, *the great majority of people, especially women, simply can't bring themselves to blind another person* partly due to a natural sense of decency in not wanting to cause such an enormous handicap to a fellow human, but mainly because of the instinctive revulsion to touching icky, slimy eyeballs.

Those are my four concerns with teaching the eye attack for self-defense: Even so, the eye attack is too potent and effective a technique to leave out of your defensive repertoire. Those of you who are small and weak won't have the power to kill or stun with a random punch or kick, and for you, a successful eye attack will disable your attacker more quickly than a blow to the throat or groin, and more completely than a kick to the knee or shin.

All you have to do is overcome certain things. Let's look first at your real-life hesitancy to stick your fingers in someone's eyes.

It will help if you know that most eye attacks *don't* result in permanent blindness. The eye is at once fragile and amazingly resilient. Very few people are ever permanently and totally blinded in streetfights. The instinctive reaction of pulling back usually prevents the eyeball from being ruptured, but the disruption of sight and the acute pain are usually enough to put that person temporarily out of the fight.

You may have been told how trained commandos thrust their rigid fingers through an enemy soldier's eye socket and into the brain for an instant kill. No way. If you look at a cross section of a human head, you'll realize that it would be all you could do to reach the frontal lobe with your fingertips before the web between your knuckles hit the bridge of the other person's nose and stopped your hand short. Considering the natural and violent backward reflex the person would execute, and the fact that you'd have to push through some pretty tough membranes and optic muscles, and you'll understand why the "eye stab" is almost never fatal.

When your fingers touch another human's eyes you'll feel something in addition to the violent movement to escape: The eyeballs seem to vibrate and flutter, like separate living entities. When you press them, they feel surprisingly firm and surprisingly resilient.

To actually put your finger through an eyeball, you have to have that person's head locked immobile against a wall, or be holding it in place yourself. They'll struggle with incredible force. It's quite unlikely that your finger will actually penetrate the eyeball. If it does, it only gets wet. It's no slimier than gelatin.

There will be large amounts of blood, and the criminal whose eyes you gouge will scream like a banshee. The pain and shock are enough that many people will actually pass out when their eyeballs are ruptured. It's tough to live with afterward, but when you realize that it's *your* life and *your* eyeballs on the line, if you don't do it first, you can do it if you know beforehand that you're capable.

I have put my thumbs into eyes, and I know what it feels like for my thumb or my index finger to pierce the tough sclera (outer eye membrane) and gouge through the aqueous tissue beneath. It's no ickier than grabbing a handful of Jell-O out of the refrigerator or pulling the gizzard out of your family's Thanksgiving turkey.

As we said, the criminal knows that all you Good Guys have been told to "go for the eyes and the groin and the shins," and he'll instinctively duck an eye attack if he sees it coming. This means that "eye stabs" are out; leave that foolishness for Larry, Moe, and Curly. What you have to do, is use a technique where he won't see your avenue of attack until your fingers are already in his eyes, and where he can't get away even then.

The system I teach is one I learned from John Keehan, AKA Count Dante, perhaps the most infamous outlaw in modern martial arts history. Keehan developed it from kung-fu movements.

Keehan was a strange man. He was one of the first promoters of sport karate in the United States but he developed an obscene fascination with the most brutal part of the arts. The son of a wealthy Chicago doctor, he had begun boxing training as a child with the famous Johnny Coulon, and had progressed through a number of martial arts, often studying overseas at his father's expense.

His obsession with violence ruled his life. He claimed to have killed men in "kung fu death matches" in Hong Kong and developed connections with the Chicago Mob, claiming that he handled their strong-arm work involving owners of porno bookstores. He was arrested, but not tried, in connection with the multimillion-dollar Purolator robbery in that city. The height of his infamy came when he convinced some friends, including the well-liked judo champion Jim Concevic, to "trash" the training hall of a rival martial arts school, the Black Dragon Society. In the melee, Concevic was stabbed to death. The mainstream martial artists hated Keehan ever since.

The fact remains that Keehan, who liked to be addressed as "the Count" and billed himself as "the deadliest man on earth," really did have a keen, analytical mind and an encyclopedic knowledge of the various martial arts. His reputation as an outlaw drew a lot of criminals and undesirables to his Chicago school.

To get in close enough to use the Dante eye attack, you charge the opponent with your hands coming up in a rising V (see Figure NT-5) to get inside his arms. Your right leg comes up to protect your groin; the assailant's right arm is now outside yours, where he won't have leverage enough to hit you hard. He could grab you by the hair, but he probably won't have time.

Your left hand slaps hard at the base of his skull, stunning him perhaps a little bit, but also giving you a firm grasp on his hair. Now, your right hand slides up over his chin, and you gouge his eyes.

That hand technique needs some explanation. It's a chilling lesson that you can learn sitting right where you are, reading this book.

Here's the exercise. Extend your right hand, shape the middle and index fingers into an eye-stabbing V, and jab them at your own eyes at gradually accelerating speeds. Stop short, of course! You'll be able to evade it easily. This shows you that it's not a technique to trust your life to, when used against a mugger.

OK, now try it again. This time, as in the figures, snake your hand *upward,* palm traveling across your chest, and try to put the same two fingers *gently* against your eyelids from beneath. *Pow!* Those fingers are *there,* aren't they?

You bet they are. Neither defensive tactics nor involuntary reflexes can start until the Bad Guy sees the fingers coming at his eyes, *and with this technique, the eyes don't see the fingers until they're already there.*

If he tries to move now, he *can't*; your hand behind his head prevents any backward movement. If you look again at the figures, you'll see that when done properly, your whole hand cups his face: His chin is in your palm, your right thumb prevents him from twisting to his right, and your last two fingers prevent him from moving to his left. Even if he's strong enough to twist his neck in a violent survival reflex, your hand is locked on his face like a Gila monster, and will just turn with him as you keep clawing and gouging your first two fingertips into his eyes.

The only shortcoming with this technique is that you may not have the strength, with finger muscle power alone, to puncture the eyeballs. No sweat; all you wanted to do anyway was hurt him and scare him, and make him stop trying to hurt you. It isn't absolutely necessary to destroy his eyes to achieve that. Indeed, *a small person's hand will be so hyperextended on a big man's face that it would be very difficult to do more than get the fingertips against the surface of the eyes!*

With this technique your hands are also in a perfect position for a neck-twist takedown, described elsewhere in this section. This is good, because the Bad Guy is going to move violently away from you anyway, and if you feel your hold on the eye-gouge slipping away from you, the fact that his balance is now almost certainly broken allows you to take a step forward, twist his neck, and throw him hard to the ground. Then run for it. It is rather unlikely that he will get up and follow you.

The Dante technique I just taught you was meant to blind people. "The Count's" disciples, who tended to come from a hard-core criminal world, used it frequently. They left some people blind out there, but they were never injured themselves. Learn from the outlaws: Dante's system was designed for the sort of person you'll face, someone who will hurt *you* without the slightest compunction.

You should understand also that the instinctive human reaction of jerking away from a strike to the eyes can help you in other ways in a streetfight. Famed martial artist Jim Arvanitis teaches the "eye flick," in which you slap your hand out quickly with all four fingers extended, toward the opponent's eyes; it won't permanently impair his vision in most cases, but it *will* snap his head back, throw him off balance, and blind him long enough for you to come in with a sucker punch or power kick to put the mugger on his back.

The reason all the people who write about self-defense recommend eye attacks is that they are devastating. The trouble is, most of those "experts" have worked only in the martial arts training hall and not on the street. When you master these simple, street-oriented techniques you'll overcome the real-life problems with the eye attack—your own inhibition about using it, and the fact that the other person is prepared for an eye attack, can defeat it easily if you try it in a conventional manner, and will instinctively protect his eyes in any case.

Depending how well you make it work, that particular rapist or mugger might also have a hard time identifying you before the jury when he tries to sue you.

31. LEARNING THE MARTIAL ARTS

Since before Christ, man has developed fighting arts that teaches him how to use his body as a deadly weapon. It has been argued whether the first scientifically developed fighting systems should be attributed to the Chinese (kung fu and gung fu), or to the Greeks, whose Pankration ("all powers fighting") was the highest purse sport in the first bloody Olympics. Some believe that when Alexander marched across the world in conquest, his *pankratiasts* sowed the seeds of scientific fighting styles in the East. The debate may never be solved.

Today, we're looking at frightened American citizens who couldn't care less about the history of "the arts." They want to feel safe, and they want to *be* safe, and so they sign up for karate classes. This is an undertaking more complex than it seems. First, you have to understand that it takes about a year to reach a decent middle level (yellow or green belt, depending on the art) of competence to defend yourself. And even then, we're talking about a serious commitment of several days or nights a week in the *dojo* ("training hall"). An extremely dedicated student can reach black belt level in two years, though it usually takes three or four. The problem is, you have to make sure you're learning streetfighting from someone who knows streetfighting himself.

In 1972 and 1973, the first great "karate craze" bonfired, fueled by the dramatic image of Bruce Lee on the movie screen. Suddenly, every ex-soldier who had taken three lessons while overseas declared himself a black belt in some style of karate, and opened a storefront *dojo*. Many signed long-term contracts (much as health spas do today), cheating their customers out of hundreds of thousands of dollars when they went bankrupt a few months later.

When the craze died out, (or "normalized," as karate people put it), a greater number of serious students were left behind as were a greater number of qualified instructors. Still, even today, you see a lot of schools that are to the martial arts what McDonald's is to cuisine—oriented to cheap, quick satisfaction and not particularly concerned with giving the best quality.

A handful of *sensei* (instructors) teach the martial arts for personal reasons; most of the rest do it for money. They learn that students pay for confidence more than anything else and that soft Americans are loathe to work hard to get beaten on.

Therefore a syndrome of karate schools has flourished where you are just about guaranteed a black belt in two years if you show up for class regularly, don't get too clumsy during the promotion tests, and pay your tuition on time. During those two years, you will never once strike another human being, nor will you ever be punched or kicked yourself.

If you reflect on this and find it troubling as you tie your newly issued black belt on over your *gi* ("practice uniform"), you might want to ask the *sensei* about it. "Have no fear," he may tell you. "Your superior martial arts knowledge will carry you through and will prevent anyone from hitting you anyway."

I don't know how you feel about it, but if a teacher gave me a line like that, I'd ask for my two years' worth of tuition back.

It's a standard joke among cons, cops, barfighters, and other people who know the hard world of the street, that a guy who knows how to take a punch and loves the feeling of somebody's else's body breaking under his punch or kick, is likely to wipe out "any fancy-pants karate jock who starts doing pirouettes on the street."

If you really want to learn martial arts, you must understand that it will take hundreds or even thousands of hours of hard work, strenuous calisthenics, bruises, and pulled muscles.

I have seen some very good "short courses" on self-defense, however. They teach you five or six easily applied techniques (including some of the ones in this book), but they also make it clear that knowing these things doesn't make you a "kung fu master of death." Properly taught, such a course is a consciousness-raising experience that puts hand-to-hand combat into a realistic context for you. If the instructor implies that it will do anything else, save your money and pass up the course.

Streetfighting is ugly and hard and brutal. You're going to be up against people who will enjoy torturing you without any compunction as an affirmation of their own manhood and strength. It's the only time in their miserable, thwarted lives that they are able to feel stronger than someone else.

If you can't imagine what it would be like to be punched in your jaw and feel your teeth coming loose, or to hit hard enough in the stomach to empty your lungs of breath, and if you're not ready to go out and get a few ribs broken in a hard-training, street-oriented *dojo*, I don't blame you. I don't like getting hurt either. If you *aren't* prepared to close in for hand-to-hand combat, you should seriously rethink whether or not you need remote-control weaponry, or a buffer on the order of a protection dog.

Those of you who are seeking martial arts training, though, have a cornucopia of styles and disciplines to choose from.

Karate or "the way of the empty hand," exists in many forms. Shotokan is a Japanese style of karate that emphasizes strength and power, with rigid blocks and potent, driving punches and kicks. Among the most destructive styles, Shotokan is also extremely hard on the practitioner because the blocks involve meeting flesh and bone directly with one's own limbs, instead of deflecting the impact. This and other "hard" styles of karate are best practiced by young, strong males.

"Soft" styles are typified by Uechi-ryu an Okinawan style founded by Master Kanei Uechi and popularized in the United States by George Mattson. For the layman, "soft" karate differs from "hard" karate in that the former emphasizes strikes to soft parts of the opponent's body that are not naturally protected, while "hard" karate teaches power techniques that will break bones and cause debilitating injury no matter where they hit. Thus, a hard style is better suited for young, athletic males, while the softer styles make more sense for older people, smaller males, and females.

This does not mean that the hard styles are superior for street combat. The circular, human-engineered movements of Uechi-ryu make it, in many ways, more realistic for streetfight training.

Koreans don't call it karate at all, but Korean karate as typified by Tae Kwon Do and Tang Soo Do, is generally considered among the harder styles. Tae Kwon Do, the most popular, emphasizes straight-line movements and high kicks (to the opponent's head), while Tang Soo Do emphasizes circular movements.

One of the most effective Korean forms is Hapkido, a

karatelike art that also encompasses grappling and throwing techniques. Never that popular outside of California, it was largely introduced to the United States by Byong Yu, who choreographed the Billy Jack movies.

Kung fu and gung fu are said by some to be Americanized terms for what the Chinese refer to as variations of Wu-shu, or simply, Chinese boxing. Bruce Lee was a kung fu stylist; the art he developed, Jeet Kune Do, translates to "the way of the sticky hands." Lee had an almost preternatural ability to evade incoming punches and kicks by simply touching the opponent's onrushing fist or foot, gently deflecting it away from his own body as the attacker helplessly followed his own momentum, going off balance as Lee counter-struck.

The Chinese, for the most part, preferred soft fighting forms that emphasized grace, agility, physical speed, and the psychomotor control to deliver a strike unerringly to a soft and vulnerable target such as the eyes, groin, or throat. In ancient China, the village *sifu* ("kung fu master") often doubled as a practitioner of the healing arts, specializing in acupuncture. This may account for the fact that these martial arts use movements and strategies that are amazingly sophisticated in light of what we now know as "human engineering."

In some respects, the Chinese influences on Kenpo karate allow it to cross the lines between the two main striking styles of the martial arts, encompassing the powerful striking techniques of hard karate with the control required to accurately strike soft targets. For many years, interestingly, the National Women's Full Contact Karate Championships was dominated by a Kenpo team coached by George Pesare. One of his champions, Linda Herzog, recently became a U.S. Secret Service agent. Were I the First Lady, I would find her presence comforting.

Savate, ("French kickboxing"), is not widely taught in America. Martial artists who have studied it after obtaining a background in the Oriental arts, acclaim it as a powerful, street-oriented discipline.

Thai boxing is considered by many the most savage form of unarmed combat presently in existence. The Thai kickboxers tend to press themselves far beyond other martial artists in physical conditioning (for instance, smashing their shins into trees until enough calcium has been built up so that they can sweep another man's legs out from under him, perhaps breaking those legs, without the practitioner feeling so much as a bump himself). The ideal among the Thai fighters is best conceptualized by Ian Fleming's Oddjob: a callused, pain-proof killing machine that has to be shot through the brain to be stopped. At this writing, I know of no Caucasian practitioners who have studied Thai boxing sufficiently to develop competitive reputations in the art.

Boxing is something you'd better understand even if you don't take it up yourself, because it's the one fighting form you're most likely to be up against on the street. Drop into a boxing gym instead of a *dojo,* and you'll enter a world of pure physical conditioning that goes a dimension beyond what you'll see in ninety-five percent of the karate *dojos* in America. You'll see men wearing protective gear—gloves, helmets, jockstraps, and kidney belts—and whaling each other with blows that will make you wince.

These guys can absorb the most powerful blows to the abdomen and then smile at you. Between tough men, hard-style fighting is simply a contrast between who has the strongest punch and the strongest abdominal muscles. This is why, for the average citizen, soft techniques make more sense: There is no known exercise to toughen and harden the larynx, the eyeballs, or the testes.

There are numerous other styles and substyles of punching and kicking; but you really have to be very experienced before you are able to analyze your own physical capabilities. As we'll explain shortly, there's more to decide between instructors than there is between styles within a given fighting discipline. For many of you, a better choice will be one of the nonimpact formats.

Judo is the best known of the nonkarate sciences, and probably the best organized of all the martial arts. Because instructors have to conform to rigid international codes set by the Kodokan in Japan, you almost never run across an inferior judo instructor the way you often do in karate, and an instructor who fakes or makes up his credentials is literally unheard-of. (I've met several *sensei* who had arbitrarily promoted themselves to tenth-degree black belts in karate).

Good judo training is available in any moderately size community that has an active YMCA. Judo is strictly a sport, with relatively little application to the street; many of the throws taught don't work on someone who isn't wearing a canvaslike, pajama-styled *gi* for you to grab onto. (Oddly enough, though, the techniques translate well to the street if your opponent is wearing a denim or leather jacket.)

One of the great advantages of judo is that it teaches you *ukemi* ("breakfalling") in the very beginning. These simple techniques allow you to be thrown to the ground without disorientation or injury, and to instantly regain your feet. Judo also teaches you the dynamics of closing full-power with another human antagonist, with much less likelihood of injury than in full power *kumite*. (In karate, *kumite* is actual sparring or practice-fighting, while *kata* is the shadowboxing technique often described as resembling ballet.) The *kumite* of judo is known as *shiai*, and is a much less painful way to learn fighting hands-on, since judo has no punching or kicking.

Jujitsu is, regrettably, one of the least-practiced of the Oriental martial arts. A layman could call it the streetfighting equivalent of sport judo. It teaches effective punches and kicks as well as judolike throwing and choking techniques, and the pain-control and joint-breaking holds and locks of *aikido*.

Aikido ("the way of the spirit meeting") is at once the easiest and the hardest of the martial arts to learn. It is truly a life study if you seek the depths of its meaning; *aikido* is generally considered the most philosophically oriented of the martial arts.

Aikido, like judo and jujitsu, emphasizes staying on the defensive and letting the attacker make the first move, thus committing his own forward momentum into a line of force. The *aikido* practitioner then intercepts and redirects that force, throwing the attacker off balance and letting his own momentum carry him pell-mell to the ground, perhaps with the *aikido* practitioner holding one of his limbs in such a way that as the attacker falls, he breaks his own arm or leg. Little impact is involved, and less physical strength. This makes *aikido*, even in its early stages of teaching, much more suitable for the elderly person, who is frail, or small in stature.

T'ai Chi Chuan is a Chinese form that emphasizes grace and suppleness. In the United States, it is taught mostly as a form of physical conditioning, and less as a combative science. Unfortunately, a number of "second- and third-generation" students of T'ai Chi teach it purely as an isometric exercise, losing sight and feel of its defensive properties.

What style to choose? Much depends on your own physique and conditioning, your age, and the degree of commitment you are willing to make to learn how to defend yourself in a hand-to-hand fight. Many of us who are seriously involved in the protection field study eclectically, taking the best of each discipline that pertains to our job, and then moving on. Many formidable streetfighters have never studied any one martial art long enough to take rank in it.

Start, if you can, with judo. The *ukemi* alone will make it worthwhile; each time you slip on ice or wet leaves or a loose step, the falling techniques of *ukemi* will come back to you instantly. I've never been hurt in a fall, be it an accident or a fight, and I attribute that totally to having been taught *ukemi* when I was about twelve. And, as we pointed out, judo is the easiest way for a relatively young and healthy person to get accustomed to full-power physical combat against another human.

You definitely want some basic study in karate, preferably a soft form. Stay through at least the yellow belt level. You will learn instinctively to block—and, in the soft styles, to block in a deflecting movement that channels the punch or kick away from you without numbing your own interceding limb with a bone-jarring impact. For instance, a 100-pound woman intercepting a 200-pound lumberjack's punch with a rigid Shotokan block is quite likely to injure her own arm seriously; doing the same with a fluid Uechi-ryu technique, she probably won't even notice the bruise until later.

In police work, I found that karate-trained street cops didn't get into nearly as many brawls as their chiefs feared they would. On the contrary, they were less likely to get into fights. If the Bad Guy couldn't tell he was overmatched just by the way the cop was standing, he'd know it quick enough when he threw his best shot and the cop simply deflected it harmlessly with a forearm block.

Hapkido is an excellent, all-around fighting style. The trouble is that you have to live in Los Angeles if you want to learn it. Mu Tau, the modern form of the ancient Greek Pankration, is probably the most devastatingly effective of the contemporary martial arts; the problem is that the only three men in the world certified to teach it are located in northern New England. I am grateful that I live near the founder Jim Arvanitis, and have been able to work out with him often. It's almost as difficult as finding a good *jujitsu* instructor if you don't live in Los Angeles or New York.

Aikido is the martial art technique I recommend for the average citizen. No, you won't make it a life study and no, you probably won't understand its deepest meaning

BAREHAND STRIKING TECHNIQUES

S-1: "Bear Paw" strike of karate. Second joint knuckles are striking surface. Fingers are curled up for reinforcement and fingers are flat with top of hand. Thumb is tucked under. Narrower striking surface concentrates force more than conventional fist punch. Ideal for striking to throat, groin, and other "protected" targets.

S-2: "Bear Paw" striking position as seen from side.

S-3: "Spear hand" strike of karate. Note that middle two fingers are flexed so (A) they're less likely to be injured and (B) all four fingertips strike simultaneously for added power. Should be used to attack soft targets, like throat.

S-4: Palm heel strike of karate. Very powerful, best used against chin (as shown, to stun), can easily break nose. Less pain to attacker than striking with fist or spear hand.

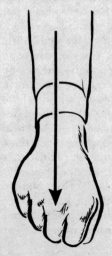

S-5: Proper fist. Line of force is straight down forearm to middle knuckle. Thumb is tucked down outside fist, *not* inside fingers or it will be broken on impact.

before you reach your deathbed. What you *will* learn is perhaps the most instinctively "human-engineered" of all the martial arts, and a number of techniques that really do work for almost anyone—*techniques you can learn and retain within minutes.*

In law enforcement, perhaps a majority of the DT (defensive tactics, unarmed combat) techniques taught to police derive from *aikido* due to the increasing number of male and female police officers who do not conform to the regulation height standards of the department. The least possible injury to the officer and the least possible training is necessary with *aikido.* If that sounds like something you can identify with, *aikido* is probably for you.

When you first enter an *aikido dojo*, you'll be put off by the flowing, dresslike robes that are generally worn instead of the macho karate pajamas you were expecting. The second thing that will put you off is that when the practitioner throws his *uke* ("human opponent"), the opponent seems to go with the flow. It looks like they're faking it. In fact, the *uke* is going along for a very good reason: If he *didn't,* his joints would be broken. A streetfighter who considers *aikido* a hoax is a man who has never been put into an *aikido* wristlock.

It works for cops; it's likely to work for you. Sure, karate will knock out guys faster, and you don't have to get as close to them *if* you're big enough and strong enough to keep them away with a savage reverse punch, backfist, or roundhouse kick to the head. Still, the high kicks emphasized in Korean karate, and which win extra points for style in any karate tournament in America, don't work on the street because the opponent can duck too easily, catch you off balance on one leg, and either grab your foot or kick you in your unprotected crotch.

Ki Whang Kim, the Washington, D.C., Tang Soo Do master who trained national champions in karate, once told me why he gave his champion fighters special lessons in *aikido.* I had commented, "*Sensei,* with so many of your top students living in the ghetto here, they must have had a lot of opportunities to put their training to use on the street."

"No, no, no!" Kim replied in great agitation. "They are too strong! They use karate; they kill somebody, go to jail! For my tournament fighters, I teach *aikido* for the street!"

Once you've decided to study, there's no easy way to find a good teacher to study with. Every karate instructor in the Yellow Pages bills himself as either a fighting master or a Korean national champion, or so it seems. If you wish to study judo, you're probably safe with anyone advertising publicly, since the U.S. Judo Association monitors that stuff to make sure that only qualified people teach. In karate, it's harder. I know one place where you can get a "certificate" as a police self-defense instructor for twenty-five dollars, and another place where the same amount of money buys you a fake "black belt." It's sort of like becoming an ordained minister through a mail-order Bible college.

First, *ask around.* Talk to people who have studied with this or that martial arts instructor. See if they felt they received full value. Ask how long they stayed with him. Some students drop out because they aren't good enough to keep up, but if *everybody* you talk to left because they didn't feel they were learning anything or because they thought it was a joke, you might want to steer clear, too. On the other hand, if they dropped out because it was too rough, that's a sign that this instructor only deals with dedicated people; if you have the courage, you'll get more than your money's worth from him.

Second, find out how long he has been teaching. If he is working solo, or as part of a very small chain, and has been doing a flourishing business for five or six or ten years, chances are that he succeeded because he's an excellent teacher. If he belongs to a chain of karate studios, ask how long he himself has had the franchise in that location,

CHOKE RELEASE

Here is the sort of practical technique you would learn at a good self-defense school.

CR-1: Attacker grabs defender in standard choke or "mugger's lock."

CR-2: Defender turns chin into suspect's elbow to release pressure from throat. Left hand grabs attcker's wrist. Right hand goes to nerve center about three inches above elbow on inside upper arm, between bice and tricep. At that pressure point, apply either strong, direct inward pressure or pinch the loose flesh firmly.

and then be doubly sure that he's giving out *real* training instead of placebo training for Walter Mitty types.

Third, review a class before you sign up. If you get pressured to sign a contract, or are told that you have to join the club before you can watch a session, leave and seek study elsewhere. This person obviously isn't confident in his ability to keep you coming by virtue of his teaching skills alone.

CR-3: Simultaneously lower head and, maintaining pressure point, rock attacker's arm forward over your head. His arm is now in position to be twisted behind his back.

(Technique courtesy John Peters, Defensive Tactics Institute.)

Finally, begin with a short-term agreement; ideally, you don't want to sign any sort of a contract at all. You're better off paying by the lesson. A *sensei* who allows you to do so is a true martial artist confident in his ability to judge potential students, and to keep them. Only salesmen make you sign contracts.

When you reach to the martial arts, reach for quality. Be honest, and state up front that you're looking for the most efficient way to protect yourselfwith street-fighting techniques that you can learn in the shortest period of time.

Maybe you're not ready to make a commitment of a certain number of hours a week over a period of years. I can understand that. When I teach deadly force, it's with the understanding that my students come to me for forty intensive hours, over five weekdays or two weekends in-

AIKIDO THUMBLOCK

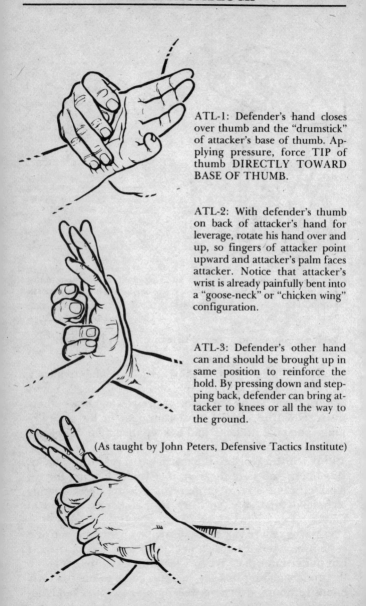

ATL-1: Defender's hand closes over thumb and the "drumstick" of attacker's base of thumb. Applying pressure, force TIP of thumb DIRECTLY TOWARD BASE OF THUMB.

ATL-2: With defender's thumb on back of attacker's hand for leverage, rotate his hand over and up, so fingers of attacker point upward and attacker's palm faces attacker. Notice that attacker's wrist is already painfully bent into a "goose-neck" or "chicken wing" configuration.

ATL-3: Defender's other hand can and should be brought up in same position to reinforce the hold. By pressing down and stepping back, defender can bring attacker to knees or all the way to the ground.

(As taught by John Peters, Defensive Tactics Institute)

THUMBLOCK RESTRAINT

TR-1: When obnoxious and potentially threatening person must be forced to leave, defender may approach from the side and apply thumblock as shown. Walk suspect out. If resistance is met, step back and apply downward pressure, forcing subject to the ground.

TR-2: Closeup of hand positioning in thumblock restraint. Done on attacker's left arm, defender's left hand is on wrist. Right hand pinches attacker's thumb into Aikido Thumblock using only thumb and forefinger.

(As taught by John Peters, Defensive Tactics Institute.)

GRAB RELEASE

GR-1: The defender (right) is grabbed by shirt or neck.

GR-2: Stepping back with left leg or forward with right leg (to protect groin from knee-lift), defender grabs with opposite hand (i.e., right hand grabs attacker's left or vice versa). Aikido thumbblock is applied.

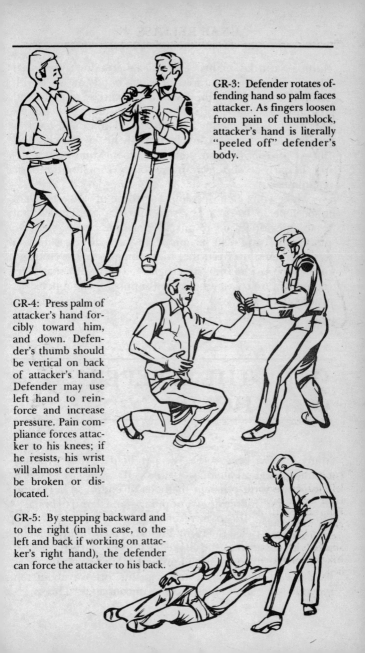

GR-3: Defender rotates offending hand so palm faces attacker. As fingers loosen from pain of thumblock, attacker's hand is literally "peeled off" defender's body.

GR-4: Press palm of attacker's hand forcibly toward him, and down. Defender's thumb should be vertical on back of attacker's hand. Defender may use left hand to reinforce and increase pressure. Pain compliance forces attacker to his knees; if he resists, his wrist will almost certainly be broken or dislocated.

GR-5: By stepping backward and to the right (in this case, to the left and back if working on attacker's right hand), the defender can force the attacker to his back.

cluding Saturday nights. The martial arts don't work that way. Teaching deadly force (of which hands-on work with a gun is but a small component) is an exercise of mind and morality that stays with you. The learning of hand-to-hand fighting demands a constant and continual level of practice in techniques involving both heavy muscles and fine-motor coordination, and the moment you stop practicing, it starts to slip away from you, except for the basic techniques.

Make your own decision. For those of you who want to be able to learn a few street-proven techniques that work, but don't want to put a lot of time into it, we have put together the next section of this book. I just want you to understand up front that these things won't even begin to make you a master streetfighter. Getting to that level requires more commitment than simply buying a book off a newsstand shelf.

32. THE SLEEPER HOLD

Many laymen believe the "sleeper hold" is just a phony gimmick used on *Saturday Afternoon Wrestling*. In fact, it is one of the most efficient methods of ending a fight, and has become increasingly popular—and controversial—among police officers in recent years.

Properly called the carotid restraint in law enforcement, it is better known as the chokeout. Judo experts have used it for years. It works on the principle that, if the supply of oxygenated blood to the brain is shut off for about ten seconds, the person will become unconscious. This is accomplished by choking off the carotid arteries on either side of the neck; these arteries carry fresh blood to the brain.

Reach up right now and place a thumb and middle fingertip on each side of your neck, just below the base of the jaw. You will feel a strong pulse. Those are your carotid arteries.

There's a simple way for you to learn the power of the carotid chokeout, *but don't try it unless you're in excellent health with low blood pressure and no cardiovascular problems or eye problems of any kind.*

Reach up to your shirt or blouse collars, taking the left collar in the right hand and vice versa. Now pull the collar tightly across your shoulders and hold them for a second. You'll feel your pulse pounding in your head, then a sensation of pressure behind your eyes. It's time to stop.

Still awake? Good. I've seen people go out with a reinforced carotid choke in under three seconds, though some can last for fifteen seconds or more if they're in good health and have muscular bull necks. They can last considerably longer if the hold has been weakly or improperly executed.

There are many cops who think the chokeout is a godsend, a magic technique that lets them put a belligerent barfighter out of action before he can hurt them, and without being charged with police brutality for lashing out with a nightstick or flashlight. Unfortunately, it's not the complete panacea everyone thinks it is. Even some police argue against the use of the chokeout in law enforcement.

In 1976, I became the first in the police sector to speak out against the chokeout in the pages of the police professional journal *Sentinel*. I had studied the technique and discussed it with numerous physicians, all of whom pointed out potentially lethal problems. Once the pressure on the neck is released, the sudden rush of blood can burst a "hardened" artery. Arteriosclerosis isn't the sole province of the elderly; it's common in the thirtyish alcoholics who so often start fights. There's also the danger of blindness, brain damage, and even brain death, plus the possibility of slipping and crushing the windpipe or breaking the cervical spine.

I warned at that time that officers using chokeouts could have a suspect wake up dead in the back of the police cruiser. This prophecy was later fulfilled by a series of deaths in Los Angeles, among criminal suspects. In virtually all of the cases, the subjects were high on drugs (usually PCP), the officers were using their batons to reinforce the chokeout, and death occurred because the frenzied suspects were struggling so hard in the almost inescapable holds that they literally broke their own necks.

I think the carotid chokeout has a very limited place in law enforcement, but a very prominent place in the civilian's repertoire of self-defense tactics because the police officer has a number of options that the civilian doesn't. If he uses a nightstick or flashlight on a barfighter who outweighs him by twenty pounds, it's considered "reasonable force required to affect the arrest"; if the citizen does the same, it's "aggravated assault" or "assault with a deadly weapon." The police officer has either a partner to back him up, or a portable radio on which to instantly call for reinforcements, and if worse comes to worse, he has his gun.

You have none of that. If you feel you're about to be overwhelmed in a fight, you have little choice but to use savage street-fighting techniques that will very likely leave your opponent permanently, and perhaps horribly, crippled.

By contrast, the sleeper hold really does look like a panacea. The street criminal goes to sleep and wakes up with a headache. Most if not all of those deaths during police custody occurred when a baton was used to reinforce the choke hold, and you won't be doing that.

Los Angeles and Kansas City, two of the largest

police agencies that train all their officers in the carotid restraint, report virtually no serious injuries when it is used bare-handed.

This is good news for those of you who are squeamish about removing muggers' eyeballs and whatnot. There are still certain side effects of the carotid chokeout that are somewhat unpleasant. Chief among these is the subject going into convulsions, what cops call *making 'em do the chicken*. The term comes from the resemblance to a flopping, decapitated fowl. Actually, what is occurring is an artifically induced brainwave interruption that resembles a *grand mal* epileptic seizure. Other problems include head injuries when the unconscious person drops to the sidewalk, and headache and nausea when they awaken.

At this point your primary concern is, "OK, if the carotid chokeout is so good, how do I do it and why isn't it mentioned in the other popular self-defense books?" Both questions have the same answer: More effective techniques have been developed only recently for physically small or medium-size persons.

The best of these methods was developed by my friend Jim Lindell, who heads the physical fitness and defensive tactics training for the Kansas City Police Department (KCPD). Jim is an advanced black belt in judo who used to run his own *dojo*, and he knows a lot about teaching the principles of movement and leverage to beginners. His specialty is developing techniques that the average cop can handle.

"The average *cop*," you wail. "Where does that leave *me?*" Well, hopefully, in about a minute it's going to leave you free of a couple of stereotypes.

The public seems to automatically assume that the average cop is young, strong, over six feet, and physically indomitable. This isn't always the case. Police work being a twenty- to thirty-year career, there are a lot of fortyish and fiftyish cops out there. Very few are required to exercise or to qualify in unarmed combat the way they do with their sidearms. The average underpaid, overstressed cop is less likely to spend his spare time in a gym than moonlighting or just collapsing in front of his TV with a few beers.

Also, there is Affirmative Action hiring, which has put a number of small-statured females and males on the streets in blue uniforms. This has given the police community its greatest impetus to develop techniques that allow small people to be able to subdue large, violent suspects.

It is from here that the Kubotan and Mo-Gem, described in Chapter 37, were developed, and it is from here that Lindell created the Kansas City method of carotid restraint. It has been in use in that city for several years. Small female police officers and fat, fiftyish cops alike have reported outstanding success with it. In hundreds of uses on the street, not one of these frail or out-of-condition bluecoats have had even the strongest suspect break out of the hold and hurt them; the worst injury occurred when a bull-like street criminal slammed an officer against the wall as he thrashed before the cop choked him unconscious.

If you're strong it's easy to choke a guy out from the front. You can use the crossed collars technique, pulling him over to one side to break his balance and keep him from hitting you as he passes out. If you have big, powerful hands, you can just reach up, grab the guy's neck, and squeeze him unconscious with one paw.

But if most of you were able to do that, most of you wouldn't have bought this book. Let's go back to the techniques designed for small female police officers and obese, aging cops.

The key to the chokeout is to execute it from a position where, for the fifteen seconds or so it can take, the guy won't be able to punch or kick you. That means you have to execute from behind.

Kansas City teaches but a single hold, the one you're about to learn. According to Kansas City Police Chief

Norman A. Caron, who authorized the development of Lindell's method,

There are several reasons for limiting this system to one kind of neck restraint. For one, this technique is the safest for the subject at all levels of control, and it provides the officer with a single sequential method of application that ensures he has performed the technique properly and safely.

The basic technique is to get your antagonist so that his chin is in the crook of your elbow, with your arm describing a V whose open top is toward you as you tighten it. This scissoring presses your bicep against one of the carotid arteries, your topmost forearm bone against the other. Both arteries must be occluded, or closed off, if the technique is to work.

To apply from the front, you have to evade the attacker's grasping hands and step around his side. You've got to be quick, but it helps that he's probably moving toward you, thus playing into your hands.

Step around whichever side of him is easiest. If that's his left side, grab his left arm with your right hand just above the elbow and push forward, as in the illustrations. (Don't worry if the guy is so strong; his arm is like an immovable tree; use it as a lever to push yourself behind him quicker.)

As you step around him, bring your left arm up with the hand in a karate-chop position, and snake your arm up into that chokeout hold on his neck. If he's much taller than you, you'll need to bend him backward; indeed, *breaking his balance toward the rear is a key to executing the technique no matter how big each of you are.*

If your height or strength aren't sufficient to lever him backward—and we're talking about getting his shoulders back at a sharp angle to the floor—grab his collar or the

CAROTID CHOKE OUT

CCO-1: Defender faces attacker with weak side forward, hands open for grappling.

CCO-2: Defender's right hand grabs attacker's left arm at bicep, pivoting attacker around "inside him," so attacker's back is to defender's chest. Left hand knifes up around right side of attacker's neck. Left foot is in position to kick back of attacker's right knee, bending leg. NOTE: IF ATTACKER IS TOO BIG AND STRONG TO BE PIVOTED, DEFENDER GRABS THE SAME WAY AND PIVOTS HIMSELF INTO SAME POSITION BEHIND ATTACKER.

CCO-3: Defender kicks rear of attacker's knee, buckling the leg. Defender's left arm is in position with top of forearm against attacker's right carotid artery, bicep against left carotid artery. Defender places cheek firmly against back of attacker's head to prevent escape. Right palm comes under heel of left hand for maximum power as attacker's neck is "scissored" by left arm.

CCO-4: Attacker is driven further downward for maximum leverage by defender as hold is tightened. Unconsciousness should begin within six to fourteen seconds if hold is properly applied. Maintain hold until certain aggressor is out. WARNING: THE CAROTID RESTRAINT IS POTENTIALLY DEADLY IF HELD FOR TOO LONG, AND *GUARANTEED* LETHAL IF HELD FOR TWO MINUTES OR LONGER. IF RELEASED TOO SOON, SUSPECT CAN RECOVER ALMOST IMMEDIATELY. THIS TECHNIQUE SHOULD BE USED ONLY WHEN FACING DEATH OR GRAVE BODILY HARM.

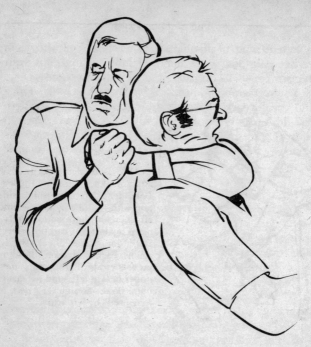

CCO-5: Close-up of hand and head positioning for chokeout. Elbow is beneath attacker's chin to create a "hollow" so larynx will not be crushed. Bony upper edge of forearm presses one carotid, bicep presses the other. Right hand helps apply strong scissoring pressure toward defender's body. Side of defender's head is firmly against back of attacker's, to prevent escape or being butted.

(Technique presented as taught by famed police self defense instructor James Lindell.)

hair on the back of his head, and jerk him backward, simultaneously sidekicking him in the knee, to fold it.

Once his balance is broken and your arm is locked around his neck, solidify your hold. Put your hip into his buttocks, and grab your choking hand with your other hand. Clasp them together, *palm to palm.* That's important;

any other type of handclasp won't give you the right leverage. Clasping your hands palm-to-palm keeps your forearms parallel with each other, Lindell explains.

You're trying to squeeze a big man's neck between a bicep and forearm that might not be so big. Raw strength won't do it for you. But, with your arms held as described and in the illustrated position, all you have to do is raise the elbow of your weak arm, and you create an isometric lock that tightens even a slender arm sufficiently to choke a man who is bigger and stronger than you.

To keep him from twisting his head and losing your hold, place the side of your head (just above your ear) *firmly* against the back of the opponent's head. In this position, you're unlikely to break his neck; Kansas City Police instructors feel that your arm actually creates a sort of makeshift, protective cervical collar.

Remember, you've got to do it hard and quickly. You've got to step around and get clear of him, and you risk taking a punch while doing so. Once you grab his arm to spin him, hang on until you've got his neck, then break his balance and tighten the hold with your other hand, as described.

You can increase the efficiency of the hold by dropping to one knee, which will cause the attacker to fall on his butt. In the standing position, he can't readily punch or back-kick you, but a big, strong man might be able to backpedal or twist. He'll find that a lot harder when you've dumped him on his rear end.

A big, strong man, or one with judo training, will probably throw himself rearward, to take you to your back, since he can't flip you forward if you've bent his legs. Even if he does go backward hard, you can retain your hold; hang on; don't worry about getting hurt; just wrap your legs around his waist, locking your feet against his inner thighs. From here, there's very little he can do before he passes out.

In the KCPD's experience, the suspect usually becomes unconscious within four to seven seconds, and awakens within five to twenty seconds. You don't want to panic and hold on forever, because that will turn a guy into a vegetable: Irreversible brain damage in the average adult begins about four minutes after oxygenated blood to the brain is shut off, and brain death occurs after six to ten minutes. *Held too long, the carotid chokeout can be a crippling or killing technique.*

You should, however, hold it long enough to make sure the guy isn't shamming. Kansas City cops are taught to lower the unconscious opponent gently, while supporting his head. You might want to consider that for civil liability reasons. You may also wish to run now because five to twenty seconds is not the world's longest head start.

Don't relax your hold just because the guy goes limp! I once choked a guy out in two seconds and released and caught him as he slumped forward. The fight was over, but in seconds he was awake and alert again, and he could have fought if he still wanted to. When this happened to me once in training, the instructor who was wrapped around my neck let go as soon as I started going limp. I caught myself, and although I was a little dizzy, I still could have hurt him, if we were playing for real.

The Kansas City officers who learn the Lindell method of carotid restraint are taught that the chokeout is but one of three levels of force in the system. First, you apply the technique and let the guy realize he's in trouble. If he doesn't give up then, you tighten the hold and let him feel some pain. Only if that doesn't work are KCPD officers taught to choke him unconscious.

Kansas City cops use it that way. Kansas City cops also have guns and batons and radios and backup partners. *If you must render your attacker unconscious, once you release him, leave immediately.* There will be ample time to reach a safe place and report the incident to police. Call an ambulance, which should always be requested when a person is out cold. If nothing else, it makes you look great in court.

You can't learn this technique just by reading about it.
Lindell recommends eight hours in basic training, and his
officers get two hours of refresher training annually. It'll
be hard to find a martial arts studio that will be familiar
with the Lindell method, let alone teach any sort of chokeout
apart from a regular, full-scale judo course.

Trying it at home is awfully tricky. If somebody slips,
somebody's neck can get broken. If you're going to do it,
though, do it very slowly, and release instantly when your
partner slaps his hand against his body, the traditional
martial arts signal of submission in practice fighting. *Above
all, make sure that a carotid choke is not applied in practice to
anyone with medical problems involving the neck, the brain, the
eyes, or the cardiovascular system.*

Once you've learned the technique hands-on, the thing
you'll probably have the most trouble with is getting behind your attacker to execute it. You'll find that the Kubotan
technique of spinning a man around and taking him down
works amazingly well, and is ideal for a follow-up with a
carotid restraint or chokeout technique.

The carotid chokeout has proven itself. The sleeper
hold works where it counts—on the street, in real-life
streetfights—and the KCPD and the LAPD among others,
have proven that it protects an out-of-shape middle-aged
man, or a small woman, as effectively as it works for a
brawny young Adam–12 type.

That's a good indication that the carotid chokeout
might, in a tight self-defense situation, work for *you* if you
take the short time required to properly learn it.

I believe the chokeout technique should be learned
hands-on from an expert. Virtually every local YMCA has
a judo instructor on staff who is competent to teach it.
Don't be surprised, though, if the instructor is reluctant to
impart such potentially destructive information to a person who lacks the motivation to take the whole judo course.

We've told you how to apply and practice the technique in this chapter because I know that some of you lack

that motivation, or for some reason can't take the proper training. *By exercising extreme care, and going through the technique gently and in slow motion the way this chapter describes,* you can safely learn this extremely potent self-defense technique. Nevertheless, because we can't be with you when you do it, I and Bantam Books can take no responsibility for injuries inflicted with this technique under any circumstances.

33. FIGHTING FLASHLIGHTS

Ever see a uniformed police officer get out of his patrol car to confront some troublemakers holding what looked like the biggest, blackest flashlight you ever saw in your life? He wasn't holding an instrument like that just so he could see them better. Say hello to the most effective and street-proven of the "makeshift" defensive tools.

That black flashlight is known to cops as a Kel-lite. Actually, that's a generic term that belongs to the one brand that a bunch of other flashlight makers copied; the original Kel-lite is made by Safariland in Monrovia, California, and is one of the best of its type you can buy.

Sometimes known to the public as police flashlights, these units are structured around a barrel made of heavy-gauge, black anodized aircraft aluminum. The barrel itself is not terribly heavy, but is rigid and unyielding. Fill it with heavy D-cell batteries, though, and you have an instrument that does a most convincing imitation of a lead pipe.

Indeed, it can inflict even more damage: The flashlight has knurling or sharp checkering on it, supposedly so that it won't slip out of an officer's hand in the rain, and these tiny, upraised bits of diamond-shaped aluminum cause fierce lacerations when the flashlight comes into contact with human flesh.

Misused, police flashlights have caused death and crippling injury. One southern police officer went to jail after he hit a guy once on the top of the head with such a flashlight and the man promptly died. Many police departments today forbid officers to even carry them.

Batons are nonlethal weapons which allow a small-statured police officer to subdue one or more larger antagonists without being fatal. The heavy flashlights do too much damage for police chiefs' tastes when used as clubs. Where a slim, twenty-six-inch hickory baton might cause a simple fracture of a barfighter's shin, the brutally heavy flashlight is more likely to cause a crushing, comminuted fracture, literally turning the bone to dust at the contact point of the blow.

Cops have learned to be very careful about hitting people with their flashlights. If they zap a guy with one and he dies, they'll inevitably be charged with using excessive force, unless the deceased had pulled a gun or knife and the cop swung his flashlight only because he didn't have time to get at his service revolver.

However, if you hit somebody with anything heavy and hard enough to cause injury, you have just assaulted him with a deadly weapon; it doesn't matter whether you hit him with a blackjack or with the ashtray from your nightstand. In the eyes of the court, you will be justified *only* if you did so in self-defense.

The only thing that could hurt you would be if the prosecution or plaintiff could prove that you were carrying something *designed* to hit people with; this could reasonably be construed as an indication of malicious intent on your part.

Among the things you can hit people with that don't

have a pure weapons connotation are umbrellas, walking sticks, and rolled-up magazines, all of which are discussed elsewhere. Interestingly, in most states you are also allowed to carry a flashlight with you, and at this writing, I know of no jurisdiction that differentiates between a two-pound Kel-Lite and a four-ounce plastic disposable flashlight.

You have, in short, a weapon that the law doesn't consider to be a weapon, yet which America's police have proven to be a most dramatic fight-stopper when wielded properly and responsibly.

In a case that made the front-page headline of the New York Bar Association newspaper, I proved in Queens County Court that a heavy-duty flashlight like a Kel-Lite or the Bianchi B-Lite used in my courtroom demonstration, was legal to carry. This was done obliquely. I was actually there as an expert witness in defense of the man who manufactures the Kiyoga spring whip, who had been arrested at LaGuardia Airport under a statute which prohibits the carrying of blackjacks, billies, and similar objects.

I won the case for him by proving that his spring whip could not possibly cause the grave injuries generally consistent with blackjacks and other forms of clubs. In one of my more dramatic moments before the bench, I laid out a couple of sets of one-inch pine boards supported by bricks. In the world of the martial arts, it is accepted that a blow that will break a one-inch pine board will break most any human bone. I whaled away at the thing with the Kiyoga, doing little more than scarring the surface of the wood, and then struck myself on the forearm as hard as I could, causing only a minor welt.

Then I picked up the four-cell B-Lite. I explained that New York law did not prohibit such a flashlight from being carried by anyone, visibly or concealed, and the judge nodded in affirmation. I then swung the B-Lite down on the board.

It shattered easily and violently. The two biggest pieces flew away, and splinters sprayed from under the contact point. Some of the wood embedded itself in the checkering of the flashlight's barrel.

My client was found not guilty. Nobody ever did anything to change the fact that it's legal for anyone to carry a B-Lite or Kel-Lite in New York, and at this writing, it is still legal.

The clubbed flashlight is potentially lethal. The blow I delivered to that numb piece of wood in the Queens County courtroom would almost certainly have crushed the skull of a human being with lethal force. This is the first caution you must undertake if you even *think* about carrying a flashlight to protect yourself: *Blows to the head may be considered lethal force and should only be struck in a situation where you are in such deadly danger that you would be justified in shooting your opponent to death.*

How do you swing a clubbed flashlight *non*lethally? At this writing, I know of only two certified courses where *cops* can learn this: one in Ohio, and the one sponsored around the country by the Defensive Tactics Institute (DTI). I do not know of any martial arts school that can teach civilians nonlethal techniques coupled with court-accepted training in the principles of this sort of forcible self-defense. However, DTI at 15 Cedarcliff Road, Braintree, MA 02148, can give limited training for civilians.

There are five levels of defensive power that you can use with a Kel-Lite. The first is *deterrent force*, simply drawing the thing and holding it firmly. Street criminals associate "the black flashlight" with cops, they know what cops carry them for, and many of them are scared to death of the thing.

The second is *blocking capability*. You can start with one hand on each end, your arms relaxed, and the flashlight horizontal at upper thigh level. By thrusting your arms out, you can stop an incoming crotchkick (he'll very probably break his shinbone against your flashlight), or thrust up and out if he strikes overhead. For a straight punch you can flip the flashlight up with either hand to catch and deflect the blow, again probably doing some definite injury to the attacker's offending limb.

Third, you have some *grappling capability*. The long flashlight can be used like a short baton to gain leverage and pivot your attacker into a wristlock or armlock, effectively restraining him without having to club him.

Fourth, you have *less-lethal blows*. The weight and mass of the clubbed flashlight delivers extraordinarily powerful force. John Peters of DTI recommends swinging against targets like the outside edge of the knee, where you're less likely to break bone. I don't recommend that for civilians; I'll teach my civilian students to smash kneecaps to powder.

Why the disparity? Again, because Peters teaches cops and I'm writing this book for civilians. Cops can use a stick on just about anybody who gives them a hard time so long as they don't bust them up too much. A civilian wielding a blunt instrument automatically becomes an aggressor with a deadly weapon *unless that civilian is in such deadly danger that he would be justified in killing or gravely injuring his antagonist.*

In that latter situation, a cop could draw his gun. So would you, if you had one. If you don't, you have to depend on your "less-lethal weapon." For a cop, an "impact weapon" like that flashlight or the baton, is considered a restraining tool. In a civilian's hands, it is a weapon *once it is drawn and turned against another human being*. You can't use a weapon legally unless you're in reasonable fear of death or grave bodily harm. And, if you are, you don't want to hold yourself back and only slightly injure your attacker.

At this writing, I am legally a civilian. I have a five-cell B-Lite under the front seat of my car, and when in New York, I have one in my attaché case if I'm wearing a suit, or slung from my belt with one end in a Levi pocket and covered with my shirttail if I'm dressed casually. I'll only pull that thing out if I'm threatened with bodily harm. But when it *does* come out, I hope to do to my attackers' bones what I once did to some pine boards in a courtroom in that city.

Against multiple, unarmed opponents, say during a mugging, my only chance to escape would be to strike repeatedly, preferably putting my attackers down in such blood-spattered screaming pain that their compatriots would either back off or be momentarily startled enough to give me an opening to break some part of *them*.

I wouldn't go against a gun with a flashlight, and if a knife was coming at me, I wouldn't try to knock it out of the guy's hand with my B-Lite. I know from experience that a light knife moves quicker than a heavy flashlight, and I'd miss. Instead, I would step outside the guy's left hip if he was right-handed, and take one fast swing for the base of his skull, hoping to crush his cranial vault with my flashlight before he could slash at me with his blade.

Obviously, that's a killing technique. You only use it if your life is in danger. If your life *is* in danger, a killing technique at your disposal may well be your only route to survival.

Very few of you are going to walk around carrying a two-pound flashlight on your belt. If nothing else, it's very handy to leave under the front seat of your car. It swings better than a monkey wrench and there's more you can do with it. In real life, you will probably use it frequently for illumination in a minor or major emergency before you ever get close to hitting anyone with it.

If you buy one with the idea of swinging it over your head and clubbing it down on somebody's skull, you have two problems: (a) If you connect, you're likely to kill that person, because no one is guaranteed to survive such an impact on the crown of his skull, and (b) an overhand swing is one of the easiest movements for any street criminal to evade and counter.

Use it to block, to jab, and to lever someone's arm into

a hammerlock once you've been taught how. If you have to, slash down with it and break your attacker's kneecap. If things are getting really hairy, you can kill a man with surprising ease using this illuminated bludgeon.

Do not attempt defensive techniques with conventional flashlights. Your basic lightweight metal Everready will probably come apart with the second hard blow, causing two problems: (a) You no longer have a functional flashlight or weapon, and (b) the very fact that you hit the person hard enough to break your flashlight could be seen in court as an indication of excessive use of force.

Buy a "police flashlight." You'll pay $20 to $40 instead of $2 for a plastic one at Radio Shack or $8 for an Everready at the hardware store, but you'll have one of the most proven defensive weapons on America's streets, and it will last forever. Due to their scientifically designed lighting globes, they're more brilliant and effective as emergency illumination than anything you'll get in a hardware store.

You'll be looking for brands like Kel-Lite, B-Lite, Code Four Mag-Lite, and Pro-Light. Sporting goods stores, gunshops, police equipment stores, and uniform stores, usually have them in stock. For women, the heavy D-cell versions are a bit too cumbersome to swing quickly; the ideal flashlight for women is the slender but still rugged C-Cell Batonlite, a variation of the Kel-Lite.

These units are made as small as two-cell and as large as seven-cell. The former are too short to do much with, the latter, too bulky to handle quickly. A three-cell is the minimum length for defense, four-cell is better, and five-cell is ideal for a "fighting flashlight."

The police-style flashlight is the most effective and destructive makeshift weapon that a civilian can legally carry without a license. It will cause more damage per blow than even a martial artist's heavy walking stick. We can't underestimate the cautions involved in fighting with a flashlight. Even a moderately light blow with one is liable to result in considerable laceration, and you can even break bones unintentionally.

Police officers have gone to jail for overzealously using their Kel-Lites. The civilian should remember this when he draws *his*. Of course, enough cops have been bludgeoned to death with heavy flashlights after they were taken away from them, that it is standard procedure in law enforcement to blow away anyone coming at a cop with such an instrument. (Some years ago, a Quincy, Massachusetts, cop was sued for excessive use of force when he put a .38 Super Vel slug into a young man who had grabbed his flashlight and was beating him with it. The court ruled in the officer's favor—as they should have—and his young attacker rolled out of the courtroom in his wheelchair and into obscurity. The cop became a minor hero to his peers.)

Still, the police flashlight is probably the most formidable defensive weapon available, without a license, to the private citizen. Before you buy one, you should check your local statutes and seek out some training in the defensive use of the instrument. You should practice with it, using grappling techniques against live, resisting sparring partners (who wear protective gear), and striking the thing against trees or other objects full-force, to get a feel of the bounceback you'll experience in a streetfight. You'll know then the awesome destructive force of the clubbed police flashlight.

Used as a bludgeon, the police flashlight can easily kill or cripple. The overhand swing is also simple for a trained streetfighter to block and deflect, and if he gets that thing away from you, he'll make you eat it.

It is best used with blocking techniques and comealong holds, and the user should know how to keep control of it during a struggle. Unfortunately, very few martial arts instructors are familiar with these techniques The two master instructors who train police instructors in these methods are:

John Peters   Eric Chambers
Defensive Tactics Institute   288 Coal Street
15 Cedarcliff Road   Middleport, OH 45760
Braintree, MA 02184

Write to each for their travel/training schedule and ask if they'll accept you. Failing that, they can refer you to a certified police instructor in your area whom they've trained. A lot of local police instructors are agreeable to teaching self-defense to private citizens who can prove that they have a clean record, and their rates tend to be more reasonable than those of nationally known instructors.

34. MAKESHIFT WEAPONS: WHAT WORKS AND WHAT DOESN'T

Almost every article on self-defense you see in the newspapers or in the popular women's magazines, offers the same advice about "weaponry." God forbid that you should use anything that could hurt someone. They recommend squirting squeeze bottles full of lemon juice or water pistols filled with ammonia, into the attacker's eyes. Hatpins to jab him with, rolled-up newspapers to hit him with, or umbrellas, sometimes with sharpened points. Car keys held between your fingers to rake his face with, or a rat-tail comb in your purse with which to do the same.

They're all useless! The people who do these stories

are writers grinding out another assignment, not experts in the field of countervailing force against criminal violence. They sketch research by talking with a few cops, and those cops are scared that a woman with a Doberman or a Smith & Wesson, since she isn't trained to the same level as his department's K–9 division or SWAT team, won't be able to handle the equipment that really works.

Among these police spokesmen, there is a term called *CYA*—"Cover Your Ass." The police lieutenant (that's usually who the chief sloughed the reporter off to) is going to think, "Jesus, if some woman loses control of her Doberman or goes crazy with a gun, they'll say she got it because of my advice. Then I and the chief and the department, can be sued jointly and separately under 'vicarious liability.' I'll just toss out a few harmless alternatives, stuff that those women won't be able to hurt themselves or anybody else with."

Let's go down the list of the commonly recommended self-defense weapons, and see what really works and what really doesn't.

Rolled-up magazines. Every article recommends these, but they never tell you how to use them. I even saw a couple of articles that recommended rolled-up newspapers (the reporter must have been in a hurry). As a result, when the trusting woman who reads the story finds herself in danger, she whales away with her newspaper as if she was trying to swat a fly. And, as you might expect, her efforts are about as effective as if she was using a flyswatter.

A tightly rolled-up magazine can be used with moderate success against your attacker if you *thrust* with it, and if you hit him off guard. Since the turn of the century, cops have known that jabbing was the most effective way of using their short billy clubs. However, those clubs are made of rigid wood or plastic, and their impact shock is focused on a narrow, blunt-end. Your rolled-up magazine is going to unfurl very quickly after impact and become useless, and even with the first blow, its wide, flimsy end won't deliver half the power of a jab from a police billy, which is illegal for you to carry.

If you must resort to this foolishness, carry a thick magazine rolled tightly and secured by a couple of rubber bands. This way, at least, you'll have a little more protection.

You can still injure your wrist if you strike incorrectly, especially with a forward jab, one of the only techniques you'll probably be able to perform if you're a woman already enveloped in a rapist's bear hug. If you must trust your life to such a feeble defense, you can at least hold the magazine properly.

The most potent blow is to jab downward and/or outward with the "butt" of the rolled-up magazine protruding from the bottom of your hand, in what we call the hammer fist strike. That's like pounding your fist on a table for attention: It's powerful and instinctive. If you're a right-handed woman in close with an attacker, swing the magazine up to your left shoulder, and then forward and butt-down to strike; go for the throat. This "windup" gives you much more impact, but you'll have to do it in a very quick, circular movement; even then, you can "telegraph" the blow, allowing the criminal to easily block or intercept it.

A forward jab will work best if you use both hands, like a bayonet thrust. If you're right-handed, you want your right hand to be in the rear, palm down on the top of the magazine, and your left hand under the front of it, palm up. Aim for a point *behind* his neck if you're going for the throat, so that the impact will penetrate.

Even then, he can slap the blow away. There's no way you can execute it suddenly enough to fake out every attacker, and you'll need the training of a combat infantryman or a police riot squad trooper to recover and keep fighting with blocks and counterstrikes if that first blow doesn't work for you.

You can often do more damage to an attacker with a hardbound book. A woman holding one across her chest the way female students do on campus, can swiftly and accurately slam the upper edge of the book into an attacker's throat; most criminals won't be watching for this sort of assault. It hits harder, too. You can thrust the book out two-handed at arm's length to ward off perhaps one punch or grab (or to smash it into his face and flatten his nose), but after that, he'll tear it out of your hands.

Magazines and books are to be *read* and you should not trust your life and well-being to that sort of amateurish attempt.

Lemon juice. Save your lemon and lime juice for fish dinners and Bloody Marys. It doesn't work for keeping predatory human beings from tearing you apart.

Sure, it stings in your eyes. You found that out the first time you squirted yourself with a fat lemon wedge at a seafood restaurant. It didn't blind you and drop you to the floor screaming, though, *did* it? In fact, it probably made you so mad you wanted to *kill* that lemon wedge. It will have about that same effect on a rapist or mugger when you squirt it in *his* face.

Don't take my word for it; ask your opthalmologist about what lemon or lime juice will and won't do as far as incapacitating a human being.

According to opthalmologist Roland Hok, it requires a fairly strong acid or alkali to cause protein to coagulate on the eye surface and cause loss of vision. Citrus juice in the eye would be the acid version of what happens when soap, which is mildly alkaline, gets in your eye. There would be only a mild irritation and some tears. I can't believe anyone believes that lemon juice in a rapist's eye would do anything but antagonize him to greater levels of violence.

About all this harebrained stunt can do for you is that after you've antagonized your rapist or mugger into beating you half to death, you can wheeze to the police, "Look for someone who smells fresh and citrus-y."

Hatpins. Even this one is dying out but people who read the advice years ago still tell younger women solemnly, "Use a hatpin for self-defense. You know, you can kill a person with one!"

And so you can. Most of the hatpin murders in recorded history exist only in Alfred Hitchcock mystery fiction collections, but you *can* kill somebody with one. You can also do it with your index finger, and more quickly and efficiently, given time and expertise.

Even if you drive the pin into someone's heart, the hatpin will create only a miniscule puncture wound that the elastic, supertough cardiac muscle will probably seal quickly, like a blow-out-proof tubeless tire. Your attacker may slowly bleed to death, in sixty seconds or sixty minutes, but he's going to take you *apart* in the interim. More likely, the frail needle will be deflected by clothing or by the breastbone. In real life, hatpins were obsolete for self-defense a long time before they became outmoded in the world of women's fashion.

Umbrellas. If you try to club a criminal with an umbrella, it will do little more damage than a slap in the face, but will certainly antagonize your opponent. If he didn't want your blood before, he will now.

Thrust with it like a bayonet? It's a hassle to sharpen the point, by the way, since you'll need special grinding tools and the cheap aluminum tips of most umbrellas are likely to fall apart in the grinding process anyway. Even if the umbrella has a spear point on it, the point only extends two or three inches: not enough to kill or disable unless you get it *right into* the throat, the eye socket, or the heart (if you can guide it between the protective ribs). There is no weight to it, so your thrust will stop almost as soon as the umbrella tip encounters the hard flesh and muscle of a burly mugger.

Pick up an umbrella you don't need anymore. See

how long it takes you to bend it, even rip it apart, with your bare hands. Seconds. Now try the same with a baseball bat or a heavy-duty flashlight or a police baton. It's still intact but you're sore, just from the effort, right? This should tell you something.

The umbrella wasn't designed to fight with, and trying to fend off a couple of muggers with one is going to be ludicrously futile.

Walking sticks. Here we're getting into some halfway protective hardware. The deterrent effect alone means something; it's a rare street criminal who'll have a more intense reaction than laughter to your clubbed umbrella, but a stout staff of hickory or cocabola wood with a heavy silver head on it will give him pause. He can visualize the impact it could deliver, and he knows that you wouldn't be carrying it if you didn't plan on inflicting injury on someone.

The trouble is, the proper use of a fighting stick requires a considerable amount of training. A cop on the Tactical Patrol Force carrying a 36-inch quarterstaff (riot baton) should have 16 to 40 hours of intensive training with the instrument.

There's a lot more to stickfighting than swinging it like a baseball bat. You have to be able to work ambidextrously, to block and thrust and parry, to sweep a man's feet out from under him with that stick. You *can* learn it, and someday in some city, a smart *sensei* is going to wake up and offer some effective training with a walking stick. After the first few well-publicized encounters with his students, muggers and rapists in that city will turn away from any potential victim they see carrying a walking stick.

But this is here and now, and all *you* know is to swing it like a bat or thrust with it like a bayonet. It is possible, however, to fold a man over surprisingly easy if you hold your weak palm over the top of the stick and thrust it through like a pool cue into his groin or solar plexus.

For most of you, though, the stick is something that a hardened street criminal can take away from you in just about two seconds. All he has to do is grab it on the outside ends and twist it, ripping it free of your fingers with superior leverage. A few years ago, a naked weirdo in Central Park murdered an auxiliary police officer with his own nightstick that way.

Besides which, if you don't need a cane to get around, you could have a tough time convincing a judge that you weren't carrying that thing as a weapon. The good thing here is that in most jurisdictions (*check yours!*) a walking stick is not listed in the statutes or the criminal code as a prohibited weapon.

If you are into the martial arts of stickfighting, or are willing to spend many hours to learn, a walking stick will be an excellent street weapon for you. But if you think you can just buy one and flail with it at anyone who comes after you, you are quite likely to wind up like that auxiliary police officer and be bludgeoned to death with your own stick.

Canes and crutches. In the pages of *Karate Illustrated* some years ago, I introduced the martial arts world to the likes of black belt master Ted Vollrath, who lost his legs in Korea.

He and other handicapped men created defensive fighting styles designed around the handicapped person's abilities. Vollrath, for instance, spent most of the fifties dragging his legless torso up-and-down stairs with his hands, developing extraordinary upper body muscles than is ordinarily seen in people confined to wheelchairs. He also developed techniques to lure an attacker to him; the attacker would bend forward, where Vollrath's lower center of gravity in the wheelchair gave *him* the edge in leverage.

He also studied wheelchair design, teaching his handicapped students how to quickly rip their armrests loose and strike with them like metal bludgeons, using the armrest as a rigid blocking surface that could painlessly deflect a full-powered attacker's best strike, then counter-attacking to drive the sharp end of the armrest handle into the mugger's solar plexus.

He knew that a seasoned mugger would try to over-turn the wheelchair in the opening moments of the assault, so Vollrath developed methods of grabbing the attacker's arms as he did so. This not only cushioned the handi-capped person's fall when he hit the ground, but created a pivoting action that shoved the wheelchair against the attacker's legs, taking him off his feet. In this way, he changed the balance of "situational dominance"; the sur-prised mugger who fell with his feet caught up in the wheelchair was now down on his back in the legless Vollrath's own environment, and if he couldn't jump to his feet, he had about as much chance of escaping Vollrath's righteous, self-defensive vengeance as you would have of slithering out of a cobra pit.

It was still a handicapped man against a full-bodied mugger, but his black belt training—indeed, the savage, tenacious survival instinct that brought him out of that mortar-blasted Korean foxhole to begin with—kept Ted Vollrath on top. His students succeeded in streetfights at a remarkably high rate; the street criminals figured they had easy marks, got overconfident, and didn't realize they had anything to worry about until the spoke of a wheel-chair armrest went through their neck. (Vollrath knew that no prosecutor would ever bring charges against a wheel-chair bound victim who maims a mugger.)

Vollrath and others experimented with crutch-fighting techniques; but the problem was, to swing a crutch with leverage and make it hit like a police baton requires a body that is so supple and athletic that it doesn't need crutches to begin with.

Oldsters who use canes can learn something from the tonfa, one of the five weapons of the savagely effective Okinawan martial art of weaponcraft, Kobu-do. The tonfa was a rice grinder, a piece of wood 20 inches long with a 4-inch handle located one quarter of the way up the shaft.

Holding a cane by the handle, with the long end of the shaft extending down the underside of your forearm, you can block or slap away punches and kicks that might break your bones if you tried to catch them on your bare arm. Slam down with it and you can break a young, strong man's arm or leg while feeling only a bump yourself.

Lon Anderson saw the *tonfa* work in Okinawa; after witnessing a local police officer putting down a small riot with a *tonfa* in each hand, he realized that here was a terrific concept for American police. Anderson created the "PR–24 prosecutor baton," now generally accepted as state of the art in nonlethal weaponry for law enforcement. A cop with eight hours training in the PR–24 can block any attack and can chop down with that reinforced arm. He can also use that short handle as a fulcrum to do some incredible armlocks and takedowns.

The PR–24, and the unique and systematized training that makes it work, is available only to police officers. However, a person who carries a cane can use many of the PR–24 system's principles for extremely potent results.

If you carry a cane and see trouble coming, *reverse it* so that the staff of the cane comes to the bottom of your fist, instead of the front as you'd normally work with it. You won't be able to move as fast, but if you *have* to use a cane, chances are, you won't be able to move fast enough anyway to get clear of the danger before you have to fight back. It's your decision: Try to escape first, but when the deadly danger is upon you, hold the cane backward.

With a flick of the wrist you can swing the shaft of the cane snug against your lower forearm. If you're under assault, get your shoulders against the nearest wall for support; that's something you should have in the back of the mind the moment you realize that muggers are stalking you, anyway.

If you feel fighting is a better alternative than submissiveness, you want your back to the wall and that cane with the shaft under your forearm. Hold your arm across your chest; that will make you look scared and helpless, and may "sucker them."

From that position, your upper body musculature is perfectly coiled for a downward slash; your cane-reinforced arm slams into the unprotected ulna bones of the attacker's wrist. You won't feel anything but a muted impact; yet he will feel intense pain, and may very well suffer wrist fractures. A downward slash of your arm will intercept his sensitive shinbone with your unfeeling hickory cane under your forearm; it may or may not break his leg, but it sure won't hurt your cane or your arm. You may be jarred backward, but *he* will be in a world of far deeper pain.

If you are grabbed from behind, you can use a cane in this position to poke the attacker out from behind you. If the cane is in your right hand (held with the shaft parallel to your lower instead of your upper forearm), you whip it up so that the shaft is between your upper arm and your chest. Now, you turn the handle of the cane sideways, so that it points toward your other arm. (This angles the blow inward to the mugger's solar plexus instead of straight back, where it could harmlessly skid off his rib cage.) Now, you quickly shove the tip of the cane *backward*.

By so doing, you deliver intensely focused impact to a vital part of his body. You're delivering roughly hundreds of foot-pounds of pressure on his diaphragm, compared to 59 foot-pounds if you had shot him there with a .25 caliber automatic pistol. You won't make a hole in him, of course (and really, that makes all the difference), but you will definitely deliver an impact that can jar him loose. When police officers use this technique with their PR–24 batons against those who attack them from the rear, the street criminals usually just fold over and vomit their guts out.

What you *shouldn't* do is lash out with your cane extended, clubbing down with it like a bludgeon. It won't hit that hard (canes taper, and you might have an aluminum one). Besides, all the opposition has to do is catch that blow on his upraised forearm, and then just rip it away from you.

Nothing that doesn't kill puts a frail, elderly person at a definite advantage with a strapping twenty-five year old, but these cane techniques make that instrument an effective weapon of defense, in methods that have been proven effective on the streets by small cops fighting big outlaw bikers and by women cops fighting male criminals.

If you were to carry a cane so that you could fight with it the way cops fight with their PR–24s, you'd want one with a 90° straight handle, like the ones dandies gave each other as engraved souvenirs around the turn of the century. If you actually need a cane to walk with, it probably has a curved handle for day-to-day comfort and balance. The techniques I have described work with such canes. Go with heavy hardwood canes if you can handle them; if you need lightweight tubular aluminum, you'll still have most of the blocking and hitting capability, though you won't be nearly as likely to break the attacker's bones and stop him from hurting you, and your cane is more likely to be bent during the fight.

35. MAKESHIFTS THAT REALLY WORK

FIGHTING RINGS

In his book *Will*, G. Gordon Liddy writes graphically and brutally about some of his experiences in prison. One encounter was with a belligerent convict who was not in as fine physical shape as Liddy. The man landed a relatively feeble punch to Liddy's forehead, and to his horror and surprise, Liddy was instantly half blinded as a flood of blood poured into his eyes. The fight was broken up before either man was seriously injured, but Liddy still couldn't believe he had been gashed that badly by such a puny blow. Another con provided the answer: "fighting rings."

Any ring with a raised, rough surface will increase the damage you can inflict with a punch or backhanded slap. Many class rings, with their multifaceted semiprecious stones and their tiny, upraised letters, are moderately effective in this sort of application. But if you're talking about serious protection against street people, you're talking about a serious fighting ring.

When I was a teenager, we'd buy a pipe holder wrapped all the way around, sharpened and secured with a screw and bolt, at the hardware store for fifteen cents. The flange on the edge was already deadly sharp, and the cops couldn't arrest us for carrying fighting tools. "That little thing, Officer? Gosh, I guess I just stuck it in my pocket after I was helping my dad with the plumbing and forgot to put it back in his toolbox."

A trip to the hardware store is one expedient. Get a pipe holder and learn to put it on, as indicated. Make sure it's a slightly loose fit, and carry one in a pocket on each side of your body where you can insert your hand and quickly slip it onto your middle finger without alerting a possible aggressor to the fact that you are "arming" yourself. Don't get it *too* loose, though, or it will be cumbersome. A ring that fits sloppily won't let you clench your fist properly, and increases the chances of your getting a broken finger when you punch, or if the opponent grabs your hand in a viselike grip.

An alternative is a professionally made fighting ring. Made of heavy metal, they are sculpted into shapes like Viking faces and wolves' heads. The Viking ring has a helmet with a sharp, raised faceguard, creating a cutting surface that will peel long, narrow strips of hide from your attacker's face. The wolf's head, with its tiny fangs protruding from its open mouth, lacerates almost as well.

These rings cost around sixty dollars and can be worn all the time so that you are constantly ready to defend yourself. Few reputable jewelers have them in stock, but some fringe-type motorcycle shops will. Failing that, you can order them by mail through newsstand magazines like *Easyriders*.

Some of you may find such rings altogether too gauche to fit your image. In that case, order them about one size larger, and carry them in your pocket.

I suggest one for each hand. They don't inhibit your grappling ability in the slightest. If you're right-handed, wear a Viking ring on your left hand, a wolf's head on the right. Most American men are brought up to box Western-style, with their weak side forward. That means the left hand will be used mostly for jabs and hooks, relatively weak punches aimed at the exposed flesh of the face and head. The superior cutting surface of the Norseman-style ring is ideal for this kind of punch.

For the same reason, the strong hand is reserved for what karateists call the reverse punch, which starts way back and travels farther, gaining maximum force. The wolf's head will optimally enhance its destructive power: The conical shape of its lupine face increases the likelihood of your punch denting or fracturing the attacker's bones.

At this writing, I know of no state or jurisdiction that considers any sort of ring to be a weapon, while virtually every state prohibits brass knuckles.

COINROLLERS

Another proven streetfighter trick is punching with a roll of coins in your fist. Since it gives weight and hardness to your striking hand, the impact is absolutely devastating.

The pennyroller is not a makeshift dreamed up by those who don't want you to really hurt your rapist or mugger. Since around the turn of the century, when coins started coming in paper rolls, hardened street brawlers have been using them to bust jaws and skulls and ribs.

Let us remind you once more that, in the eyes of the law, *anything* becomes a weapon when you hit somebody with it. The secret of the makeshift fighting tools is that it is perfectly legal to wear them, while you can be arrested for possession of a prohibited weapon if you carry brass knuckles, even if they're in the form of a novelty belt buckle.

Most people who carry coinrollers for purposes more serious than patronizing vending machines use pennyrollers, simply because they only cost fifty cents. However, they're harder to explain, and they're too big for many women and too small for a lot of men.

For a very small female hand, a roll of dimes is about the right size, and doubles as an ample supply of emergency payphone change. Most men will find that a roll of quarters fits their hand more comfortably and these also make good phone-food. Big-handed men will hit hardest with a roll of half-dollars, and if anyone asks why you were carrying them, you can explain that it's for the tollbooths.

It's a good idea to exchange your coinroller once a week for two reasons: It's less likely to fall apart in your hand after a couple of punches, and it doesn't look as if you've been carrying it around for weeks, waiting to punch someone out with it.

This last is an important consideration. If you break a mugger's jaw with a coinroller in your fist, he's likely to find a sleazy lawyer to sue you. That lawyer can make a better case against you if he can convince the jury that you were carrying the coinroller as a weapon. The jurors will know that a coinroller is too bulky and heavy to carry around for any purpose other than hitting people. The fact that you only planned to hit criminal aggressors won't do you much good in court; the street criminal's lawer just wants to establish the fact that you were an armed person.

36. THE KOBOTAN AND MO-GEM

With the exception of the cane and walking stick, comparable in use to the fighting staffs of the Orient, none of the martial arts weapons are legal for street carry and self-protection. These include the *yawara* stick (a short piece of wood designed to reinforce a punch or an edge of fist strike, also used in Bo-Kibo fighting techniques to hook into the corner of a man's mouth, punching out his teeth and then ripping his cheek open to the ear). Often improperly called a judo stick, the *yawara* is more often taught to *jujitsu* students.

Another is the *nunchaku*, one of the five components of Kobu-do, the Okinawan martial art of weaponcraft. A favorite of youth gangs and motorcycle clubs, who call them *nunchuks* or *chakas* or karate sticks, these consist of two twelve- or fourteen-inch pieces of wood, plastic, or metal chained or tied together. When first marketed to cops, they were known as nutcracker flails.

This was a very apt description. If you hold one of the sticks and swing the other, the momentum is awesome and lethal. Used like a giant nutcracker, the *nunchaku* can break wrists or legs or necks in its crushing blunt scissors; SEALS in Vietnam found them ideal for the silent killing of enemy sentries.

In New York, it's illegal to carry such weapons; in Boston, it brings about the same penalty as an illegal gun only not mandatorily. Almost everywhere in the country they are considered illegal, deadly weapons ... and if someone comes at you with one, you *are* justified in shooting him down. They're considered deadlier than knives by most martial artists.

Shuriken and *shaken* ("throwing darts" and "kung fu stars") are also illegal, and frankly, they're not that effective for street defense anyway. The *tonfa*, the bulky instrument that inspired the modern police PR–24 baton, is impossible to carry concealed and doesn't work as well as the PR–24, which is sold only to police. Illegal for civilians on the street? Yes.

I love to work out with *nunchuks*, and when I was a police officer, I would have sooner gone to work without my pants than without my PR–24 baton. As a civilian, however, I can legally carry neither. Police don't issue permits for anything but guns, because they perceive blackjacks and clubs to be gangster weapons, while for centuries, bankers and lawyers and doctors have been carrying pocket pistols for defense. I do not foresee the martial arts weapons being socially legitimized in the near future. That's why I recommend either the tiny Kubotan or Mo-Gem or the heavy police-style flashlight for the individual who wishes to learn martial arts techniques with an effective less-lethal weapon that is "street legal."

If whistles and makeshift weapons like car keys and water pistols filled with ammonia don't work, there are equally unobtrusive protective devices that have proven to be extremely effective in violent confrontations.

The systems that work are systems *developed* by professionals in fighting, to be *used* by professionals in fighting. During his career a street police officer will be involved in numerous physical encounters, from scuffles to brawls to full-fledged riots. Anything introduced as a police weapon gets street-tested quickly and if it doesn't work, it gets dropped by the wayside. Chemical sprays are a case in point.

If the cops accept a defensive tool enthusiastically, it is because the instrument works on the street. Two such street-proven devices, available to civilians and generally legal to carry without a permit, are the Kubotan and the Mo-Gem.

THE KUBOTAN

The Kubotan is a cylinder 5½ inches long and ⅝-inch in diameter, made of Monpac Plastic or Lexan. It is named for its designer Shihan Takayuki Kubota, universally recognized as one of the world's leading figures in the martial arts. *Shihan* is a Japanese term that loosely translates as "master instructor"; and the title belongs to only a handful of men in the world.

The Kubotan was an evolution of a previous system developed by Kubota called pen fighting. Seeking a simple self-defense method that could be used by average American citizens with little training, Kubota built techniques around solidly constructed ballpoint pens.

The principle was not impact, but pain control. The student learned the location of easy-to-reach pressure points on the wrists, hands, and up and down the torso. By placing the rigid body of the pen over the exposed ulna bone of an attacker's wrist, the student could gently wrap his other hand around it, and with a gentle forward-and-down turn of the wrist, inflict excruciating pain that would break the assailant's balance and spin him around, and force him to his knees.

There were two problems. These are still only ballpoint pens, and not built for that sort of punishment; it was found that they could bend or break if the subject struggled violently. In another sense, the pen worked almost too well: On a downward jab against unprotected skin, even if the ballpoint was retracted, it could puncture flesh and have grave legal (and medical) ramifications.

Kubota eventually came up with the Kubotan. Its almost unbreakable construction and flattened ends solved both the problems, and its greater thickness gave the student much better leverage for restraining and takedown holds.

In January of 1979, at the Ohio State Peace Officers Academy, I was among the first 58 American police officers to be certified as instructors of the Kubotan. All of us were experienced cop-teachers, and all of us had grave doubts that this little black plastic Tootsie Roll could do anything except give our officers false confidence.

In very short order, Kubota proved how wrong we were. Kubota has taught the police of Tokyo and Los Angeles to name but a few, and his feeling is that "Kubotan works on principle of pain control, so you must feel all the pain it can give."

Kubota who stands about 5 feet 4 inches, singled out his first victim: Stan Kubas, one of the top police instructors in the Chicago area. About 6 feet 4 inches and 260 pounds, the muscular Kubas, a karate practitioner, had just won the gold medal for weightlifting at the national Police Olympics, and had recently been the Illinois State Champion in police combat shooting. Altogether, not a man on whom to attempt "chicken" defensive techniques.

Kubota ordered Kubas to come at him, and the big police officer, not one to lose face in front of 57 peers, did so. We all knew in that instant that Kubas was serious, and that he was quite literally capable of picking up the small Japanese with one hand and bouncing him off the nearest wall.

Instead, Kubota's little black wand flickered. Kubas let out a sound like a wounded wolf, and the floor shook as he was slammed to his knees. With a brisk step to the side, Kubota placed himself out of reach of Kubas's other monster arm, while he kept the huge left wrist trapped firmly between his own two small hands, and the Kubotan.

The giant police officer's face had contorted into an involuntary grimace. The teeth exposed back to the gums; sweat burst out on his face. Finally, with his free hand, he slapped his own body twice in the universal martial arts gesture of submission. The encounter had lasted perhaps six seconds.

A hush fell over the academy gymnasium. It was a silence soon to be replaced with grunts and curses as we spent the rest of the day practicing the sixteen Kubotan techniques. By lunchtime, we were covered with bruises, and the smarter ones skipped lunch and drove to the nearest drugstore to buy Ace bandages to wrap around their wrists. They didn't help.

At day's end, not one of us had escaped swollen or aching hands, or the bluish-green bruises that dotted our chests and sides from the pressure point takedowns. They didn't fade for weeks.

Since that time, the Kubotan has been widely accepted by U.S. law enforcement agents. It is especially popular among court bailiffs, youth corrections personnel, prison guards, and others, who must use low-profile methods that will restrain violent subjects in an environment where they are forbidden to draw or sometimes even possess, firearms.

The Kubotan is equally adaptable to civilians. A physically weak person, conceivably even someone with mild arthritis, can make it work. The excruciating wrist-takedown, for example, requires less force to be exerted by your hands than it takes to snap a stapler. The secret is that as your hands go into position, you roll your wrists forward. *He* feels pain like an electric shock; *you* feel none whatsoever. Then you just step back and lower your hands, and he drops.

In the necklock takedown, also illustrated in these pages, the key is to move quickly and then to drive the bottom end of the Kubotan *straight down toward the floor* once it is in place against the pressure point on the opponent's chest. You have to have it applied to you to understand why it works.

When your assailant drops to his knees or his buttocks in a Kubotan technique he is moving toward the line of least resistance in a desperate, instinctive effort to escape or alleviate the pain. No system is foolproof, including this one. A drug-crazed criminal, or one with an unusually high natural pain tolerance, may be able to withstand it. Anyone can escape it if you move slowly, hesitantly, or halfheartedly—something true of any other defensive fighting system, for that matter.

There are no test cases on the books as yet, but at this writing it appears that the Kubotan is legal to own and carry anywhere in the United States. Pending changes in the law, I would venture (as a certified expert witness in this area) that the Kubotan should not legally be considered a prohibited martial arts weapon under the same laws that now control weapons such as *yawara* sticks and *nunchaku*. It only roughly resembles the *yawara* in shape, and due to its different length and thickness, would be less effective than the real thing if applied with *yawara* techniques. These may, of course, be used with the Kubotan, but that's true of numerous other instruments, including a Bic pen.

Buy the model with a keychain on the end, and use it for your car keys (*not* your house keys, in case the Kubotan is lost or dropped in a fight). Some martial arts instructors purport to teach the Kubotan, capitalizing on its fame among those who know weapons, but cheat the student by only teaching a few *yawara* techniques, and advising that the device be used as a handle to slash the car keys across the attacker's face.

If a martial arts instructor teaches you such techniques, you should ask for your money back. They are weak and ineffectual. Only the Kubotan training system developed by Kubota and his protégé John Peters will work decisively on the street. It requires four hours of hands-on training to learn these techniques, after which you become certified with the instrument and with the system. This builds practical confidence and a defense in court, to boot.

The original training manual that came out with the Kubotan was very poorly done, and you won't learn a thing from it. Read the new one published by DTI (Defensive Tactics Institute). Even then, you won't really have a functioning security instrument until you've been trained, hands-on, by a certified instructor. You can locate such an instructor in your area by writing to:

Shihan Takayuki Kubota   John Peters
Kubotan Institute   DTI
1236 South Glendale Avenue   15 Cedarcliff Road
Glendale, CA   Braintree, MA 02184

Paul Starrett
Monadnock Lifetime Products
Route 12
Fitzwilliam, NH 03447

The improved Kubotan manual is also available from DTI for $5.95. The instrument itself can be bought for $4.95 in Monpac from Monadnock Lifetime Products, or $3.50 in Lexan from DTI. I prefer the black whether it's Monpac or Lexan, because it looks more intimidating when you pull it out. The day after I left my Kubotan course in Ohio, I drew mine on a street criminal in Indianapolis. He did a double take when I pulled it from my belt, took a step back, stared at it, and literally threw up his hands and walked away. The deterrent effect of the Kubotan had kept one street person and one law-abiding citizen from getting hurt, and had saved one street person from the danger of being legally shot to death by an off-duty, out-of-state cop (me) thwarting a mugging.

The Kubotan is best carried in the front waistband of slacks or skirt, with the keys hanging outside. If you need to make a quick escape, your car keys are where you can reach them instantly without fumbling through a purse or digging into the pocket of tight jeans while you're running. Indeed, you're better off to have the Kubotan keychain in your hand when walking through a danger zone to your car. It is quite comfortable in the belt-carry position, though, and won't fall out unless you forget it when you drop your pants.

The Kubotan is an extremely useful self-defense tool. It leaves, at worst, a bruise on the person you have to deal with, making it excellent for those low-threat level situations (mashers, grabby drunks at parties) whom you have to restrain but don't want to seriously injure.

Still, I can't emphasize strongly enough that the Kubotan works only for the man or woman who is properly trained with its technique. If you just buy one and stick it in your waistband, you're just buying false confidence.

THE MO-GEM

Late 1980 saw the introduction of a new defensive tool, Jim Morrell's Mo-Gem. Morrell is a karate instructor in New Jersey, with a clientele divided about equally between police officers and security officers, and preponderantly female classes of scared citizens.

Morell feels that the best answer for a cop in a streetfight is a PR–24 baton, but also realizes that in some low-profile situations, the use of a big stick could be inflammatory. His female civilians couldn't carry serious weapons under New Jersey's strict laws, and even the guards in the Atlantic City casinos are forbidden to carry batons, let alone guns.

For them, he developed the Mo-Gem, a cylinder of aluminum 8¼ inches long and 1 inch in diameter. It has a

KUBOTAN WRISTLOCK

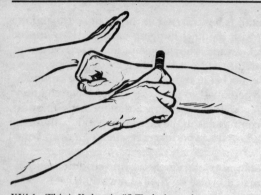

KW-1: This is Kubota's #2 Technique, the strongest Kubotan wristlock. Kubotan is hooked over suspect's wrist, with defender's thumb beneath the wrist. Defender's other hand, in same position, comes in on other side of attacker's wrist.

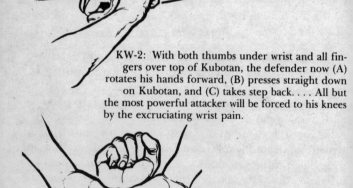

KW-2: With both thumbs under wrist and all fingers over top of Kubotan, the defender now (A) rotates his hands forward, (B) presses straight down on Kubotan, and (C) takes step back. . . . All but the most powerful attacker will be forced to his knees by the excruciating wrist pain.

KW-3: Underneath view of Kubotan wristlock. Note that webs of defender's hands are tightly against attacker's wrist, creating "gasket seal effect" that prevents him from wriggling loose.

built-in bulb and two AA batteries, so that a flick of the wrist can turn it into a penlight.

The Mo-Gem isn't swung in the manner of a Kel-Lite-style police flashlight. As the illustrations show, the only blow taught with it is an underhand flick that Morrell calls a cobra strike.

No physical strength is needed for this blow. You hold the Mo-Gem vertically, with the niche on top resting against the web of your hand. Then cock your hand at the same angle as if you were playing with a child and making shadow images of a duck on the wall. Then, just flick your hand toward the target.

The lower end comes flying out with an impact sharp enough to make deep dents in wood; though you're unlikely to break bones, the impact will be extremely painful. Your little finger then catches the lower end as it reaches its fullest extension, snapping it back to striking position. The way to practice is to put a few big nails into a pine board and, while you're watching TV, practice hammering the nails through the wood with these little cobra-flicks of the Mo-Gem.

I personally prefer the grappling and restraint techniques Morrell teaches with the instrument. While a Kubotan works with the long end extending up from the thumb-side of your hand, the business end of a Mo-Gem projects downward from the bottom of your fist.

As the illustrations show, the Mo-Gem differs considerably from the Kubotan in shape. While the latter is smooth, with only edgeless grooves to keep it from slipping in your hand, the Mo-Gem is as sharply checkered as a Kel-Lite police flashlight. You won't be hitting anyone with the checkered part if you're trained properly.

What does happen, is that when you hook someone into a wristlock, as illustrated, you're going to take a little bit of meat off him. It's nothing that would qualify as maiming; he probably won't even notice it, because the

MO-GEM BLOCKING TECHNIQUE

MGB-1: Attacker (left) begins to throw punch against defender armed with a MoGem.

MGB-2: As blow comes in, defender begins circular block.

MGB-3: Fist is deflected upward; note that defender's other hand is in blocking position to protect face and head.

MGB-4: As blow is dissipated, defender easily forces attacker's arm upward, hooking MoGem against unprotected ulna bone at attacker's wrist. Delivered forcefully, this can break attacker's wrist, or trained defender can continue into a wristlock.

MGB-5: Continuing to wristlock. Maintaining MoGem in position over ulna bone, defender grabs attacker's left wrist and pulls it toward him, hyperextending (locking to full length) the attacker's arm.

MGB-6: Maintaining MoGem hold at wrist, attacker now leans forward and presses his forearm over the upraised knob of attacker's locked elbow. If attacker continues to fight, downward pressure will break or dislocate his elbow.

(As taught by Jim Morrell of International Police Academy, Inventor of the MoGem.)

pain of the lock on his wristbones and nerve centers will be so much more intense.

The first time I worked out with Morrell on the device, he put me in a wristlock and I resisted. A few seconds later I was on my knees. Only afterward did I notice eighteen tiny lacerations on the back of my hand, in the exact pattern as the Mo-Gem's checkering. Two weeks later, those marks were still readily apparent to the naked eye. They remained for two months.

This creates good evidence. If everything goes well and the mugger gives up the assault the first time you torque his wrist and bounce his kneecaps off the sidewalk, you're still going to want the cops to be able to find him and identify him later.

Indeed, after the workout I found tiny shreds of my own epidermis embedded in the chekering of the mean little "flashlight." My friend Bob Lindsey, a leading police defense instructor and a captain in the Jefferson Parrish Sheriff's Department that encompasses tough New Orleans, teaches in his weapon retention classes that the officer should rake the suspect's hand or wrist as he rips his service revolver away from the attacker's grasp. The particles of human flesh that are embedded on the grooves and checkering of the gun's front sight or hammer spur, Bob has found, can be used by lab technicians for positive identification if the suspect escapes and is captured later.

With a Kubotan, you have to block with your hands, not the instrument. With the Mo-Gem you can swing, and hook an oncoming fist harmlessly away from you. From there, you either apply a wristlock and take the person all the way down, or grab his hand and swing the Mo-Gem behind his neck, hooking him forward and off balance. *This, however, is a potentially lethal technique, and should only be resorted to when you are facing great danger.*

How does the Mo-Gem compare with the Kubotan? You can hurt an attacker more with the Mo-Gem, and you have more blocking capability and of course, it *is* a flashlight. It's also bulkier to carry, and downright uncomfortable in the waistband; cops carry it in the "sap pocket" sewn into their uniform trousers at the back of their thigh.

At this writing, the Kubotan taught coast to coast is by far more effective since numerous real-life struggles have been documented in which it has worked. The Mo-Gem is newer and without a national training organization, its use has been limited to the New Jersey area where it is racking up an excellent record. I spoke with one motorcycle cop on the Atlantic City Police Department (ACPD) who told me, "I've used my Mo-Gem on the street and it's terrific. If it's a full-scale fight, I'll use my PR–twenty-four baton, but the Mo-Gem has done the job for me every time I had to subdue a 'rowdy,' or fold a guy's arms up and take him out of a bar."

The Mo-Gem costs $9.95 at this writing, and is sold by Monadnock Lifetime Products. As with the Kubotan, you won't be able to do anything with it unless you're properly trained. Inventor Morrell has a manual coming out, and is now in the process of training instructors around the country. Drop him a postcard at 76 Green Drive, Toms River, NJ 08753, and he can direct you to someone who can teach you how to use it.

I have both, but favor the Kubotan because of its ubiquitous unobtrusiveness: I can carry the little thing everywhere without inconvenience, and it's a fraction of a second away from my hand. My wife, trained on both, prefers the Mo-Gem; though she packs a gun, she just doesn't like a Kubotan *or* Mo-Gem in her waistband. She carries her Mo-Gem in her pocketbook, next to the spare clip of 9mm Luger ammo for her automatic. At the same time, even Jim Morrell carries his car keys on a Kubotan. You build your defensive system around your own personal life-style. Some of us carry both; during my last days as a cop I carried a PR–24 and a Kubotan, just as that ACPD motorcycle cop had a PR–24 and a Mo-Gem.

Either device offers you a level of self-defense against

unarmed assault that is worlds beyond rolled-up magazines, two little car keys between your fingers, or any of the other junk recommended to you by people who never get into streetfights. The Kubotan and the Mo-Gem are used routinely by the police, and if they *didn't* win streetfights, they would have abandoned them as quickly as they did the chemical sprays.

37. TIPS ON TEAR GAS SPRAYS

Though often referred to as aerosol incapacitants, tear gas sprays shoot out in a stream rather than an aerosol mist, and they are properly labeled "irritants." There are three kinds: CS, CN, and pepper formulas. The latter are useful only as dog repellents and have little if any effect on humans.

The debate still rages among police officers as to whether CS or CN is better, a moot point since most street cops don't trust either one. That's cool for cops, who have guns and nightsticks and portable radios on which to instantly call for help from their brothers in blue. When you have none of those, Mace and similar products start looking good.

In layman's terms, CN is *tear gas,* and CS is *choking gas.* Quantity for quantity, CS is about ten times more powerful. CN may have no effect on a drunk or an enraged man with a high-pain tolerance, but CS usually will. The problem is that CS can take as long as thirty seconds to work if it is not sprayed directly into the eyes, while CN causes an intense burning sensation the instant it comes into contact with unprotected human flesh.

When I carry such units I generally use CS because I'm trained with it and am confident that I can get it right into my attacker's eyes. The person with less training would be better off with CN. Paralyzer is the most popular CS brand, while the original Mace is your best bet in CN.

For those who don't feel they could physically handle martial arts training or defensive tools like the Kubotan and Mo-Gem, there is something to be said for Mace and its competitive sprays. The device is simple to operate, works by remote control, and has received so much publicity that most civilians who carry it are quite confident. However, you should by all means study and practice before trusting your life to such a product.

The great majority of "Mace schools" at this time are conducted very poorly, as was confirmed in a dramatic 1981 exposé produced by Glenn Winters for ABC's *20/20*. At this time, Smith & Wesson (producers of the original Mace) offer such training only to police, though some in the organization are pushing for civilian classes.

Their five-day course, Chemical Agents Administration, concentrates on the tactical use of gas grenades, tear gas projectiles, Pepper Foggers, and other large-scale delivery systems designed for mob control and sieges on barricaded gunmen.

However, the program does include half a day of excellent training in the use of Mace. Says S&W academy instructor Hank Kudlinsky,

We believe that Mace can be extremely useful in a number of police scenarios, including one-on-one encounters with unarmed suspects who resist violently. We believe that, on the ladder of escalating force, Mace is somewhat below the use of the baton or nightstick.

Like this writer, Kudlinsky is fond of quoting Arthur Lamb of the Boston Police Department, the legendary baton instructor who taught officers to smash their antagonists across the kneecap with the nightstick *and then take a step back,* "to give the suspect an opportunity to reconsider his negative attitude." Says Kudlinsky,

This allows you a second or two for the CN gas to take effect. One reason Mace is produced only in the CN formula is that it works that quickly; we find that CS, while some believe it is more potent, takes longer to work when not sprayed directly into the eyes.

As per factory instructions, the academy teaches the user to spray the Mace at the suspect's chin and lower face, carefully avoiding the eyes. Kudlinsky agrees that the old method of spraying the shirtfront and waiting for the vapors to rise, simply didn't work against violent suspects on the street.

The person who carries Mace as an all-purpose defense mechanism against muggers or rapists should consider the first thing Kudlinsky teaches his cops and police instructors: "Mace is *not* to be used in life-threatening encounters! It would be extremely foolish to use Mace on a suspect immediately capable of employing a deadly weapon. That is simply not what it was designed for."

When you attend a two- to four-hour training course, you would be well advised to take it from a source that does not sell chemical substances as a business. Otherwise, you're liable to be oversold on the effectiveness of the tear gas. If at no time in the course are you exposed to actual tear gas, you should justifiably wonder if you have been "trained" at all. The course should also allow you to use spray canisters filled with an inert substance, duplicating the spray patterns of the real thing, so that you can develop a realistic idea of how accurately you can "Mace" a man, and at what distance.

If no such class is available to you, consider purchasing an inert canister, available through many of the deal-

ers who sell the real thing. They are manufactured by
S&W and others.

The practice will be educational. I find that I can, in
practice, easily hit a motionless silhouette target in the face
at ten or more feet with my Curb CS units, but Kudlinsky
wisely suggests six feet as the optimum distance. He and
his police students find that, in a fast-breaking situation
where both Good Guy and Bad Guy are moving rapidly,
it's hard to get an accurate "hit" of the chemical spray
much beyond that distance, even after intensive training.

The inert sprays allow you to practice face-to-face
action with a friend. This is the only way to learn if you
can *really* apply the substance quickly enough to incapacitate your opponent in real life. Work out different
scenarios—such as getting grabbed from behind—but be
sure that you're in a "soft" environment where you're not
likely to be hurt if you fall, and make sure that both you
and your partner don't exceed your own physical skills and
endurance with too-rough "practice."

Don't cheat yourself: It is a must to practice each
scenario starting with the Mace unit where you normally
carry it—in your pocket, purse, or wherever. You'll quickly
find that you only get it out in time if you have your hand
on it when the confrontation begins. A number of manufacturers now produce keychains with tiny chemical sprays
in a leather pouch at the end—a very sensible approach
for the private citizen, one that also keeps the means of
escape readily at hand. You may not be able to find an
inert practice canister this small, but you still shouldn't do
face-to-face practice with active ingredients. Inert Mace
canisters are available through any Smith & Wesson dealer;
check the Yellow Pages for gun retailers and police equipment stores.

The vast majority of those who rely on chemical sprays
haven't given much thought to what they should do after
they've "Maced" their attacker. They all seem to assume
that the mugger or rapist is going to crumple into a

helpless, sobbing heap, allowing them to leisurely saunter home. Wrong. You have to assume the worst: that your attacker is going to be either unaffected or enraged when you Mace him. Be prepared to move backward. Kudlinsky and I both teach cops to use the "Lamb Technique," which requires one step backward—but remember, our police students are required by duty to hold their ground regardless, until the Bad Guy is subdued and in custody. Our students also have guns and clubs, and the authority to use both if it becomes necessary. *You*, in all probability, have no such options; as a civilian, the law requires you to retreat as soon as possible.

Your best tactic may be to spray as you retreat, hoping that he won't be able to follow you with his eyes and throat burning.

When you work out with your partner, *practice* spraying as you move back. After a solid "hit" in his face, quickly divert your movement—sideways if you had been going backward, or vice versa. This helps keep him from blindly and instinctively grabbing you if he continues his charge and aims at the position where last he saw you.

If you don't walk with your hand in your "Mace pocket" or while holding a chemical-spray keychain, you'll be hard put to get at it while you're grappling to break free of an attacker and ward off his blows, or just keep your balance as he throws you around. The relatively few police officers who still carry Mace and similar substances usually have them in a belt pouch, often fastened in with a safety strap or flap.

Those who carried pistols learned more than a century ago that a holster was the quickest way to gain access to it and very shortly realized that having to unsnap a flap first could be fatally slow. While some officers do carry their Mace in open-top, quick-draw pouches, most don't mind the flap. If they need their *gun*, they need it in a hurry, but if things have gotten so dangerous so quickly that they need to speed-draw their Mace, the situation has already probably progressed to the point that they'll be reaching for their gun or their club instead, anyway.

If Mace is all you *have* to reach for, though, a holster may be your best bet, assuming that you normally wear a belt to hang it on. Do yourself a favor and cut the flap off with a sharp knife. You may also want to carve a niche in the outside upper part of the holster body, to give your fingers a surer hold if you must reach for it in a hurry when there's no time to fumble. Always carry your canister *head-down* in a holster or belt pouch. This does two positive things for you: It greatly reduces the likelihood of an accidental discharge that doses you as you hastily draw, and it makes sure that the spray will work full-power on the first press of the activating button.

Those of us who have the training and authority to carry guns can afford to wrinkle our noses a bit at the thought of trusting our lives to a little canister of irritant chemical spray. When I was an assistant professor of law enforcement teaching Weapons and Chemical Agents to full-time, in-service police officers, I became well aware of the fact that many veteran street cops hold the chemical sprays in contempt. In the eight years I carried a badge I very rarely bothered with a chemical sprays. I was physically fit, well trained in hand-to-hand restraint, and equipped with a PR–24 baton, either a .45 automatic or a .357 Magnum service revolver, a .38 Detective Special in my hideout ankle holster, and a combat shotgun locked to my patrol car's dashboard. Police reinforcements were a radio call away and I was backed with the authority to use them all at my trained discretion.

A little less than a year after leaving my New England police department, I found myself doing more on-the-street research work for the Patrolman's Benevolent Association, New York City's police union. It was not legal for me, as an out-of-state civilian, to carry a gun or baton there. It was not legal for me to even have Mace, and there was some question as to whether my little Kubotan might be considered similar enough to a *yawara* stick to be a "prohibited martial arts weapon."

I wound up walking the streets of New York with one legal-length, razor sharp folding knife in my trouser pocket and another in my jacket, and carrying a five-cell Bianchi police flashlight. All were legal; all could have been used lethally; but none gave me a lot of middle ground for dealing with a violent physical assault that didn't involve deadly force. In that period, I would have found a can of Mace comforting, indeed.

It's all a matter of perspective. Mace, under some circumstances, is every bit the "instant chemical incapacitant" the ads claim it to be. In other cases, it could be worse than useless. Properly labeled an "irritant," it could "irritate" a mugger or rapist enough to kill you in anger. Many cases will be in between: It will help to incapacitate your attacker, but you would be foolish not to have a Plan B of retreat and a Plan C of hand-to-hand fighting to fall back on.

If you have a chemical spray keychain, you might want to take it with you when you're traveling, but there are a number of things you'll have to be aware of first. *Never* fly with Mace or any other such product, even if it's locked in checked baggage. Changing air pressures at high altitudes can cause the canisters to leak.

Pocket-size canisters to fit your keychain holder can be purchased in many cities and generally sell for under ten dollars. Trying to economize by bringing your own on a plane trip can cost you a lot more. A pocket-size canister of CS (which tends to contaminate permanently) contains about twenty-two grams of the substance. If that lets go inside your suitcase, your entire travel wardrobe could be ruined. You'll certainly have to give it a good airing out and multiple washings before you can wear it again, even if you were only carrying CN.

I've attended many police demonstrations where large volumes of CS and CN were released with grenades, and after you've walked through it a few times, you *do* want to get your clothes off and air them out. After washing (I recommend twice) the students and I can wear those clothes again, but remember, we were out in the open air. The close confines of a suitcase could allow your clothing to be permanently contaminated.

An episode that happened to me illustrates the dangers of taking tear gas canisters aloft. I had flown to Des Moines to interview the first class of Affirmative Action trooper recruits in the Iowa State Patrol, and chucked a small canister of Curb CN into my suitcase. As soon as I reclaimed it from baggage check I slipped the unit into my pocket, got into my Rentacar, and drove to the State Law Enforcement Academy at Camp Dodge.

I was halfway into a round table interview with the academy director and several female recruits when I noticed that some of them were sniffling and rubbing their eyes. After a bit—I had a cold—I smelled an all-too-familiar odor. About that same time my own eyes started to sting and so did my leg. I suddenly realized that my CN unit, in the de-pressurized baggage compartment of the plane, had spring a slow leak.

I rapidly excused myself and headed for the men's room. Once there, I found an open window, sprayed the remaining CN from my leaking chemical weapon into the open air, and threw the empty canister to the bottom of a trash receptacle. Then I whipped off my trousers.

At that point, a couple of young recruits walked in and were treated to a strange sight: a man standing in his skivvy shorts, holding his right thigh over the sink as he poured cold water on it from the faucet, full blast. I managed to wash most of the chemical out of the slacks (thank God I was wearing Navy blue!) and was able to return and finish the interview for *Trooper* magazine, but it was the last time I ever flew anywhere with aerosol tear gas.

Incidentally, the reason it took me longer to notice it even though I was closer to the leaking unit had nothing to do with my cold. As a police instructor I had frequently been exposed to CN, and one *can* build up a physical tolerance to the stuff. This is no reason to purchase CS, which hits just as hard every time, since it is most unlikely that your mugger has been Maced often enough to build up a CN tolerance.

You may or may not be able to legally buy it in every city. Mace and its imitative sister products are banned in New York City; you can buy it in Chicago ostensibly for home defense, but it's against the law there to carry it on your person; in Los Angeles, you can pick some up, but can't carry it without a permit. While as a police instructor in Weapons and Chemical Agents I am certainly more qualified to do so than someone who only had a two-hour course as provided by California state law, even I would still be subject to arrest for carrying tear gas spray in that state if I didn't have the state permit.

Place a phone call to the office of the attorney general or district attorney in the place where you're headed. They can tell you quickly about the law. Between the phone call and the chemical spray you buy and dispose of there, this temporary protection could cost you twenty bucks, but decent protection is never cheap.

Before you fly back out, it's your responsibility to dispose of the unit properly. Children getting hold of your discarded canister could be blinded or suffer serious lung damage from misusing it even from the residue in an "emptied" unit.

I either give mine to a police officer or spray it where there are no people, where the spray goes with the wind to disperse, and where there is cold running water readily available in case there's an accident. I then chuck the empty canister down a sewer or someplace else where children won't get at it, wash my hands thoroughly in cold water, and head on out.

38. SHOULD YOU HAVE A GUN?

Every book on self-protection as well as every article on the subject in newspapers and general-interest magazines seems to agree on one thing: Never keep guns for self-defense because you're more likely to have a family member killed by accident or in a domestic act of rage than you are to shoot a burglar. Besides, the intruder can get the gun away from you and kill you with it.

That's mostly propaganda. In nearly every rape defense article you find there's a quote from some senior police officer about why women in particular should never carry guns. Why does the cop tell the reporter that? There's a little bit of elitism in the world of law enforcement, and very few cops think civilians are as capable of dealing with crime as they are. Some police officers sometimes harbor a little bit of resentment for someone who wants to get his or her own gun and "play police officer," for self-protection.

Besides, the cop giving the antirape interview is probably scared to death that some neurotic woman might buy a gun, then panic when someone touches her in a subway, and start firing wildly, wasting a few innocent citizens. Is he going to have that dumped on *his* doorstep? No way.

"No guns for rape victims" is standard advice in police circles, and only one hard fact saves it from being pure hypocrisy: In a good police academy the officer will receive forty-hours training in firearms as well as instruction in the legalities of applying deadly force. In a good police department he'll also have to "qualify" with his weapon two to twelve times a year to prove that he can shoot straight without endangering bystanders with wild shots. No civilian at this writing is required to have that level of training before buying a gun.

For the person who is emotionally capable of dealing lethal injury to a violent, criminal attacker, the gun has a very real place in the world of self-defense. But that place is a very narrow and limited one, and it exists only at the highest threat levels of danger to innocent human life and limb.

In more ways than one, guns kept for self-defense are a major reason why you're reading this book. I first came to the attention of Bantam Books because of the response generated by my privately published book, *In the Gravest Extreme: The Role of the Firearm in Personal Protection*. Appearing late in 1979, the book was in its fifth printing within eighteen months, almost unheard-of for a privately published book with practically no advertising. It was widely endorsed by cops, lawyers, even judges.

Gravest Extreme did not proseletize, and I am not one who believes that every God-fearing man and woman should have a gun. The book spoke only to those who had already chosen to carry or keep firearms, but who didn't fully understand the complex legal, moral, and ethical parameters that govern the use of deadly force in self-defense.

This book is different, because *you* haven't yet necessarily made the decision to go "all the way" in self-defense. Before we talk about what gun to buy, where to keep it, and how to shoot it, we have to seriously explore the question of whether you, the reader, should even be armed with a lethal weapon.

I'm sure you've heard the arguments from those who don't believe any citizens should have guns: Most murders are committed by people who know each other; very few shootings involve criminals who are slain by law-abiding citizens in self-defense; a lot of children are killed in tragic accidents when playing with their parents' guns.

Accidents are a serious concern. That's why this book has a separate chapter on how to safely keep guns should you choose to rely on them as a component in your defensive system.

As for the rest of the arguments against law-abiding citizens, I'll leave it up to your own common sense to decide after we've looked at the facts. True, most murder victims knew the person who killed them. However, that statistic includes dope dealers murdered by other dope dealers, would-be cop killers shot in self-defense by police officers who had arrested them before, and estranged wives who had begged for protection from their psycho ex-husbands only to find that there aren't enough cops to stand bodyguard duty for everyone who's in trouble. They never told you *that* when they ran those statistics by you, did they?

If someone tells you, "You shouldn't have a gun in the house because you and your wife are more likely to shoot yourselves with it in a fit of anger than you are to shoot a robber," perhaps you should ask that person one question: "Are *you* so mentally and emotionally unstable that you might grab a gun and murder your wife in the course of some silly argument?" If he's not that unstable, where does he get off implying that *you* are? And if he *is* that unstable, why doesn't he check himself into an asylum instead of presuming to tell normal, well-adjusted people how to handle life-or-death stress situations?

I don't say *everybody* should have a gun. But I don't say that *nobody* should. If someone wants to turn the other cheek when facing deadly danger, that's his business. I just don't want him telling me that if the newest incarnation of Charles Manson chooses me for a victim, *I* have to roll over and turn butt-up in submission. I believe that those who wish to ban the ownership of guns by other law-abiding citizens, in a world where violent crime against the person is spiraling further and further out of control, are being a bit too presumptuous with their self-righteous morality. End of editorial. Let's look at *you*, and whether guns will or won't fit into your protective package.

—Be honest with yourself. If you are an abuser of alcohol or drugs, if you have a violent temper, or if you are subject to periods of extreme hostility or depression, guns are not for you. Indeed, federal law prohibits the sale of firearms to alcoholics, drug addicts, and former mental patients, just as it does to convicted criminals.

—If you sleepwalk or experience episodes of dream-active sleep where you actually act out the dreams (that is, punching your wife when you have a nightmare about being mugged), you do not want a loaded firearm anywhere near you. Jerry Usher, head of weapons training for Westec Security and a former member of the U.S. Practical Pistol Team, tells his civilian clients who are deep sleepers that they should store their weapons unloaded and a distance from their bed so that they'll have to wake up and perform a complex sequence of acts before they can actually put a loaded gun in their hands.

—If you are one of those people who can honestly say, "I could never take another human being's life under any circumstances," then *forget about having guns for self-defense.* In Hunter S. Thompson's classic book, *Hell's Angels,* he offers documented proof that many armed citizens have driven predatory outlaws off at gunpoint, but that God's mercy is required for the guy who pulls a gun on a Hell's Angel and doesn't pull the trigger when the bluff is called.

There are two basic aspects about the deterrent effect of firearms upon criminals that you'd better understand up front: A gun scares Bad Guys more than Dobermans, Mace, or anything else, *but* it only works when you are demonstrably prepared to use it.

There is a lot in those two basic truths that needs to

be explained to people who don't understand just how firearms function in lawful self-defense.

First off, you always hear that statistic about more homeowners being killed by criminals than vice versa. Of course. Criminals come in tight and poised and hyper, already prepared to kill to get what they want. The citizen reacts from "a state of peace," and even under the worst circumstances is reluctant to take the life of a fellow being. The home invader might kill his innocent victims and even enjoy it, but the homeowner may have to work himself up to "dropping the hammer" on an intruder who wields a knife.

Besides, killing burglars isn't the main idea; remember, for every one shooting thirteen to fifteen criminals are deterred or driven off just by the sight of the gun, and this fully accomplishes what the homeowner bought the gun for in the first place. When you also consider the fact that only about one out of four people who are shot actually dies, you realize that for every home intruder shot dead by the resident, there are ninety-nine others who don't get killed, but who give up their assaults.

You must remember also that you have to understand the enemy and operate on the basis of a "worst possible case" scenario. Let's assume you're facing a man who has already killed and who would kill *you* with absolutely no compunction. He can smell fear as keenly as a dog and he can recognize fear symptoms in your body language and in your voice. If he can tell by your actions that you *won't* pull the trigger, he'll lunge for your gun, and if he's right, he'll get it away from you and most likely will kill you with it. Very possibly, he'll also murder everyone else in the household: They're potential witnesses, and they can send him to jail. In most states he knows he won't die for murder anyway. If he kills in a state like Illinois, he knows that in less than twelve years he'll be eligible for parole whether he kills one person or thirty.

The ironic truth is that a loaded gun in your hand

will stop trouble most of the time just by being there. But *you'll need to make it clear in your words and in your body language that you are fully prepared to shoot this transgressor to death*. If you can't do that—if you really believe you couldn't shoot another human being to death in self-defense—then, guns are not for you.

I might support laws that ban all guns if all guns could be banned. But they can't. There are two hundred million of them floating around the country now, and anybody with a Bridgeport lathe and a year's training in the prison metalworking shop can build a functional imitation of a Sten submachinegun for about thirty dollars.

Even if there were some fantastic, giant electromagnet that was able to pick up all the guns, what about all the criminals with knives and clubs? What about the packs of muggers or multiple rapists who, by force of numbers, prey on the lone innocent? Mace won't deter all of them, and certainly not squeegees of lemon juice or any of the other joke "weapons" that writers on self-defense piously tell you to trust your life to. Whenever you reach the higher threat levels of deadly danger, only countervailing deadly force is going to bring you back from the brink and keep you safe, and most of the time, the sincere threat of that force is enough to accomplish it without bloodshed. I resent "experts" who have never faced deadly threat, yet who tell me—and you—that we should not consider a response of equal power against those who threaten our lives.

A major problem with all the "experts" who've been telling you how to protect yourself, is that they're just like that cop who tells you to carry a whistle so as to protect yourself from a rapist. They're looking for something that isn't there: a soft, gentle, harmless way of fighting something that is hard and vicious and brutally destructive.

You don't battle cancer with cough drops; you fight it with radiation and chemotherapy and even surgical amputation: things that hurt you and make you sick, but keep you alive. When you face the possibility of being murdered, you'll also have to do things that hurt you and sicken you so that you can stay alive—things like taking the life of the criminal who placed you in unavoidable and inescapable peril.

The choice to use deadly force for self-defense is an intensely personal one. Ask yourself if you could pull the trigger of a gun and extinguish the life of a human being if that human being had placed you, your spouse, or your children, in immediate and otherwise unavoidable danger of death or grave bodily harm. If your answer is no, then you should not have guns.

The average citizen makes one terrible, frightening mistake when he buys a gun for self-defense. He sees the weapon as a talisman that magically wards off evil. In fact, it is nothing of the kind. The defensive firearm is much like the fire extinguisher in your kitchen. It is there to deal with a limited, specific band in the spectrum of threat to you and yours. Within that narrow band, properly handled, it will protect you better than anything else. But you need the courage to face danger with it and *use it*, and you need to be trained in its proper employment. Otherwise, you'll fill yourself with false confidence that can get you and yours killed. And, unlike the fire extinguisher, if you use a gun injudiciously you can be criminally charged and sued.

In the following chapters we'll explain how and when to use the various levels of lawful, countervailing force against violent criminals and come out alive and safe, instead of in a prison cell or in a coffin.

39. THE SHOTGUN FOR SELF-DEFENSE

Of the relatively few books and articles that endorse fire-arms for civilian self-defense, a large percentage recommend short-barrel shotguns. This advice is also prevalent among a number of gun dealers. It makes sense on the surface, but the more deeply you explore the actual dynamics of real confrontations between homeowners and criminals, the more problems you begin to see.

Let's consider both the cardinal arguments and the prevalent *myths* in favor of the shotgun for home or store defense, and examine them one by one.

MYTH #1—*The shotgun has utterly decisive stopping power.* There's little argument here, so long as you're talking about a 12-,16-, or 20-gauge gun at close range, but criminals have been known to take three blasts of buckshot and keep fighting.

MYTH #2—*You don't have to aim a shotgun, just point it and the spreading pattern of the shot charge hits the target.* At seven yards, the longest combat distance you're likely to face in a household, even a shotgun that is "choked" OPEN CYLINDER for the widest shot dispersal will hit a target about the diameter of two shirt buttons. *The shotgun does have to be aimed to be effective.*

MYTH #3—*The shotgun is the simplest weapon to learn to shoot effectively.* A 12-gauge shotgun with a full combat load kicks hard enough to knock you off your feet if you aren't braced for it. Female police recruits dread it, and even big men flinch when they fire it. When you flinch, you jerk the

330

muzzle away. The shot you intended for the kidnapper or armed robber may kill your child or a store patron.

All currently available pump and automatic shotguns have tubular magazines, which are awkward to remove shells from and which are harder to check for remaining shells. Pump guns have mechanisms that lock closed once they've been pumped, and the only way to get the shell out is to either fire the gun or to remember to press a small, unobtrusive slide release latch. Undertrained people tend to forget these things under stress, a syndrome that has led to a fair number of accidents among both police and hunters—people far more accustomed to handling shotguns than *you* may be.

Double-barrel and single-barrel single-shot shotguns *are* perhaps the simplest of all firearms to safely load, fire, and unload, so long as they do not have exposed hammers. Ironically, exposed hammers are touted by some "experts" as safety features. In fact, they pose a greater danger: Once the gun is cocked, it's very easy to fumble when you're easing the hammer down, and the gun could go off by accident. If you choose a single- or double-barrel shotgun, select a "hammerless" design which can be rendered safe via a safety switch.

Because of the relative awkwardness of the controls, and the fact that it's difficult to see if their firing chambers and tubular magazines are empty, *most repeating shotguns are actually more complex and more dangerous to manipulate under stress than revolvers or even automatic pistols.*

MYTH #4—Nobody ever argues with a shotgun. Street-wise people know that a shotgun blast at close range generally means instant death, and they *are* less likely to mess with you if you're so armed. But if they don't think you're going to shoot anyway, they don't care if your gun is a machine gun or a .22. If they are convinced that you *will* shoot, they don't want to be shot with even a .25 pistol.

MYTH #5—*If you load your shotgun with birdshots, you'll discourage the burglar you shoot, but you won't kill him.* Within ten feet the charge of tiny birdshot pellets has just started to spread out and is still an almost solid mass of lead. It may actually tear a bigger hole than buckshot or slugs. Old movies show farmers "dusting a watermelon thief's backside" with birdshot. Try that in real life and you'll shatter his pelvis and probably kill him outright. *Never delude yourself that any firearm, let alone the devastating shotgun, may be used with impunity to wound instead of kill.*

Those are the myths. Let's consider some of the practical realities of using the shotgun for home or store defense, and the reasons why I recommend *against* choosing it as your primary defensive weapon.

It's difficult to activate shotguns quickly. The shotgun is a two-handed weapon. A police "riot gun" with a stubby, barely legal 18-inch barrel is 40 inches long, while a duck-hutting shotgun is 1 foot longer. A folding combat stock cuts 12 inches off that length, but also reduces considerably your ability to fire accurately.

You can drop a hand down to the hidden pistol at your bedside or at the edge of your cash register and surprise your assailant when you come up shooting. It's most unlikely that you can bring a shotgun out of concealment that quickly when a life-or-death confrontation is upon you. More probably you'll be blown away before you even get your gun up.

Shotguns are awkward to maneuver. If someone comes up on your right flank when you're holding a shotgun in the conventional "port arms" position (the butt is against the right hip and the muzzle is near the left shoulder), you'll have to take two steps or a pirouette to bring your gun to bear. With a handgun, you would only have to pivot your hips 90° or less to defend yourself and probably wouldn't have to move your feet at all. This makes the difference between death or survival when you're attacked by surprise.

It's easy for a criminal to take a shotgun away from you. Remember, you only have to shoot the Bad Guy once out of fifteen times. The other fourteen times, the bulk of the instrument can endanger you more than its gaping, intimidating yell will protect you.

Let's assume that you've caught your burglar, and perhaps his accomplice, at gunpoint. If you can't get a spouse or roommate to call the police, you're going to have to march them to the nearest telephone and do it yourself. *This will occupy one of your hands, leaving you holding the shotgun one-handed.*

It is easier to get a shotgun or rifle away from someone than a pistol even if they're holding it with both hands. As any military recruit has been taught, all you have to do is grab the barrel and the stock farther out than the person holding it, and you have enough leverage to twist it out of their grasp. It is far, far easier to do this to a homeowner who has one hand on the shotgun and the other hand occupied by the telephone.

By contrast, you can hold someone at gunpoint with a pistol (or search your house with it) holding the gun tucked tightly against your hipbone. It's not extended where anyone can reach it, and you can fire into them before they get a good hold on it if they do lunge for your weapon. (It is rather widely accepted in court that if a criminal suspect attempts to take a gun away from a citizen lawfully holding him at gunpoint, the citizen has the right to fire.)

When you come right down to the reality of it, there are only three advantages of the shotgun over the handgun as a home or store defense weapon. First, an acceptable-quality shotgun generally costs a bit less than an equivalent handgun, especially when purchased used. Second, in cities like Washington and New York, where local gun laws make it a major hassle to legally purchase a handgun, shotguns require much less red tape since they are considered sporting guns and are less strictly regulated. It is of course equally illegal for a convicted felon to buy a shot-gun *or* handgun.

The last, and most significant advantage of the shot-gun comes that one time when you do have to use it: It delivers an awesome, fight-stopping impact shock. Unfor-tunately, it also has a proportionately high rate of lethality. If you are shot once at random with a pistol, chances are about one in four that you'll survive. With a shotgun, your chances drop radically. Remember that one murdered cop in five is killed with his own gun that was snatched away from him.

Thus, the only real purpose of a shotgun (or if you can afford a good handgun instead) is to give you one-shot stopping power if your back is to the wall and you have no choice but to shoot. This might seem to make it a good choice for the back room of a store, but there you're talking about a shot pattern that could spread sufficiently to endanger innocents.

I keep a shotgun in my bedroom. It is strictly a "secondary" weapon, to be used in one of two scenarios. First, if our sleeping area were under direct assault (alarms going off, doors kicked down, dog barking and biting downstairs) I would assume a totally defensive posture, using the shotgun with the assumption that it's going to be a battle instead of just a confrontation.

Second, if I were to go downstairs to check out a noise in the kitchen, I would take handgun and flashlight and bullet-resistant vest while my wife would sit by the phone with the shotgun and the children, whom I would have isolated in the "hardened" master bedroom before going downstairs.

If I were to be disarmed and killed, it would be entirely possible that the intruders would go over my corpse and head for the staircase to finish the invasion and perhaps to exterminate the household and its witnesses. They would very likely assume that they already had the only gun in the house and would hit the staircase quickly and maybe carelessly.

They would surely die there. My wife is trained with guns, and she would have either taken a protected position above and behind the staircase, or secured herself in the hardened master bedroom; in either position, she controls both conventional lights and strategic spotlights that would blind an intruder.

This information on the use of lights means little in terms of protecting your unoccupied home from burglars. But when you and your family are there, and the intrusion thus becomes a far more serious "home invasion," your control of lights allows you to dominate the situation both tactically and psychologically, assuming you have the force at your command to back it up.

A shotgun is a last-ditch fighting tool. Police consider it an offensive weapon; soldiers from the Philippines to Malaysia to Vietnam found it deadlier in jungle fighting than machine guns. It is perhaps the most efficient close-range killing machine in the world's arsenal of small arms. But it has only a limited place in home defense. If you choose to purchase a shotgun for that purpose, the following is a distillation of the advice of experts.

Avoid a single-shot or bolt-action shotgun. If you face more than one antagonist, you won't be able to fire a second shot before the first dead criminal's vengeful accomplice is upon you.

Double-barrel shotguns are recommended by some because of their ease of manipulation, and the intimidation factor a felon experiences when he looks down those twin, 2-caliber barrels, both of which can be fired instantly. It's true that NYPD detectives use stubby double-barrel shotguns on all their raids because the department thinks the conventional police-style pump repeaters are too complex to be handled without special training. It's also true that no detective in the history of the NYPD has ever needed more than the two shots in that gun to get the job done. However, consider the fact that the detectives raid en masse, and that all those detectives carry at least one loaded revolver for backup.

The double-barrel shotgun does have certain advantages. Old ones that are still functional are available dirt cheap in gun shops that carry used merchandise. Once the barrel is cut to the legal minimum of 18 inches (go with 18½ inches to be safe), it's handier to manipulate than a pump or automatic shotgun since the receiver, or firing mechanism, is shorter. Finally, it *is* the simplest firearm to manipulate: A swing-lever behind the breech opens the gun harmlessly and hammerless "doubles" have simple, sliding thumb safeties: switch forward means FIRE and back means SAFE. Avoid the often-recommended Rossi Coachman double-barrel; though made with quality, this gun has outside-hammers that most people will fumble with while trying to uncock, which can create a hazard during or after stressful moments. Outside-hammer double-barrel shotguns were considered obsolete by serious gun-users well before the turn of the century, as any firearms safety instructor can confirm.

Pump shotguns are the choice of most police because they're relatively cheap, they're so ruggedly built that little can go wrong with them during ten or twenty years of abusive service, and they can fire four to eight rounds as fast as an officer can pump the slide and pull the trigger. Firearm safety instructors have considered double-barrel shotguns obsolete for serious gunfighting for decades.

You can get a good pump gun for half the price of a good automatic shotgun. There is also a built-in safety feature: Pump the empty shotgun (thus cocking it over an empty firing chamber), lock the safety switch on, and then load the magazine. To fire the gun, someone will now have to (a) find and release the unobtrusive slide lock lever, (b) pump the action, and (c) push the safety switch into the FIRE position before they can pull the trigger and make the gun go off.

Automatic shotguns are much more expensive than manually operated repeaters. They pay for themselves with superior human engineering: You don't have to do anything except pull the trigger for each shot, and if you buy a gas-operated model, the recoil is considerably softened, so that you're less likely to flinch and jerk your shot off target, and you can fire with a maximum rate of speed and accuracy. Automatics are harder than pump guns to clear if they jam, but on the other hand, they're less likely to in real life.

One reason why police use pump guns instead of automatics for patrol is reliability. That's because the shotgun in a police car is exposed to dirt, temperature changes that cause rust, and even chewing gum down the barrel when they're mounted on the dashboard (traffic offenders seem to think that's a cute way to get even with the cop who gave them a ticket, if he turns his back long enough).

In real life, though, people who aren't trained with a pump gun will often "short-stroke" it when under stress; that is, they'll pump the slide only partway through the cycle. This means that when they pull the trigger again, with their life on the line, either the gun will click impotently on an empty chamber or it will be hopelessly jammed. When your nerves turn to Jell-O, you're better off trusting the engineering of firms like Remington that have been making highly reliable automatic shotguns for decades, than trusting your own hands to operate an unfamiliar pump shotgun mechanism.

Which models to buy?

Double-barrel shotgun: Stevens 311. The most cost-effective, reliable, and safe double-barrel shotgun for your dollar, by far. It's made with some investment cast parts and less expensive wood, which is why tradition-conscious sportsmen trade them in as soon as they can afford to in exchange for guns that are more hand-built, making the Stevens available dirt-cheap on the used gun market. It's hammerless and has been proven effective for decades among sportsmen as well as on the streets of New York. Have the gunsmith cut the barrels to 18½ inches and reinstall the front sight. Put a Perry Ammo sling on the stock, keeping 5 spare shells where you can reach them so as to be able to reload quickly. The Perry unit is about $10 in gunshops.

Pump shotgun: Mossberg 500. The Mossberg was designed for economical manufacture and costs only about 70 percent of what the "fancy brands" go for. Yet it was built for rugged reliability—being kicked around in the bottom of duckboats for a lifetime of waterfowl hunting— and has a good reputation for "standing up." Like the premium Remington, it has double-"action bars" in its pump mechanism for smoothness and durability.

More important, it has a safety switch on the top of the action that slides back and forth, as on a hammerless double-barrel shotgun. Most other pump shotguns have crossbolt or "dual push-button" safety switches. The trouble is that most people can't remember which way to push the buttons when they're under pressure. I've seen relatively highly trained police officers fumble with crossbolt safety switches.

The NYPD and the LAPD use the Ithaca because it's trim and light and slick-handling, but the most popular pump gun among police and gun experts is the superbly made Remington 870. I use the latter myself with a folding stock, but unless you constantly hunt with it, shoot trap or skeet with it, or take refresher training with it several times a year, you're more likely to fumble with the safety switches than if you had a Mossberg.

Automatic shotgun: Remington 1100. The Remington is the most popular gas-operated shotgun in firearms history, and the most proven in terms of reliability. Point gun; pull trigger; and it goes off. You're talking big bucks, but if cost is not an object, you can fit it with an extended magazine of 8 or 10 shots, available from Choate Machine Tools (your local gunshop can order it). It bolts right on in your kitchen and you can take it off for hunting season. At close range you can pump 10 shots into silhouette targets in under 4 seconds once you get skillful—firepower beyond what you could get with a submachinegun. Choose your gauge or shotshell size carefully. Police use the 12-gauge for maximum stopping power against men. On a safari, a 12-gauge shotgun with buckshot is what the professional hunter will take with him if a lion or tiger is wounded deep in the bush and he has to go after it.

A 12-gauge shotgun has a brutal recoil few men are comfortable with, and it terrifies most women. Yet the tiny .410 gauge is too puny. Perhaps a better choice for the novice male who weighs under 150 pounds, or for the female, is the 20-gauge. You're talking about 70 percent of the 12-gauge's power with about 70 percent of the "kick." A 20-gauge shotgun is still more devastating at close range than even a .44 Magnum revolver.

There are three types of shotgun load: birdshot (hundreds of tiny pellets), buckshot (8 to 34 lead balls ranging from .22 to .35 caliber), and slugs, which in the 12-gauge means a monstrous .72 caliber projectile weighing a full ounce.

Slugs are terrifying manstoppers, but will usually exit a human body and go on to strike down any bystander behind the felon. Buckshot looses its effectiveness for defense at around 50 yards, but in close, its multiple wounds are devastating; cops and soldiers alike consider it the optimum shell for moderate-range antipersonnel work. Birdshot, designed to kill a tiny feathered grouse or a duck at ranges of 15 to 60 yards without tearing up the meat, won't reliably stop a human opponent except at very close range.

For home defense, the choice should be buckshot or birdshot. Fine birdshot (number 6, or the smaller number 9 or the even tinier number 12 pellets) are recommended by many for home defense on the theory that the shots won't penetrate walls to endanger children or neighboring tenants. I know a lot of seasoned cops who use birdshot when going in on drug raids, prison sweeps, or other missions where ricochet and overpenetration could endanger brother officers. These men, however, have backup officers and backup handguns in case their tiny projectiles fail, and they know that even then, their birdshot could penetrate Sheetrock and kill a child in the next room.

I have number 1 buckshot in my own home defense shotgun; my wife and I know the fire angles and simply won't fire if the shots would endanger an innocent person in our home. I want to be able to shoot through heavy furniture if I have to, or even through a wall if an armed home invader ducks behind it. *But you have to be an expert to be able to deploy buckshot firepower that coolly.* My wife and I, due to our intensive training, are able to make that tactical decision. You probably aren't qualified. For most, number 6 or smaller birdshot would be the best choice for a close-range home defense shotgun.

If you can handle the recoil, use a 12-gauge. It is by far the most fight-proven of the combat shotguns. If recoil is a concern, go with the 20-gauge. Thousands of small women use them when hunting game every year without flinching.

The shotgun was not designed for capturing criminals and holding them at gunpoint by yourself. Any police department's manual of operations requires that the officer with the shotgun keep the suspects at gunpoint while other officers handcuff and search the prisoners. That's because they know how easy it would be for one of the Bad Guys to get the shotgun away from the lone officer, even though he is intensively trained.

Keep that in mind when you consider a shotgun for home or store defense. It's a formidable weapon that will protect you when the gunfire is flying, or when you're under assault and there's nowhere to retreat, but if you rely on it primarily for the situations where you might have to hold a criminal at gunpoint and call the police, you'll be leaving yourself open to some serious problems that you wouldn't have with the more maneuverable handgun.

The superb Benelli autoloading, 8-shot police combat shotgun retails for $500, while the excellent Remington 1100 autoloader costs $430. Remington's well-made 870 pump shotgun retails for $305, while the rugged Mossberg 500 equivalent costs only $215. The best buy in a short, double-barreled defense shotgun is the Stevens 311 at $214. Mossberg's bolt-action hunting shotguns retail for $130; if you must choose one, get the unit with a detachable 3-shot box magazine.

Purchased second-hand from quality gunshops that will make good on any gun they sell, new or used, an autoloading shotgun in acceptable condition can be purchased in the $200-range. Many used, short-barrel pump guns are available for $110 to $130, an excellent value. For those with a minimum budget, used bolt-action shotguns can be purchased for under $60.

All these prices are for the powerful but popular 12-gauge guns. Lighter recoiling 20-gauge weapons are more scarce and usually demand higher second-hand prices, though prices are comparable in new models.

40. RIFLES FOR SELF-DEFENSE

The rifle is not well suited to the sudden, close-quarters deployment and maneuvering that is required of a defensive firearm. On the battlefield, yes. In close civilian combat, no way.

Fire a high-powered rifle in an enclosed room and the blast is literally deafening: the muzzle flash looks like a grenade explosion. It will stun and disorient the user and can even cause some degree of permanent hearing damage. The bullet itself is quite likely to go through the intruder's body and the interior walls behind him, into a child's room or another apartment. And, like the shotgun, the rifle is too bulky for maneuvering through doors and hallways, too long to quickly and surreptitiously pick up when the attacker drops his guard, and too easy for a criminal to take away if the homeowner's attention is diverted.

The .223 (5.56-mm) assault-type rifle typified by the AR–15 is sometimes used by SWAT teams hitting a building, but on home searches for felons they usually favor shotguns or handguns. These men are heavily trained and come in four-men strong at least.

An autoloading rifle such as the AR–15 or the .30 caliber U.S. M–1 carbine, can quickly be loaded via its box magazine. Even the .30 carbine, however, has excessive penetration with most loads, though it has little recoil and, weighing only 5½ pounds, is easy for women to handle. The AR–15 might make sense due to the enormous close-range destructive power of its light, softnose bullet that travels at 3,200 feet per second and shatters inside bodies, in the hands of a rich homeowner who could afford to silence it. However, a silencer would make it a foot longer. (Silencers are legal if your state statutes allow it, and if you get a special $200-license from the Federal Bureau of Alcohol, Tobacco, and Firearms. An AR–15 with a Sionics sound suppressor sounds like a .22 rimfire rifle being fired without a silencer. Of course, .223 bullets that miss the opponent can still rip through several walls.)

For those who are extremely sensitive to recoil and muzzle blast, a .22 rimfire rifle makes some sense. Get an autoloading ("Automatic") model of good quality. If the gun is to be kept loaded, buy one with a tubular magazine slung under the barrel, which will hold 15 or more shells; given the feeble stopping power of .22 rimfire bullets (a 39-grain slug at 1,200 feet per second velocity), you may well need all 15 shots.

A nonatypical situation was documented by a female officer of a Texas police department when she won *Police* magazine's story award for her account of a gun battle. Arriving at a domestic disturbance she saw a crazed gunman murder a woman; before she could respond, the man shot her in the chest with a .38, blasting her out the door. She lay helpless as she watched a neighbor empty a .22 rifle into the killer; the neighbor then had to club the madman down with the empty rifle, again and again, before he succumbed.

Since your rifle should be kept unloaded for reasons of home safety, your best bet is a .22 autoloader, kept empty with the detachable box magazine (commonly called a clip) stored separately in an equally secure location. Under stress you'll have a hard time inserting 15 tiny cartridges into the gun; instead, you can slap in a preloaded clip of 8 to 10 shots, jerk back the chambering mechanism, and be ready to fire.

In a tube-magazine .22 auto rifle, the best quality is found in the $140 Remington 552, though at under $90 the Stevens, Savage, and Marlin models give acceptable reliability at a lower price. For a clip-fed .22 rifle, your best dollar value by far is the $115 Ruger "10/22." Use the factory-supplied 10-shot magazine; the 25-shot "clips" made for this gun by other firms don't always function reliably.

Quality .22 rifles are among the best bargains in the used-gun racks at your local gun shop. New guns can often be bought through discount stores like K-Mart or through Sears Roebuck, which often has Marlin and similar guns manufactured more cost-effectively under Sears's trade name, J.C. Higgins. (This is also true of the Stevens 311 double-barrel and Mossberg pump action shotguns).

In a .22 rifle, use high-velocity hollowpoint bullets.

Though they deliver little pure impact shock, they ricochet and explode inside the body, causing dramatically destructive wounds. Also, their outside-lubricated slugs pick up fouling from the gun barrel and dirt from the attacker's clothes, creating a highly septic wound that is extremely difficult to treat. I would rather be shot with a round-nosed .38 Special police bullet than with a high-speed .22 hollowpoint.

You want your .22 rimfire chambered for a ".22 Long Rifle," not .22 Short or .22 Long cartridges which are less reliable in feeding and have even less power. The .22 rimfire Magnum causes somewhat more impact damage but is more expensive. One of the good things about a .22 rimfire defense gun is that ammo is so cheap that you can afford lots of practice with it. At this writing, you can buy 100 rounds of .22 Long Rifle hollowpoints for $2.55, while that quantity of factory-made ammo would cost $12.88 for a .22 Magnum, $29.50 for a .38 revolver, $60 for a 12-gauge shotgun, and $68.25 for a high-powered .30/06 hunting rifle.

A rifle makes sense only in a jurisdiction where the citizen finds it a monstrous legal hassle to buy a handgun. A .30 carbine *with hollowpoint bullets* offers adequate stopping power and less likelihood of the bullet dangerously exiting a rapist or home invader's body.

The .22 rifle has a place in home defense since it is among the cheapest of the functional firearms (often around $50 for a good used .22 autoloader, sometimes only a little more than that for a new one on sale at Sears or at K-Mart during hunting season). Ammo is cheap, encouraging you to practice so as to build up skill and confidence. The blast and recoil are the mildest of any firearm, making the .22 more acceptable to many women and senior citizens. Be sure, however, that your .22 has a fairly high cartridge capacity and an autoloading mechanism—and be prepared to empty this low-powered gun into an attacker before he goes down.

Remington's light Nylon 66 .22 autoloader costs $115 Marlin/Glenfield's 70 with a detachable 7-shot box magazine (desirable for quick loading) is $86, or the same for the carbine model with a less desirable tubular magazine; Ruger's top-quality 10/22 (10-shot .22 caliber) with a detachable magazine is $112. The Universal military M–1-style .30 caliber carbine, firing 15 to 30 shots, lists for $200. The Commando Arms carbine, resembling a submachinegun in appearance and taking the .45 caliber automatic pistol cartridge, is a good home defense choice at $200. Modern combat-style weapons not really suitable for inhouse defense use include the Colt AR–15 at $475 and the Ruger Mini–14 at $250, both firing the military 5.56-mm NATO (.223 caliber) cartridge from 20-to 40-shot magazines.

41. WHY A HANDGUN?

Where allowed by law, the average private citizen who has only one gun for protection is almost always better off with a carefully selected, good-quality handgun than with a rifle or shotgun.

It is commonly stated that rifles and especially shotguns are better for home defense. These statements are based almost entirely on battlefield experience by war veterans; on the fact that it is easier to hit a target with a rifle or shotgun than with a pistol no matter what the level of the user's training, and that the long guns are, in the calibers selected for big-game hunting or military use, far more powerful than any handgun.

All three of those arguments are true, *as far as they go.* The average person under stress won't be able to hit a man-size target at ranges much beyond 25 yards.

Held in two hands and braced against the shoulder, and with a long barrel and "sight radius" for precision aiming, long guns are indeed more accurate than shoulder guns whenever significant distance is a factor. It is equally true that high-powered rifles and shotguns within their range, cause damage to human flesh and bone that far exceeds the destruction that a pistol bullet can wreak.

However, *when you understand and consider the human dynamics involved in defending yourself against violent criminals, the handgun immediately becomes the logical choice in terms of real-life tactics and strategy.*

For you, it won't happen on a battlefield where the nearest Soviet soldier is 600 meters away behind a French hedgerow. For you, it will happen at point-blank range. Studies by the FBI show that the great majority of shoot-outs occur at a range of 7 yards or less, and more commonly at about 7 *feet.* And this is among police, whose statistics include running gunfights on the highway and long-distance gunfire exchanges with snipers and barricaded felons.

The civilian, almost always, will fight his opponent face-to-face. In that close space he won't be able to bring a rifle or shotgun up before the attacker can take two steps forward and stab, club, or disarm him, or fire his own illegal gun. The battlefield-proven "combatability" of the rifle and the jungle-warfare shotgun are meaningless in American crime-defense scenarios.

For the same reasons the greater accuracy of a hunting-type rifle or shotgun is useless to a citizen fighting a would-be killer 7 feet or 7 yards away. Partridge hunters use their shotguns at small, flying birds 15 to 40 yards away, and duck and goose hunters fire at ranges up to 65 yards; deer hunters typically shoot their rifles at bucks 50 to 300 yards away. *Any* physically normal adult can quickly learn to empty a pistol into a target the size of a man's torso at 7 yards and do it much quicker than with a rifle or shotgun.

Handguns can, where legal, be carried on the person. With a limited amount of training they can be drawn and, if necessary, fired as quickly and reflexively as you can draw a ball-point pen from your shirt pocket. To grab a 5-to 10-pound rifle or shotgun that is 36 inches long and swing it to bear on a close-quarters rapist caught momentarily off guard is almost impossible.

Those of us who carry guns for self-defense don't want to *kill* our attackers; we only want to *stop* them; whereas our attackers, if they shoot or stab *us*, want us dead so that we can't testify against them.

At close-combat distances, police studies (conducted by the NYPD and the Police Foundation, among others) indicate that a deliberately inflicted handgun wound will result in death only one time in four. By contrast, a wound deliberately caused at that range with a shotgun or high-powered rifle is almost certain to cause death.

The massive destruction caused by rifle and shotgun projectiles is one reason why some favor them for self-defense: The reasoning is that this will instantly stop the offender. I can't argue with that. If my bedroom is under assault by home invaders I'll reach for my secondary weapon and unleash eight to ten rounds of 12-gauge Magnum buckshots.

But, in real life, 14 out of 15 times when a citizen *or* police officer draws a gun on a criminal, the deadly threat ends there at least for the moment. Only 1 time in 15 will you have to call the massive, killing firepower of a shotgun into play. *The other 14 times, you have to march the offender to someplace where you can use a phone, or at least, hold him at gunpoint.*

In the hard, cold light of reality, you're probably going to be looking at a hardened criminal only a few feet away who desperately wants to take your gun away from you and kill you with it.

Police officers armed with rifles or shotguns hold their suspects at gunpoint several yards away and wait for backup officers, who will come in to do the handcuffing, to respond to a call from the radio on their belt. The citizen doesn't have this luxury. In a typical apartment, average-size house, or the counter area of a retail store, the citizen will be within a few feet of the criminal. A quick lunge will bring the latter within reach of the gun.

With a pistol, all you have to do is fire. It was *designed* to be a one-handed weapon, one that could follow a target's movement with only a slight flick of the wrist. Not so with a rifle or shotgun. Even if you have two hands on it, a man who can reach it and duck under the muzzle or to the side of it, can take it away from you in a second or two.

This is taught to every military recruit in every branch of the service in Basic Training. All the Bad Guy has to do is grab the barrel and stock and he can twist the gun away from you like taking candy from a baby.

Conversely, the average street criminal who grabs at your handgun won't have as much leverage as you have; you can quickly learn to slap his hands away or twist your gun clear, or you can simply fire.

I am certified through Smith & Wesson's Training Academy and the Criminal Justice Training Institute, to teach Weapon Retention to police officers. I have taught this discipline to police officers and I can tell you unequivocally that it is far easier to keep hold of a handgun when a criminal grabs for it, than to keep control of a rifle or shotgun, and that a short-barrel revolver is perhaps the hardest gun for anyone to take away from you.

It is extremely awkward to fire a rifle or shotgun one-handed if the criminal jumps you when you reach with the other hand for the telephone, even if you have your eyes on him. All he has to do is move his body sideways, clear of the gun barrel; the gun is so awkward and the leverage of its heavy barrel is working so much against you, that he can almost certainly evade the first shot. Then he'll have his hands on the gun and will probably destroy you with it. Not so with the handgun.

If you hold a criminal at gunpoint, keep him in an awkward position. If you have to march him somewhere, take your time: Make him interlace his fingers atop his head, and shamble forward on his knees, while you stay ten feet behind.

When you've reached the point where you want him to stay put, keep him facedown, his ankles crossed, and his hands outstretched to the side, knuckles down; you want his face away from you so that he can't see what you're doing. If he makes a threatening move that a reasonable man would interpret as being intended to take your gun away from you and kill you with it, shoot him and keep shooting.

For the person who requires a gun in his/her place of business or on the street, the handgun obviously will be available instantly where the nearest rifle or shotgun would be steps, or miles away. Even if the liquor store owner can maneuver to the point where he has carefully cached his short-barrel shotgun, he'll have to reach down with both hands to pick it up, a signal that will trigger the criminal to kill him. A handgun can be grabbed one-handed with a flickering movement and can be fired before the homicidal criminal even realizes that he is being counterattacked.

In Texas recently, a young manager of a 7–11 store was marched, along with other innocent people, into a backroom by an armed robber. The manager knew that the only reason for such an action would be the quiet murder of himself and the others; the criminal would have simply ripped out the phone lines and used the manager's keys to lock the doors behind him, if his only concern was how soon police would be called.

No way on earth could that young man, at gunpoint, have gotten to a concealed rifle or shotgun and made it work in time. Instead, his hand flashed down to his hidden pistol and the surprised would-be killer died in a hail of defensive pistolfire before he could hurt any innocents. The 7–11 parent company fired the young man, on the grounds that he had violated the corporation's policy of passive acceptance of criminal victimization.

After what that young manager had been through, I imagine that his firing was no more than a gratuitous slap in the face, compared to what the alternative would have been. I'm told that more realistic shopowners tripped all over themselves offering him new jobs at better salaries. But none could have offered him a benefit more dear than what he won for himself: his life and the lives of the innocent people under his protection, preserved by a courageous action he couldn't have duplicated with any other life-saving instrument but the handgun. Neither a shotgun nor a rifle would have helped him, or the innocent customers.

42. SELECTING A HANDGUN

Countless books have been written about how to select handguns for personal protection. I do this sort of thing for a living, so let me try to narrow it down for you. There are two sorts of handguns suitable for defense: double-action revolvers (which can be fired by a straight pull of the trigger instead of having to thumb-cock the hammer first like the Frontier Six-Shooters in cowboy movies), and semiautomatic pistols. The revolver holds 5 to 9 cartridges in a rotating cylinder that moves a fresh round under the firing pin each time the trigger is pulled. The "automatic" uses the recoil pressure of the cartridge going off to slam an operating slide back and ejects the spent shell casing causing a fresh round to be stripped off the magazine, or clip, and into the firing chamber as spring pressure slams the slide back into the BATTERY, or firing position.

Revolvers tend to be a bit bulkier due to the thickness of the cylinder. Automatics are flat sided and, with 6 to 18 cartridges stored vertically in the magazine inside the "handle," tend to be more compact than revolvers of the same power levels. They hold more cartridges, too.

Because an automatic self-cocks its firing mechanism, it usually has a trigger pull requiring only 4 to 6 pounds of finger pressure to make the gun go off. With a double-action revolver, the trigger has to exert leverage through about 18 contact surfaces to not only drop the firing pin on the cartridge, but to rotate the cylinder into a firing position. This requires a trigger pull of 9 to 12 pounds of pressure. In other words, it is not very easy to pull the trigger of a double-action police revolver.

This means that, in the hands of someone less than expert-level, the revolver is much less likely to be accidentally fired. On the other hand, this also means that if you have to fire, it's easier to shoot the automatic rapidly under stress and have the bullets go where you want them to.

According to a Police Foundation study American law enforcement agents only hit the Bad Guy they're shooting at 25 percent of the time, and 99 percent of American law enforcement agents use double-action revolvers. But when I studied the gunfight record of Illinois State Police, the only large domestic police agency that issues service automatics (9-mm Smith & Wessons), I found that approximately 70 percent of the shots they fired in action struck the intended target.

In a sentence, *revolvers are easier and safer to manipulate when you're routinely loading or handling them, but automatics are easier to shoot straight when you're under stress.* The heavy trigger pull on the double-action revolver—12 pounds of pressure exerted on an instrument that only weighs 1 or 2 pounds—tends to jerk the muzzle off target.

On a pistol range, that would only be embarrassing, but on the street, it could be tragic: The bullet that misses your assailant could hit an innocent child a block away.

On the other hand, the revolver is safer to manipulate. Pressing the cylinder release latch, you can swing the whole cylinder out of the gun to easily determine if it is loaded or empty. The automatic hides its cartridges in its magazine and firing chamber, and only a trained user can *really* be sure if the weapon is loaded or not. The saying among gun experts is, "You have to be incredibly stupid to have an accidental discharge with a double-action revolver, but only a little stupid to have one with an automatic."

There are two reasons why 99 percent of America's cops are issued double-action revolvers. First, it is assumed that the average recruit has never fired a gun before signing up for the job and therefore requires an instrument with maximum simplicity and safety of operation. Second, the revolver is much less sensitive to abuse or "owner misunderstanding," and therefore is more reliable when the chips are down.

Any revolver that is in proper mechanical condition will fire any cartridge of the caliber it was designed for—light target load, round nose service bullet, or hot hollowpoint. But the automatic is dependent upon the cartridges "self-loading" into its firing chamber as a result of recoil impulse. A light load might not move the operating slide back enough against the pressure of the recoil spring to properly cycle the weapon: A wide-mouthed hollowpoint bullet might catch on the "feed ramp" that guides it into the firing chamber; or the metal lips of the magazine or "clip" might be bent sufficiently to make the cartridge enter the chamber at the wrong angle. If any of those things occur, the feeding cycle will be interrupted and the pistol will jam, becoming unfirable.

Certified gun experts carry automatics with full-power loads, with "throated-out" feed ramps and firing chambers that guide hollowpoints into place, and with expensive, proven cartridge magazines. Our automatics don't jam. A factory automatic out of the box from a sporting goods store *could* very easily jam in a number of situations.

If you *are* a qualified "gun expert" and choose to carry an automatic—I carry a Colt .45 automatic most of the time as do most of my colleagues—you will have no problem cleaning it once a week and religiously checking its magazines and its ammo. But if you're *not* ready to make that commitment, you are better off with the revolver which feeds any ammo it's chambered for and can function even if it's covered with accumulated balls of dust.

Sophisticated martial arts weapons like the *nunchaku* karate sticks are only taught (in responsible *dojos*, anyway), to students of brown belt or black belt rank. So should it be with automatic pistols. For the "expert" and "master" shooter, the brown and black belts in combat shooting, the automatic, with its greater firepower (number of rounds available instantly) and its greater, more "human-engineered" ease of accurate rapid fire, is the weapon of choice.

For the expert or master, the most combat-proven automatics are the Army-style Colt series and the Browning Hi-Power. Firing eight .45 slugs or fourteen 9-mm bullets respectively, they have earned a reputation for total reliability in military, police, and civilian combat. "Double-action" automatics, which fire the first shot with a long, revolverlike trigger stroke and then self-cock themselves for easy follow-up shots, are almost universally scorned by combat masters, because the radically different transition from a hard-pulled first shot to an easily pulled second shot causes problems in delivering accurate fire on the street. I have to agree with this: On the street, Illinois State Police's double-action S&W 9-mm's have shown that the officer frequently misses the first shot and connects with the second. These guns are also somewhat more fragile mechanically.

For the person just getting into guns, the double-action revolver is the obvious choice. It offers safety and reliability a dimension beyond the over-the-counter automatic pistols, and the five or six .38 or .357 rounds they hold will be all you'll need in most personal or home defense situations.

You should select the same weapons that have been proven effective for decades in law enforcement. Most police departments allow only double-action revolvers manufactured by Colt, Smith & Wesson, or Ruger, in calibers .38 Special and .357 Magnum.

For the person who is not into guns, the recoil and "blast" of the .357 Magnum will be more than they can handle in a fast-breaking, close-in situation where their accurate delivery of gunfire is the only thing that stands between them and death at the hands of a violent criminal. We who teach combat weapons for a living consider the .38 Special the bottom-line minimum for "stopping power" against a violent antagonist, but when loaded with high-performance $+P$ hollowpoint bullets, they get the job done at a rate that, coupled with the weapon's safety and controllability, makes it optimum for general use.

Those who carry concealed guns may wish to go with the "Detective Special" genre of snub-nosed .38's, small-framed revolvers with 2-inch barrels. For a home or store defense gun, the full-size 4-inch revolvers carried by most uniformed police work out well. For men, I recommend the service-size revolver. For the average woman, I favor the snub-nosed. The short-barrel, small-frame gun is not human-engineered for accuracy so much as the bigger revolver, but its size is scaled down to the female hand; most police service revolvers have been "human-engineered" for men with average-to large-size hands. Another advantage of the small-frame, short-barrel .38 is that if you and a criminal are ever wrestling for your gun, that revolver gives *you* all the leverage. If you held a larger, long-barreled gun, the criminal could grab the barrel and exert enough leverage to twist the weapon out of your hand. If he tries that with you while you're holding a snub-nosed revolver, his palm will slip over the gun muzzle, and with a pull of the trigger you can blow his hand away.

The .38 and even the .357 are taught every day in America to the smallest female recruits who never fired a gun before. What scares women about guns is that they "kick" and that they're loud. Indeed, that's what really intimidated several generations of military recruits with the .45 Army automatic.

It's no problem if you understand that the kick of a revolver in the hand is no more painful than playing pat-a-cake with a srong child. The blast is definitely sharp, but if bird hunters have been able to inure their dogs to gunfire for hundreds of years, is there any human being who has an excuse to be afraid of a sharp noise? Use muff-type ear protectors when practice-firing, and the sound of the shot won't scare you—in real life, you'll never even hear the shots as they go off under stress, and if you doubt that, ask any hunter you know if *he* ever was startled by his own gunshot.

If you choose to buy only one gun for home or personal protection, I believe it should be a handgun.

There are hundreds of handguns presently on the market. Let's look at the ones professionals have found to work best.

Snub-nosed .38: The Colt Detective Special. Almost as

compact on its .38 frame as the Smith & Wesson equivalent Chief Special series, a 5-shot .38 on a little .32 frame, the 6-shot Detective Special combines the compactness of a pocket-size revolver with almost the handling and shooting characteristics of a full-size police service gun. Selling for about $340 at this writing, its trigger is lighter and its sights bigger and easier to see than its S&W counterpart, making it more likely that a man *or* woman will be able to shoot it effectively under stress.

Full-Size .38 Special Police Service Revolver: Smith & Wesson 10. This weapon is America's most popular police service revolver, due to its smooth action and ideal balance in the hand of the average man. As inherently accurate as S&W's much more expensive target models, this gun also has a reputation for durability and longevity. The price is $195 as of 1982, or $210 in the stainless steel 64, which better withstands owner neglect. Buy it in the 4-inch heavy barrel configuration for better balance and less recoil when fired.

.357 Magnum Revolver: Ruger Police Service 6 Reasonably priced, compact, and more rugged than its Smith & Wesson Combat Magnum counterpart due to its heavier cylinder, the Ruger has surpassed Colt to become the Number Two brand of police revolver's behind S&W, and is closing that gap fast. Its reputation for accuracy, durability, and smoothness is excellent. The price is less than its competition. The all-stainless steel version is slightly more expensive than the blue steel model, and worth it for its corrosion resistance. The state police of Pennsylvania have adopted it, among others, because of its superior design. The price runs in the $230 range. The short-barrel, round butt version doubles as a gun that's easy to conceal, and hard for a criminal to wrench away from you in a face-to-face struggle. Like any .357 caliber revolver, it also fires .38 Special ammo for less-expensive target practice and for reduced recoil with .38 service loads.

9-mm Automatic: The Smith & Wesson 439. The first S&W 9-mm automatics were flawed weapons, but the 439 represents the third generation of development, with greater durability and reliability. Unlike the earlier 39 and 39–2, it won't go off if you drop it on its muzzle by accident. You can carry it ready to fire with a double-action trigger pull, instead of fumbling for a safety switch; the safety switch is also there to confuse someone who gets the gun away from you, if you wish to leave the lever in the SAFETY ON position. One of the safest automatic pistols to handle, it sells for $360 or so, and is easy to carry with its light-weight aluminum frame. The all-steel version (539) is bulk-ier to carry but also kicks less. It fires 8 shots; the 459 and 559 series have 15-round magazines inside fat handles that are hard to hold.

.45 Automatic: The Colt Government or Combat Commander. This is the modern commercial version of what the mili-tary calls the U.S. Pistol, 1911A1. It is the only weapon ever to pass a U.S. Army Ordnance test 100 percent, and has been proven since the first world war as the most reliable and hardest-hitting military sidearm ever made. Best carried with seven rounds in the magazine and an eighth in the firing chamber, with the hammer cocked and the thumb safety ON, they're surprisingly easy to shoot accurately with the proper hold, but for safety reasons should only be carried by very well-trained and competent people. With less muzzle flash than any hot-loaded .38, 9-mm, or .357 Magnum, it is an ideal weapon for shooting at night, when most violent encounters take place. An untrained criminal who gets a cocked and locked .45 away from you will probably have to fumble for several seconds to figure out how to make it go off, but a trained person can fire it instantly. At around $400 for the full-size Government model, the shorter all-steel Combat Com-mander, or the Lightweight Commander with aluminum alloy frame, it is the choice of champions, but suitable only

for experts. In their hands it is the ultimate gunfighting pistol.

Inexpensive Handguns. Because of media publicity about "Saturday Night Specials," the public thinks functional handguns can be bought for $37.50. In fact, there are very few cheap handguns that work reliably and none are high-powered weapons: It takes expensive, modern metallurgy to engineer a weapon that will withstand the 35,000 or more pounds per square inch pressure that are generated when a .357 Magnum cartridge goes off inside a firing chamber.

The Raven .25 automatic, retailing for about $75, is one of the few cheap handguns that work without jamming. It fires an impotent cartridge, however, and many gunshops prefer not to sell it because of its "cheap" image. In fact, though, it outperforms .25 automatics that sell for three times the price. If your gunshop doesn't have one, try an Army-Navy store or pawnshop.

In a low-priced revolver of caliber .22, .32, or .38 S&W (the so-called .38 regular, less powerful than the minimum-rated .38 Police Special), the Harrington & Richardson brand is the most durable and reliable. You're talking about $110 to $160. You may have to shop for them in a hardware store that sells guns. They have rough trigger actions and are therefore hard to shoot, but they're sturdily made and last forever.

Your best bet for a low-priced gun of fight-stopping power level is a second-hand model. Shop *only* at a store whose owner makes his living selling guns, and can't afford to compromise his reputation by selling junk. The full-time gunshop owner, unlike most part-timers, has a test range where he checks out each used gun before resale to make sure it works properly. Be sure to ask if they'll make good on a bad gun, *and test-fire it yourself before trusting your life to it*. I recommend 200 rounds of full-power ammunition for test-firing before the gun is assigned to self-defense duty, even with a brand-new sidearm. Some brand-new revolvers will malfunction out of the box, and automatics need to have their parts "worked in" with a couple of hundred rounds, like driving 500 careful miles on your new car's engine to "seat the parts."

Buy the best gun you can afford: Your life may literally depend on it one day. But remember, the gun you buy is only the fourth consideration when preparing to defend your life against armed criminal assault. Most important is mental awareness and preparedness; the second consideration is a knowledge of tactics that will allow you to evade and defeat armed attack; the third consideration is skill with the safety equipment (in this case, your ability to shoot well under stress), and only after all that has been achieved does it matter whether you're carrying a Harrington & Richardson .22, or a Smith & Wesson .44 Magnum.

There are also hundreds of cartridges manufactured for dozens of calibers of guns. Books have been written about that, too, and the U.S. government in 1976 paid half a million dollars through the U.S. Justice Department for a study of "relative incapacitation index," or stopping power, as delivered by popular police handgun ammunition. The results of that study are highly suspect among those of us who deal with guns for a living. The tests were conducted using ballistic gelatin and other "tests" have been done on bullet performance upon "wetpack" (water-soaked newspaper), plumbers' duct-sealant (Duxseal), the ubiquitous gelatin, and other materials that supposedly duplicated the bullet resistance of human tissue.

But in real life, you're not going to be attacked by a Jell-O monster or by a wet newspaper. In real life, you'll be attacked by a violent, possibly drug-supercharged human being who is made of tough, elastic flesh and muscle and wants to kill you. The only thing you can trust is firepower, proven on the streets by America's police officers, who face that sort of threat daily.

Here are the loads that I've found, in ten years of intensively debriefing cops who were in gunfights as well as from officers who deeply investigated gunfights, to be the most reliable in terms of taking a violent criminal *out of the fight.*

.38 Special: 158-grain all-lead semiwadcutter hollowpoint bullet at +P (additional power, factory-accelerated) velocity. This load was adopted in 1973 by the FBI and the year after, by the Chicago Police Department. The FBI is extremely happy with its performance in gunfights involving its 7,000 agents. The Chicago Police Department, the second largest law enforcement body in America with 13,000 officers, is the *only* metropolitan police agency requiring .38s whose street cops don't complain about not having guns powerful enough to sledge down criminals who are trying to shoot them. John Dineen, president of the Chicago Police Department's Fraternal Order of Police bargaining unit told me, in 1978:

We used to get a lot of complaints about having to carry thirty-eights, but that stopped when the department went to the (lead hollowpoint +P) cartridge. Since then when one of our officers shoots a Bad Guy, the Bad Guy goes down.

+P loads should be fired only in modern, steel-frame revolvers guaranteed to withstand the additional pressure of the hotter cartridge. These include Colt, Smith & Wesson, and Ruger for all their steel-frame .38 Special revolvers.

9-mm Parabellum (9-mm Luger): 115-grain Remington, jacketed hollowpoint. Most 9-mm automatics are designed for military use, with long, round-nosed, fully copper-jacketed military ammunition. In 9-mm, while such bullets may conform to the Geneva Convention, they do not work well at all in street gunfights. The pointy, hard bullets tend to knife through the criminal's flesh with a wedge effect, pushing his muscles and arteries aside and allowing them to snap back into place and resume function a moment after the bullet has passed through. These bullets also, almost invariably, exit the felon's body, traveling on to perhaps strike down an innocent person who was standing behind him.

There are a bunch of 9-mm guns out there, and you should understand that we're talking about modern-made loads for modern-made guns, not hot-loads to stick into 1942 war souvenir pistols. Even modern guns are built for military-style full-jacketed ammo, not the hollowpoint antipersonel bullets that tend to be more decisive in street shoot-outs. Remington makes a 115-grain jacketed hollowpoint that won't deform as it slides into an automatic's firing chamber, but usually will mushroom when the fired bullet strikes a criminal's body. Reliable "feeding in the weapon" and proven performance within its caliber range on the street make the Remington 115-grain jacketed hollowpoint the load of choice for those who trust their lives to 9-mm pistols.

For street defense against criminals, the 9-mm requires a hollowpoint bullet that expands as it enters. This means that the bullet slows down and stops, in most cases, before it exits the perpetrator's back and endangers bystanders. If the bullet stops inside the felon's body, it also delivers all its inherent kinetic shock potential making it more likely that the suspect will be punched backward and knocked out of the fight without having to fire additional bullets that will tear more of his body organs open and further reduce the likelihood of his survival.

.357 Magnum: 110-or 125-grain semijacketed hollow point bullet. When this caliber was introduced in 1935, it developed a reputation for extreme penetration. With old-style bullets that date back to those years, that would still be a concern, but modern hollowpoint designs actually utilize the extra Magnum velocity (almost double the speed

of a .38 slug) to mushroom the bullet more quickly, therefore making it more likely that it will stay inside the criminal's body while delivering roughly 200 percent of the kinetic shock you could transmit with a .38.

Recoil is sharper with a .357 than with a .38, by a considerable margin, and the blast and muzzle flash are *much* harsher. The .357 Magnum should be used only by those who have substantial training in "combat pistolcraft."

.45 automatic: 185-grain Remington jacketed hollow-point. There are a lot of old, U.S. government-issued .45 automatics that were bought as surplus by vets, and a lot of commercially made equivalent guns that were built to military specifications. The military only expected the gun to feed round-nose, fully jacketed "ball" ammo, which on the street has a tendency to penetrate more than it should. Only Remington makes a hollowpoint cartridge that, while likely to stay inside a felon's body, still feeds through the cycling mechanism of even a crudely made pistol designed to work with full-jacketed loads only.

A novice would not be wise to trust his life to a caliber other than what we've discussed here. "Exotic" cartridges like the .38 Superautomatic and the .41 and .44 Magnum are for experts only. Twenty-five-and .32 and .380 caliber guns don't hit a street aggressor hard enough.

Remember: The only time you'll ever fire a gun into another human being's body is when you feel totally justified by every law of God and of man and of society, to end his life.

You can't always do that with a bullet of less potency than the .38 Special hollowpoint. That fact has been proven in hundreds of documented police gunfights.

The interesting thing is that the harder you hit him with the first one or two shots, the less likely he is to die. Forty-five or hollowpoint, .38 slugs are more likely to knock the guy down after one or two hits. If you are firing Geneva Convention bullets they'll rip through him giving him a lot of pain but no impact shock. To stop him from hurting you you'll have to fire again and again until he goes down. By that time, with the so-called humane bullets, you'll have drilled so many holes through so many vital organs that this guy couldn't possibly survive.

The fact of life is that the Defender keeps firing at the Aggressor until the Aggressor either falls down or otherwise makes it clear that he's not going to try to hurt the Defender anymore. In defensive gunfights the signal to stop your defensive fire is usually the sight of the Aggressor falling down.

This is a basic human dynamic long overlooked by those who would legislate high-performance handgun ammunition away from police. What you have, in real life, is a choice: The Bad Guy gets shot once or twice with hollowpoint bullets or he has to be shot numerous times with "conventional" bullets. The more wounds a combatant sustains in a shoot-out with the Good Guys, the lower the likelihood of his survival.

Thus, although hollowpoint ammunition is excoriated as "killer dum-dum bullets" by people who know little about weaponry and less about the actual dynamics of violent human confrontation, hollowpoints are actually safer for all concerned.

They are much safer for innocent bystanders. The bullet is less likely to rip through the offender's torso and go on to slam into an innocent person who couldn't be seen behind the suspect. Also, this type of bullet is more likely to shatter harmlessly when it hits a wall, instead of ricocheting wildly and endangering noncombatants.

Finally, they are safer for *you*. The whole idea of shooting another person is to immediately stop him and hit him hard. Bigger bullets (.45), faster, higher-energy bullets (.357 Magnum), and at all levels, hollowpoint bullets, do that more effectively.

One of the hardest things for the decent, law-abiding

human being to understand when he or she picks up a gun is that there is no way for this inherently lethal weapon to be used with limited force. You don't aim to "wing 'em," "get him in the leg," or "crease his scalp." Under great stress and facing a moving target, it's all the best-trained gunfighters can do to hit their opponent somewhere in the torso. "Shooting guns out of people's hands" is simply not realistic.

If you cannot accept the fact that a person you shoot may die, you should not have a gun, because the day may come when you'll hesitate on the trigger and be killed by your opponent. You can't give someone a "boo-boo" with a firearm. If you're not justified in killing the person, you're not justified in trying to shoot him in the leg, either. Unlike on TV, bullets through the arms or legs or shoulders tend to cause crippling or even fatal injuries.

CARRYING THE HANDGUN

In many jurisdictions, it is possible for the private citizen with a spotless record to acquire a permit to carry a concealed weapon, a document generally known as a CCW. Check your state laws, which vary widely on this. Illinois and Missouri have no provision for issuing CCWs. They're all but impossible to come by in southern California but are issued somewhat more freely in the northern part of the state. In New York, they're so tough to get that there are attorneys who devote their entire practices to handling permit applications. Yet in New Hampshire, police chiefs are required by law to issue a carry permit to any qualified applicant within a week or ten days, and in Vermont, no permit is required for a person with a clean record.

In most states (again, check the law where you live!) it is legal to carry a concealed weapon in your place of business. The practice is becoming routine among pharmacists and liquor store owners because of the ever-present danger of holdups. Physicians and attorneys are among the highest occupational categories of civilians requesting gun permits because of the danger of assault by criminals or deranged persons in law offices and emergency rooms. Psychiatrists report an enormously high rate of violent assaults on them by patients.

If you make the decision to carry a gun, there are a few things you'll have to learn to live with. One is that you are no longer free to shout angrily or make obscene gestures when, for instance, a motorist cuts you off in traffic. As an Armed Man, the court will hold you to what is called a higher standard of care, that is, a greater responsibility not to do anything that could be interpreted as escalation of a potential conflict. That is one reason why philosopher/science fiction novelist Robert Heinlein once noted wryly, "An armed society is a polite society."

Most people are alarmed by the sight of firearms in public, except on the hip of a uniformed police officer or guard. (Some lawyers even request that uniformed police witnesses not wear their guns into the courtroom on the grounds that the practice intimidates witnesses and jurors.) Thus, the person lawfully carrying a concealed gun in public is mandated to practice discretion above all.

Even a full-size police service revolver or a .45 automatic can be carried discreetly. Numerous books have been written on how to select holsters, perhaps the best being *Blue Steel and Gunleather* by John Bianchi, $9.95 from Beinfeld Publishing, Inc., North Hollywood, CA. For our purposes here, let's look only at the more common methods of carrying your gun.

Probably the best concealment rig is an inside-the-belt holster. Because the weapon is inside the trousers, the snout of the gun barrel or its holster is less likely to protrude under the hem of a jacket or sportshirt. Also, the gun is tucked in closer to the body (much less bulge), and the material of the trousers "drapes" the holster, blending the outline in to the body's silhouette much more naturally.

For $10 or so, you can buy the popular suede-finish style, which fastens to the belt or the waistband of beltless trousers or skirts, with a spring clip. It is probably the single most popular holster among plainclothes cops and others who carry concealed weapons daily, due to the ease of taking the gun and holster on and off.

A compact revolver in a proper holster is no more cumbersome than, say, a beeper on your belt. Within a week or so you will grow quite accustomed to its presence.

With an inside-the-belt holster, the gun can easily be concealed under a sweater, or under the tails of an un-tucked sportshirt. If you're wearing a dress shirt and will ever be taking your jacket off where people can see you, a belt holster will be too indiscreet.

Alternatives in that case include pockets, ankle holsters, and "belly band" rigs that resemble money belts which are worn beneath a tucked-in shirt. Most of you will feel a bit too James Bond-ish with the ankle holster, and in any case, it's hard to get at the gun in a hurry when it's that far from your hand. Pockets are not good. The weight of a pocketed gun feels pendulous, and modern-cut slacks will fit too tightly: The gun will be distinctively silhouetted by the taut material, and you might not be able to get it out of the tight pocket smoothly. The Bianchi belly band holster, discussed in the chapter on defeating pickpockets, doubles as a money belt, is supercomfortable and superdiscreet, and allows you to get at the gun rapidly. It's my favorite for when I'm wearing shirt-sleeves when coupled with a quality .38 snub-nosed revolver.

Shoulder holsters make a lot of people feel like Mike Hammer. There's a certain "squad room mystique" to them. You're constantly aware of the gun's presence because its weight is literally hanging under your arm from the harness that wraps around your shoulders. Still, the gun *is* accessible to either hand, and is easy to get at (in some models) through a partially buttoned topcoat. A lot of women are partial to shoulder holsters, simply because all the good belt holsters are designed for men.

This is more of a problem for women than one might think. High-riding hip holsters that bring the gun butt up to about the kidney-height on a man, shove the handle awkwardly up past a woman's floating ribs. That's because females have higher pelvises and shorter torsos than men. They're also less likely to be wearing belted slacks. A good shoulder rig, or the simple belt-clip waistband holster, is generally the best bet for the female who has chosen to go armed.

Shoulder holsters do have one practical advantage, which is not as humorous as it sounds. Anyone who anticipates taking their pants down in a public restroom is going to have problems with a belt gun. Did you ever notice on the syndicated reruns of *Barney Miller* that the only detective wearing the shoulder holster was old Sergeant Fish, who had to go to the bathroom every ten minutes?

Cops and others who routinely carry guns, have nightmares about someone in the next stall reaching under the partition and grabbing the gun from the lowered waistband. The gun can fall out of the belt holster, or the holster can slide off the belt. In New Jersey several years ago, an officer set his gun on the toilet tank as he prepared to drop his pants; the weapon slipped off and discharged when it hit the floor. The bullet passed through a wall and killed a child.

There are other rules for those who "wear steel." Do not carry a gun into a place where liquor is served. In many states that's a Class IV felony or a misdemeanor. Saturday Night Specials got their nickname from their frequent employment by drunks spending their paycheck in bars. If you fear attack in your local lounge, seek a better class of drinking establishment, or drink at home—just don't pack your gun in a gin mill.

You must also learn not to wear a belt-holstered gun under a short jacket; reaching for an item on a high shelf in the supermarket will raise the jacket enough to expose the weapon. Don't wear a hip holster with a side vent jacket, or before the end of the day, your gun butt will be visibly protruding. If you have a concealed gun on your hip, learn to reach under your jacket for your wallet, instead of sweeping the jacket back as you reach toward your hip pocket.

Some people, when they carry a gun for the first time, feel a perverse urge to display their newfound "power." It comes, I suppose, from growing up in a society where armed men are glorified in the entertainment media. It is something to be avoided at all costs. We in the trade call such people gun flashers, and like a sexually exhibitionistic act in a public park, it is done consciously or subconsciously to shock and intimidate people.

Neither the police chief where you live nor the firearms licensing bureau, want you to be going around shocking and intimidating people with your gun. Wanton exposure of the weapon is, in must jurisdictions, grounds for revocation of your permit. This is as it should be.

We cannot state strongly enough that while having a weapon in your home may be your right, carrying one in public is a privilege. The only ones who deserve that privilege are responsible people who have been trained in the legal, practical, and ethical parameters of using a firearm in a public place.

When you apply for your gun permit ask the licensing officers about training courses. You can take such courses under police supervision at a departmental range or at bona fide gun clubs.

Remember, however, that while almost any gun club can do a fine job of teaching you gun safety and marksmanship, very few have staff people qualified to teach the judicious use of deadly force in self-defense. As happened with dog breeders and alarm installers, a flood of unqualified people have offered self-defense training with the firearm in the wake of "the fear boom." The majority have never been properly trained themselves and are passing on some frightening misconceptions about what is and is not legal and proper to do with a deadly weapon when you are attacked by a vicious criminal.

At this writing, I know of only four private academies that can give the civilian proper grounding in the use of firearms in self-defense. Chapman Academy (P.O. Box 7035, Columbia, MS 65205), is run by Ray Chapman, a former World Champion who has served as a police officer and has seen combat in WW II. Defensive Training, Inc. (Route 2, P.O. Box 207A, Elroy, WI 53929) offers training from John Farnam, a police officer and a fine instructor. The American Pistol Institute (API) (P.O. Box 401, Paulden, AZ) was founded by Jeff Cooper, one of the pioneers of modern combat-shooting methods. The fourth is my own Lethal Force Institute (P.O. Box 122, Concord, NH 03301).

A good 5-day, 40-hour course should cost $300 to $500. The API and the Chapman Academy teach on-site (there is also a Chapman Academy South facility in Clewiston, Florida). Defensive Training and the Lethal Force Institute offer training at their home bases and at selected sites around the country. Write for schedules.

Be certain that you're getting a true self-defense course and not a "pistolcraft" course in which you merely learn to draw fast and shoot straight. You want a program that encompasses your civil liability in the wake of a shooting, your proper interaction with witnesses and responding officers, and the proper way of handling yourself in the aftermath.

If you are not able to immediately take such training, one of the best short-term approaches would be to read my book on the subject, *In the Gravest Extreme: The Role of the Firearm in Personal Protection,* available for $7.95 post-paid from Gravest Extreme, P.O. Box 122, Concord, NH 03301. It covers the legal, ethical, moral, and practical considerations of having a loaded gun in home, shop, or holster. The Chapman Academy, Defensive Training, ISI, and of course the Lethal Force Institute, use it as their exclusive textbook for defensive firearms training.

The use of the firearm in public, by a law-abiding citizen against a violent criminal, is an act of social and personal enormity. It is, quite literally, a matter of life and death. You would not attempt to perform a tracheotomy if you didn't have the proper emergency medical training just because it happens to be legal for you to go out and buy a scalpel and a plastic airway. It follows that you aren't ready to handle a lethal threat encounter just because you went out and bought the most expensive custom combat pistol that was advertised in the latest issue of *American Handgunner.*

An increasing number of law-abiding citizens are carrying guns to protect themselves from criminals. I have no quarrel with that. It has been a tradition in my own family since the turn of the century, and at various times that tradition has kept myself, my father, and my father's father alive. But over the years my family learned something on the street. We learned that the privilege of carrying a gun in public demands great responsibility in terms of self-control, discretion, and above all, training in the use of deadly force to ward off deadly threat.

43. EFFECTIVE COMBAT-FIRING

In conventional marksmanship where the gun is held stock steady and you hold your breath and sque-e-eze the trigger hoping to hit a bull's-eye the size of a nickel fifty feet downrange at the gun club, the pistol is the most difficult weapon to shoot accurately. This has been misinterpreted to mean that you can't hit anything with one when your life is on the line in a panic situation.

Wrong. With the *proper* training, effective combat shooting with the pistol is about as easy to learn as 35-mm photography. Combat shooting as opposed to target shooting utilizes both hands to steady the weapon, and simple, effective isometric techniques to lock the gun on target in rapid combat fire.

Literally dozens of books and pamphlets have been written about combat shooting. Most are hopelessly outdated. Here's a proper grounding in the latest techniques that have been proven to work on the street.

We'll start with the basic hold, *always using unloaded guns in the early stages of your practice until you've had certified safety training*. Grasp the gun with your second, third, and fourth fingers around the grip. The thumb is curled down, and the gun is held with about the same pressure as a firm handshake. The rear edge of the grip should meet the web of your hand.

At this point the gun barrel should be parallel with your arm. If it isn't, the grips or the gun itself may be too large or small for you. With a revolver your index finger should be in contact with the trigger at the first joint. If it doesn't reach that far, you'll be pulling with your fingertip, and if you're right-handed, that will throw your shots to the left. If your finger goes farther into the trigger guard than that, you'll be "choking up" on the gun, pulling your shots to the right. With an automatic, since it has a shorter and lighter trigger stroke, you don't need the leverage of pulling with the first joint of the trigger finger; pressing with the tip of the finger is often preferred with the self-loading gun.

Now, we bring up the support hand. The two-hand hold is, for anyone short of master level, mandatory if you want to have effective control of the handgun when under stress. There are half a dozen such techniques, but the best is the "wraparound." The support hand wraps itself around the strong hand that is already holding the gun. The weak hand's fingers slide into the grooves created between the strong hand's fingers. This hold gives you maximum strength and leverage to hold the light gun steady on target against the heavy trigger pull, and to control recoil or "kick" and snap back on target for a fast second shot.

Students wonder at this point what to do with the thumb of the support hand. Unless the gun is very small or your hands are very large, your best bet is to curl the thumb up tightly, right in front of the curled strong thumb. This is better than crossing the thumb over the back of the shooting hand. For one thing, the latter position would put the thumb in the way of an automatic's recoiling slide and cause a thumb injury and a jammed pistol. Besides, since the human hand was made to work off the opposing thumb, your four fingers can squeeze more tightly when the thumb is curled up.

Now, point the gun in both hands at the target, shoving the weapon straight out in front of you until your wrists and elbows *lock*. You'll want to be leaning slightly forward. This hold won't give you quite so much recoil control as the Weaver stance popular among gun buffs (the elbows are sharply bent to create a shock absorber effect). However, to shoot straight, the person using the Weaver hold must precisely execute five to seven isometric aspects, from the angle of the elbow bend to the placement of the feet. Unless one practices almost daily, that's too complicated to work under stress during a surprise attack.

The straight-point method, called the Isosceles hold because the arms describe that shape of triangle in relation to the chest, is more instinctive. Under stress, you thrust the gun straight out in front of you (an instinctive reaction in most cases anyway), until it won't go any farther, and you are automatically in the correct position.

While foot placement is critical in some of the isometric shooting techniques, it doesn't have to be that way if the shooter couples the Isosceles hold with the McGee Turret position. This position was popularized in this country by Frank McGee, the legendary chief instructor of the NYPD.

Finding that the simplest, strongest techniques were what worked best under stress, McGee taught his officers to lock their head and neck, allowing the torso to become a gun turret that rotated at the hips. Thus, foot position became inconsequential: The feet would find their own balance without thinking about it, and the officer could turn instantly toward the threat.

This training was inaugurated around 1970. Many of the officers resisted it because of the old myths about the gunfighter's crouch being the best way to shoot, or that firing with one hand was quicker than firing with two. But street results soon convinced the police officers that it was easier and more natural to fire from the two-handed turret position. Their hit potential in shoot-outs with armed aggressors increased enormously.

Since that time, NYPD officers have been involved in more than 6,000 firearms incidents. With McGee's training they've gone from an unacceptably high casualty ratio to a situation in which their officers are winning eleven out of twelve gun battles. Note that the average New York cop probably never saw a gun before he came on the job, and police regulations only require him to take practice fire twice a year.

If you must fire, experts agree that you should aim for the center of your opponent's torso mass and keep firing until he is unable to shoot back. That point of aim is used partly to deliver debilitating gunfire, and partly because it allows a wide margin of error for your shot, but it can still hit the antagonist in some vital part of his body. The saying in law enforcement is, "We don't shoot to kill or to wound; we shoot to *stop,* and the center of the torso is the likeliest aiming point to stop the felon's violence." This is excellent advice for the law-abiding private citizen as well.

You'll also want to do some one-handed shooting to practice for very close-quarters encounters. The best technique is with the inside of your wrist against your side. This keeps the gun out of a criminal's reach, and at close range, your fire will be directed into his belly and pelvic area. The lower abdomen is the second most liquid part of the body (after the brain), and a high-velocity pistol bullet there sets up hydrostatic shock waves that help put the attacker out of the fight. A bullet that shatters the pelvis breaks down the body support structure, usually causing the subject to collapse.

This is also a good position when you are searching for prowlers or holding a suspect at gunpoint. The Bad Guy most definitely *is* thinking about taking your gun away from you, so you want to make that as difficult as possible.

Contrary to the old-time gunfighter myths, you'll generally have enough time to bring the gun to eye level and aim before you fire. The human eye can recognize images, in this case a "flash aim," in as little as a thousandth of a second. All the speed records in pratical shooting matches belong to people who used both hands and took a quick aim, instead of firing blindly from the hip. There is a saying among the shoot-out veterans: "You don't win a gunfight with the first shot; you win it with the first *hit*."

Experts agree that the most efficient mode of defensive fire is usually a two-shot burst. In practical shooting, this is called the double-tap. You take quick aim, fire the first shot, and immediately trigger the gun again as soon as it goes off. You'd think the second shot would go wild, but that won't happen if you have a proper, two-hand hold on the gun. Recoil will only have pushed the muzzle up a very short distance, and the pressure of your two locked arms is already forcing the gun back on target when the second shot breaks. Within seven yards—the width of a typical room, and the range within which more than ninety percent of recorded gun battles occur—the first bullet should strike in the solar plexus, the second in the middle of the chest. The double-tap does, however, require considerable training and practice.

For those of you who use shotguns, there are other "old gunfighter myths" to be dispensed with. Shotguns were designed to be fired with the buttstock tucked into the shoulder, and when you shoot one from the hip, you lose your aiming coordinates. If you fire right-handed from the hip your whole shotgun blast is likely to go over the attacker's right shoulder. As any bird hunter can tell you, it takes only a fraction of a second to throw the shotgun to your shoulder and point it properly for a surer hit.

If you insist on a shotgun, you may find the recoil too brutal when fired from the shoulder, especially in a 12-gauge weapon. This is especially true for women and for men under 160 pounds or not well muscled. The pain of the recoil creates what shooters call flinch, a tendency to automatically cringe at the moment of discharge, jerking the muzzle off target. People who are afraid of shotguns will flinch wildly with them when under stress.

An alternative for those who can't abide handguns is to use the shotgun in the arm-tuck position. The top edge of the stock goes under the armpit, where it is held in place by the upper arm. When the gun goes off, it now slides between the chest and arm, delivering no impact whatever. The gun is high enough in this position to point the muzzle for a good visual index on the target. It doesn't work with autoloading shotguns, which have to be held firmly against the shoulder if their mechanism is to cycle properly, but takes the discomfort out of firing manually operated shotguns, even the rugged 12-gauge, at close-combat distances.

IF YOU ARE HIT

If the situation has deteriorated to the point where you're shooting at someone, it's probably a panic scene in which they're trying to kill you with an equal level of destructive force. The possibility exists that you'll take a bullet.

The sensations vary wildly in gunshot wounds depending upon how big you are, whether or not you've had time to reach an "adrenalin high," and whether your feet are properly balanced. Expect a deep pain and a burning sensation (they don't call it hot lead for nothing), and a feeling of stunning shock.

Ignore it and keep fighting. You have to, because there's no turning back at this point. Your chances of dying from a random gunshot wound in a shoot-out are about one in four, or less. But if you give up, there's an excellent chance that your angry antagonist will walk over and fire a certainly fatal coup de grâce into the back of your head.

A recent Pat Caudell poll indicates that, in 1981, some 3.8 million Americans had used a gun for self-defense. Very few of them got shot. Very few of them had to shoot anyone else, either. In the great majority of cases, the very sight of the gun in the determined citizen's hands is more than sufficient to make the criminal break off his assault and either flee, or wait like a good puppy for the police.

But the Catch-22 is that if you're *not* prepared to go all the way, to back up the threat of your gun with the promise of using its power, the criminal is likely to sense your hesitation and challenge you. Guns do scare a lot of criminals away, but only when the criminal senses that the citizen is fully prepared to do something worse with that gun than just scare him with it.

If your assailant is so doped up or deranged that he ignores the implied threat of your deadly weapon, or if his assault is so brutal and sudden that there is no time for warning gestures, you are now caught up in a lethal force encounter, and it's going to be the most hideous and terrifying moment of your life. The only thing more hideous and terrifying would be to go through it without the equipment to fight back and short-circuit the threat to you—to lose instead of win.

Time will seem to go slowly for you. Don't let that fool you. Don't try for blinding speed or you'll fumble. You want positive movements. As world champion practical pistol shooter Ray Chapman says, "Smoothness is five sixths of speed."

Stay in the fight with maximum controlled aggression. Don't be afraid. Your gun isn't called an equalizer for nothing, and if you've had professional training, you'll be more than equal to your attacker. But your own will and your own determination, is even more important than your marksmanship.

There are four priorities to lethal threat survival. First is mental preparedness, the resolution that you will fight and that you will do as you've been trained to do. A champion marksman with the most expensive pistol will be killed by a mugger if, at the crucial moment, he hesitates to ask himself the question, "Can I *really* shoot another human being to keep him from killing me?"

Second is tactics. Keep a constant scan of your surroundings when danger even remotely threatens. Know the escape avenues, and know where you can take cover from gunfire. An unarmed man who takes cover and has an escape route handy is more likely to survive an armed attack than a SWAT trooper with a ballistic vest and machine gun who gets caught in the open.

Third is skill with your emergency safety equipment, that is, your gun. Those New York cops with their little .38s win 11–1 against Bad Guys who have shotguns and high-powered automatics and Magnums because those cops take cover and fire with more telling accuracy. A New York cop who had been in more than one shoot-out told me with a wink, "Shooting straight with my thirty-eight beats them giving me jive with their forty-five."

Only when the first three priorities have been achieved do we come to the fourth concern, the choice of instrumentation. In trained hands, the added shock power of a Magnum or a .45 gives you a definite survival edge, and under some circumstances, so can the additional firepower of a 14-shot 9-mm automatic. But if you haven't learned to handle that level of performance with total competence, you're better off going "smooth and straight with a .38." There has long been a saying in the world of firearms: "A hit with a .22 scores more than a miss with a .44 Magnum."

Let us say it one more time: *Training in safety and in the proper use of defensive deadly force is imperative before one resorts to the firearm as protective equipment.* If everyone had safety training before getting a gun, and then followed what they were taught, there would never be any gun accidents.

44. KEEPING FIREARMS SAFELY

For many, the primary reason for not keeping firearms as self-defense weapons is that they might be accessible to children, thereby setting the stage for a tragedy. It is a valid concern. Yet firearms rank only about forty-sixth among causes of accidents, according to the Consumer Product Safety Commission's Product Hazard Index. The reason for the relatively low accident ratio is probably most because people who keep firearms are sufficiently cognizant of their destructive potential to take common-sense safety measures.

There are two approaches to gun safety. What we'll call Level One is taught by the National Rifle Association, your state Game and Fish Commission, and organizations such as the National Shooting Sports Foundation. At Level One it is assumed that the firearm is kept solely for sporting purposes and the gun is therefore completely neutralized. It is empty, locked in a cabinet preferably with a chain through the trigger guard, and an additional lock is on the gun cabinet door. Ideally, the gun has been disassembled with its bolt, cylinder, or other vital mechanism stored separately. Ammunition is also stored in a separate and locked location.

From the protective point of view, there is a huge problem with Level One gun security: If you need the gun for self-defense, chances are that you won't be able to get it unlocked, put together, and loaded in time to do you much good. Remember, we're talking here not about sporting equipment, but about emergency safety equipment to protect against homicidal threat. You'll have all the time in the world to get ready for the opening day of the hunting season or for a weekend skeet shoot, but trying to assemble a lifesaving machine from Level One security can take altogether too long if you are in immediate need of that sort of protection.

You don't have to compromise your family's safety if you want to have a defensive weapon quickly at hand. This is Level Two firearms security. Any hardware store or gunshop can sell you gunlocks; these fit inside the trigger of an unloaded *or* loaded firearm and prevent anyone from pulling the trigger if they don't have a key, or the tools to break the lock.

There are two types of gunlock that I *can't* recommend. Some designs use a combination lock, and if you've just woken up after you heard a window break, you'll be hard pressed to remember the combination, or to dial it in the dark. Another unit relies on adjustable finger pressure, which supposedly can be set so that an adult can pinch it open but a child can't. Don't underestimate your child's strength or ingenuity: He or she can press a pen or something against the button to release the pressure lock.

The best lessons are learned from the half-million people who have guns at home and often feel nervous if they aren't loaded and near at hand. These are America's police, and they've come up with some very simple and proven-effective methods of making a loaded revolver reasonably child-proof. *Their* guns are usually kept loaded and ready at Level Two of deadly weapons preparedness.

A favorite trick is to use a pair of handcuffs. One bracelet is locked through the trigger guard of the loaded revolver, *behind the trigger,* which prevents the weapon from being cocked or fired. The other bracelet goes around a night table leg, a radiator, or a solid and inexpensively installed wall bracket. This offers relatively little deterrence to burglars, but children who are curious won't usually bust up their parents' furniture to get at that fascinating handgun.

A padlock inserted behind the revolver's trigger will work the same way. I prefer the handcuffs. While legitimate stores in most states won't sell them to civilians, cheap but effective models can be bought in "adult" bookstores or by mail order from men's magazines. If worse comes to worse, and you capture a burglar during a blizzard when the phone lines are down, handcuffs give you a means of securing your prisoner during the *very* long wait for the police.

At this point you will probably ask, "If I'm not going to have time to get my gun out of a cabinet and load it, how am I going to have time to find a *key*?" Remember the chapter on locks: If you have maximum security double-cylinder locks on your doors, and keylocks on your windows, you want to have those keys immediately at hand when you sleep so that you can escape in case of fire. *Put the gun key on the same ring.*

If the gunlock key is the only key you feel you need handy with your particular security system, you can simply put it on a chain around your neck and sleep with it. The key can also be taped to the inside of a wide watchband. Wherever you place this and other vital security keys, *make it a ritual to always have them in the same place, where you can find them instinctively.*

If your budget can handle it, there's something a dimension beyond anything else, which combines the instant readiness of a loaded handgun with the extreme safety precautions insofar as children are concerned. It's the Magna-Trigger conversion of a double-action revolver.

This device was developed by an inventor named Joe Smith, who was shocked and sickened by the number of police officers being murdered with their own service revolvers. His reasearch was partially funded by the International Association of Chiefs of Police. Smith cuts away the front part of the grip frame and inserts a module that makes the Ruger or Smith & Wesson police-style revolver incapable of being fired, unless a powerful magnet comes within an inch or so of the module, causing the internal safety switch to be released. This potent samarium magnet is worn on a ring, with the magnet-side inward. When the person wearing the ring grasps the gun in the normal manner for firing, the revolver instantly becomes "live."

It works, and since mid-1980, my primary home security gun has been a Smith & Wesson .357 Combat Magnum with a Magna-Trigger conversion. Both my wife and I wear the activating rings. My four-year-old daughter and her little friends and cousins who sleep over, have no idea how the gun in Daddy's bedroom works, nor why he and mommy wear those plain stainless steel rings to bed. Good: By the time they figure out the system, they'll be old enough to have learned gun safety. The system also gives you a definite edge if you're ever grappling with a burglar who tries to get your gun away from you. When that happens, the criminal usually concentrates for a few seconds on pulling the trigger; this gives you plenty of time to retaliate.

I trust my own life to my ring/gun system. When I appeared on ABC's *20/20,* one piece that was left on the cutting room floor was a shot of me starting with my back to three targets, and then shooting each four times with my Magna-Trigger .357, pausing only to reload, all in 9.3 seconds. Had I thought the gun would make me fumble and look like a fool, I would have used something else when facing a projected audience of 42 million people.

The Magna-Trigger can be installed only on double-action Ruger and Smith & Wesson revolvers. The alteration costs $150 as of 1982 and the rings (be sure they're properly fitted) are $25 apiece. I had my revolver done at a time when I had recently received two serious death threats and had a three-year-old daughter, and I consider it a bargain. Contact the Magna-Trigger Safety Company, 10090 N. Blaney, Suite 6, Cupertino, CA 95014.

Don't put your gun somewhere obvious, like on the top of your nightstand. You don't want a cat burglar or an invading rapist to spot it before you do. Don't keep it under the pillow (it'll shift around and be pointing at your head half the time), nor under the mattress (you won't be able to get at it if the rapist is on top of you).

Rather, you should affix a holster to the *bottom* of your nightstand or under your bed. No one who isn't crawling on the floor can see it there (one reason you have it there *only* when you sleep, since children often *live* at that level). You'll be able to reach it by surprise if an intruder catches you off guard in the bedroom, and it's also somewhat protected from dust.

Even if you have a Magna-Trigger gun keep it out of the reach of your children when you're not actually in bed. When your child is home alone, keep your gun at Level One security, dismantled and under double-or triple-lock and key, and make sure the keys are with *you*. If you think there's anyplace in your home where you can hide something from a child left to his own devices, you've probably forgotten your own childhood.

Rifles and shotguns can also be secured by trigger locks. If you keep any weapon loaded with a keylock on it, you should still keep the firing chamber empty. A presistent child jiggling the gun might otherwise make it go off, especially if the lock doesn't fit perfectly. This shouldn't be a concern with a double-action revolver, since this requires a long rearward movement of the trigger in order to cock or fire it.

If your children are *very* small, you can keep a loaded pump action shotgun with relative safety. Keep it the way cops carry theirs in patrol cars: The action is pumped on an empty chamber, and the safety switch is locked, so that one has to first release the slide lock lever, pump the mechanism, and then release the safety switch before the gun can be fired. But even this won't deter a child left alone with a gun for long; I put my pump shotgun on an inaccessibly high closet shelf when my daughter turned three, and invested in a Magna-Trigger for my main-protection firearm.

Don't think that even the most normal, average child can't make the gun work. Before I was six, I was able, under my father's supervision, to operate any gun he owned—pump, automatic, lever action rifles and shotguns, or revolvers and automatic pistols. He taught me and my sister to do that so that we'd know how to de-fang those deadly weapons; we never got bitten by them.

Really, there is no way to childproof your guns one hundred percent. What you have to do is gunproof your children. Once they reach an age of responsibility, explain to them how your gun works, and most important, *show them how to clear the mechanism and engage the safety switches.* Guns are so glorified in the entertainment media that children find them irresistably fascinating.

There is never safety in ignorance, and the stern warning, "Stay away from the gun or I'll tan your hide" just isn't enough. Take the child to the shooting range some-time and satisfy his natural curiosity. Consider it a safety valve that drains off dangerous curiosity.

If you have a child (or grown-up, for that matter) in your household who has serious mental or emotional disturbances, *you should not have guns there* unless there is a *reasonable, clear, and present danger that makes them mandatory.* "The stranger within" is far more likely to harm you with those weapons than a random burglar.

Level One gun security refers to guns that no one can fire without several minutes of searching and lock picking and door breaking. Level Two gun security refers to weap-ons that you can muster quickly to your defense, without endangering children in your household.

Decide for yourself which you need, but you must understand that this is no place to scrimp. Your child will never kill himself with your lock or your burglar alarm. Your protective firearm, like your protective dog, works by destroying or by convincingly threatening to destroy human life forms that jeopardize your existence. Like the dog, it can't tell the Good Guys from the Bad Guys by itself. It is your responsibility to make sure that neither ever draws blood from a person who hasn't waived his own right to life and health by threatening to criminally deprive you and your family, of yours.

IV. POSTVENTION

45. THE AFTERMATH OF VIOLENCE

Once you have been involved in a violent encounter you'll find that it doesn't all end when the immediate danger ends. It's a nightmare that takes a long time to wake up from.

If you have been injured, your first priority is medical assistance. You may have to care for yourself. If you've been stabbed or shot, your most immediate concern is hemorrhage and the traumatic shock that results from it.

Heavy bleeding is controlled first through direct, firm pressure on the injury site; it it's a limb, it will bleed less if you can elevate it so that the wound is above the heart. If the hemorrhage presists, use pressure points. Only in the worst cases will you require a tourniquet, which if improperly used can cause gangrene or death.

No one can teach you these techniques effectively in a book. Every responsible adult should be trained in at least basic first aid. Contact your local Red Cross; the training is inexpensive and something you'll be using in home and family emergencies for the rest of your life.

If you think you might pass out, especially if you're bleeding heavily or if it's very cold, you *have* to get help; if you don't, it could be fatal. Take a moment to gather your wits: Where is the nearest payphone, or the nearest friendly source of human beings?

If you're alone and bleeding badly, you have to make a decision no one else can make for you: whether to stay there or to attempt to go for help. Physical activity at this point is going to make your heart race faster, increasing the blood loss; you're likely to get dizzy and collapse, thereby losing your pressure hold on the wound and causing even more blood flow. Chances are that with such uncontrolled hemorrhage you'll *exsanguinate* ("bleed to death").

If it is reasonable to assume that a rescuer will happen along soon, you may be better off to put yourself in a "shock position," that is, flat on your back with your legs elevated, and with some garment wrapped around you to keep you warm. If there's nothing to rest your feet on, bend your legs sharply and lock your toes against a wall or something similar; it's important that you keep them in that position if you pass out. This insures that as much blood as possible will remain available to your vital organs.

Pneumothorax is a condition that occurs with a sucking chest wound, that is, an injury where the chest wall has been punctured and its internal vacuum violated. Outside air pressure squeezes the lungs empty and eventually presses down on the heart, causing death. Try to seal the sucking chest wound with plastic. A plastic driver's license is adequate if you're going to be awake to hold it in position, but something more flexible like a piece of Saran Wrap or the cellophane from a cigarette pack, is ideal. The sticky blood bonds this substance to the edges of the wound, creating an airtight seal even if you pass out.

If you've suffered a piercing wound of one lung, roll over onto *the injured side*. It sounds unnatural, and it's going to hurt, but this prevents the good lung from being shut down from the pressure of spilling blood (hemothorax) inside the chest cavity. Press your cheek to the ground. This turns your head so that if you lose consciousness, blood or vomit can flow out of your mouth without causing suffocation.

If you've sustained a broken bone, a Basic First Aid class will have taught you the principles of applying traction. This dramatically reduces pain and therefore lessens the likelihood of going into shock. If it's a compound fracture (bone splinters driven through the flesh), then traction will slide the bone ends back into place and allow you to more effectively reach down and stop the bleeding with direct pressure.

If the break occurs at a joint, *don't* try to straighten it, just immobilize it. A half-rolled magazine or newspaper makes an excellent splint.

A broken collarbone is best treated by taking the right hand (if the right collarbone is fractured) and lifting it with the other hand until the right fingers can firmly grasp the lapel. This holds the affected limb at an angle that considerably reduces pain.

Remember: You can't learn first aid from a book. Red Cross first aid training is dirt cheap, and something that will always be useful to you. You should have a decent first aid kit in your home and another in your car. You can even make up a small one for your coat pocket or purse, including flat sterile dressings, a small roll of gauze bandage (which easily folds flat), and perhaps a Velcro-adjustable tourniquet kit. Keep it in a plastic bag; this can be used for sealing sucking chest wounds.

One of the most useful and street-proven "trauma dressings" is the common sanitary napkin. A box of Kotex is standard issue in many police cars and ambulances around the country; the product has been proven almost unbeatable for absorbing blood while remaining firm enough to still apply direct pressure to a wound site.

Above all, remember to stay calm and rational when you are injured. Panic won't do anything except kill you by contributing to a more rapid pulse, higher blood pressure, and therefore more serious shock and hemorrhage side effects.

Pain is transitory. It will go away. Pain can even be mentally overridden. Most physicians agree that there is a point of extreme pain where the human brain says, "This is enough; we can't take it anymore," and just shuts off the pain sensation.

If you are in the grip of the "fight or flight reflex," strengthened by the sudden dump of adrenalin into your system, your survival instinct may shut out most of the pain. We frequently get reports of people shot or stabbed in the heat of an attack, who didn't realize they had been injured until after they had put their attacker on the ground. If you're a man who has been in a few streetfights, you can probably remember taking a punch to the jaw that you just shrugged off because you were concentrating on slugging back.

AFTERMATH OF RAPE

If you've been the victim of sexual assault, there are some basic things to consider before you start thinking about learning to live with the aftermath. Number One, make sure that you've escaped from your rapist. At the same time, give yourself first aid for physical injuries.

It's a terrible time to be alone. Get to someone you know and who you can trust. If that's not possible, immediately call a Crisis Hotline; they can coordinate assistance for you swiftly. It might be wiser to call the police if there is the slightest reason to believe that you are still in danger.

Rape victims feel sullied and have an overwhelming urge to bathe and douche. It is an urge to be resisted. It destroys vital physical evidence of the rape, and may be seen by a skeptical detective as the act of someone "giving a false story and covering their tracks." Most experts still recommend that the woman report the assault immediately. But you should first consider these estimates by rape crisis specialists:

Of every 1,000 rapes, only 100 will be reported. Of those, only 50 of the subsequent investigations will lead to arrest. Of the suspects arrested, only 30 will be prosecuted. In half of those cases, the accused will be acquitted or charges will be dropped. Of the 15 out of 1,000 rapists actually convicted for their crime, only 2 or 3 will go to prison.

These are terrible odds. Add to it the fact that if the rapist is innocent until proven guilty, it follows that to many intents and purposes, the victim who accuses him is guilty until proven innocent.

The police do not torment rape victims in the manner seen in *A Case of Rape*, the Elizabeth Montgomery TV movie that left half of America's women terrified to report sexual assaults. Investigating officers will, however, seem "cold and uncaring." This is merely because they are trained to be detached and objective; if anyone thought they were taking your part in the matter, they could be accused of having conducted a prejudiced investigation, and the rapist they arrested could go scot-free on that alone.

It is imperative that you go to the hospital. You may have received injuries in the assault that are more serious than you realize, such as internal bleeding from a torn vagina. This is surprisingly common. A woman's vagina seems to dry out instantly when she's in a state of fear, and rapists tend to be extremely brutal in their penetration, sometimes even using blunt or sharp objects as surrogate penises. Also, there is always the danger of veneral disease. The quicker the antidisease steps are taken in the aftermath of the rape, the less likely she is to suffer long-term problems.

Pregnancy may be a possibility. A D&C was once standard medical procedure, but now the "morning after pill" ensures safety from unwanted pregnancy, with minimal side effects that are acceptable in any case when you consider the alternative.

It is up to you whether you wish to submit to the "evidence gathering." Semen samples will be taken from the vagina and from the mouth and anus if indicated. Don't brush your teeth or wash your mouth after being forced to perform fellatio; as gross as it may seem, this is necessary to preserve the evidence, and the basic truth is, "No evidence, no prosecution." The whole reason you're going through this ordeal is to put the perpetrator behind bars.

It gets ugly. You'll be able to handle the scraping from under your fingernails (in case you clawed him and have skin samples that can identify him), but the removal of semen samples from your vagina and anus require a dry speculum so that the evidence won't be "contaminated." If you find routine internal examinations unpleasant when the gynecologist lubes his Sani-spec with K-Y surgical jelly, you can imagine how it feels when it's dry.

No one can make the decision for you as to whether or not you should prosecute. The fact remains that once you've reported a rape there are only two or three chances in a hundred that the guy will actually go to jail. It *is* possible that he'll lie about you, and that he'll find liars who will perjure themselves on the witness stand and insist you were a slut who led them all on. It is *quite* likely that the rapist's attorney will attempt to make this implication; it's probably the only desperate chance he has of doing his job and getting his client off the hook.

Going through the Rape Report System is a moral decision you have to make for yourself particularly if you feel strongly about getting your rapist caught so that he won't harm anyone else. Project yourself into that situation while you weigh your commitment to self-protection which might prevent a rape and *then* ask yourself if good locks and alarms aren't worth the price, and if the ownership of a protection dog or the possession of a lethal weapon is *really* something you couldn't cope with at any cost.

POSTVENTION·

Prevention is when you keep something from happening. Intervention is when you interrupt something that's happening, and are hopefully able to stop it in time. Postvention is when it's too late; everything is all over and all you can do is pick up the pieces.

Part of postvention includes surgery and physical therapy to help you recover from whatever physical injuries you suffered in the criminal act that victimized you. A more subtle part is counseling. Pain goes away after a time, but the thing that never leaves you is that overwhelming sense of helplessness.

When I was younger, I knew an executive of about forty-five. Frank was a quintessential leader: He advanced without being ruthless, he did his job superbly, and he built around him a staff of confident, rising stars in his field. All of them fed off his self-confidence and control.

One night, at a convention in a major city, Frank returned to his hotel late. He was attacked outside the lobby by a gang of street criminals. They beat him savagely, stomping fragments of his dentures into his gums and kicking him in the testicles, and they took his wallet and watch away from him as he lay crying and wetting himself, and begging them not to hurt him anymore.

Very few of his co-workers ever knew what really happened to Frank. Most just knew that he had been mugged; he went back to the office a week late with new teeth and the bruises muted and laughed it off. But something had changed in him. He lost his initiative. The up-and-coming protégés he had cultivated now seemed an object of fear to him. He no longer asserted himself. He walked with his shoulders sagging. The last time I saw him, Frank was fifty-five and had been sidetracked as a management analyst. It was a job he could do alone without having to interact with people because his supervisors knew that he couldn't handle that anymore. He looked as if he had aged twenty years instead of ten, and he never smiled, and he himself wasn't sure why anymore. Frank had become a zombie of sorts. A Victim.

There are ways to dig yourself out from under that sort of thing before; like "Frank," you bury yourself too deeply in the aftermath of fear.

Seek out help. Not from your brother or a buddy from the Marines, but from a professional. Here again, the Crisis Hotline can come through for you. Dial their number, tell them you're a crime victim who's having trouble coming to terms with it all, and ask what counseling is available. Don't worry; they won't be tape-recording you, and they don't care if you don't give them your right name.

If they don't have people within their own organization who specialize in your problem (many hotlines deal mostly with suicides or battered wives), they can always refer you to a professional who can help. If you're nervous about giving out your phone number for a return call, they'll understand, and will arrange for you to call back at a time of your choice.

They and the professionals they'll put you in touch with can help you sort out a lot of things. They can quote you statistics, for one thing, and that's always healthy: The person who is victimized always seems to feel that he's the only one who ever went through this and must have done something awful to be singled out for this fateful punishment. It helps to know just how many others are victimized, too.

If you feel inadequate for not having fought off the assault, they can help you deal with that, too.

I have mixed feelings about consulting spiritual advisors for advice in the aftermath of such encounters. Some just tell you to turn the other cheek. Fortunately, most modern spiritual advisors are experienced in the subtleties and realities of dealing with people in crisis situations, and some of them can help you more than any psychiatrist.

Psychologists and hotline workers are virtually unanimous in recommending that you not prepare to violently defend yourself "the next time." They assume that you're still too disturbed to handle it and in some cases, they may be right.

Once you and whoever is counseling you agree that you've gotten it together in the aftermath, and that hysteria or overreaction is no longer a concern, *then* think about trying someplace like my Lethal Force Institute. Only then will you be ready for what it teaches. If you don't have your act together when you come, the intensive training program—five days "on the dark side of the force"—can do you more psychological harm than good. Once you've accepted that what happened to you wasn't your fault, and that it doesn't make you a weak, helpless, and unworthy human being, *then* you're ready to responsibly deal with the fear that it can happen again.

Fear control goes beyond the arcane martial arts concepts of *sanchin* and *ki*. It can be understood and acquired at a logical and modern level of thought. For example, if you had been in a car crash and were now afraid of driving, the best therapy might be a driving course with either Tony Scotti or Bob Bondurant, both ex-race drivers who teach very advanced, high speed auto maneuvering, where for $1,500 to $3,000 you spend a week slamming a car through hairpin curves and into tire-screaming bootlegger turns. You come away having mastered that piece of iron and you aren't afraid of it anymore. Nobody at the school will tell you that you got hurt in your previous accident because you were stupid; you figure out for yourself that if you had known these skills going in, you would have been much less likely to get hurt. And, when you leave you won't be afraid to get behind the wheel anymore.

Martial arts teachers see this syndrome repeated again and again. A layman walks in off the street after having been beaten up, and spends the time to learn confidence in controlling an antagonist hand-to-hand. If the victim knows that he or she has the strength and the knowledge and the general wherewithal to control "it" if "it" happens again, they are well on their way to recovery. Psychologist Walter Gorski, one of the pioneers in treating psychological symptoms among police officers who have lost violent encounters, finds that martial arts training is one of the most successful forms of "outpatient therapy."

To control fear, you have to go beyond the symptoms. The symptoms are common legend: "Scared stiff" and "a chill down the spine" are not merely Agatha Christie catch-phrases.

The sensation down your spine (doctors call it a thrill, and so did Alfred Hitchcock, for different reasons) is a physiological indication that your fight or flight reflex is kicking into gear. Losing control of your bladder and bowels is nothing to be ashamed of, either. As the fight or flight reflex takes hold, blood rushes to your visceral organs with greater pressure and pulse-drive, causing them to clamp down and empty themselves. Even vomiting can occur in the face of bare fear. The stomach closes in upon itself with the general tightening as the body prepares to run or do battle, and jettisons its excess baggage.

Ask someone who skidded into an accident and *then* went into advanced driver training if he's still afraid it will happen again. He'll tell you, no. That person has now learned how to countersteer, how to master the principles of rolling traction, how to take advantage of every nuance of his vehicle's movement.

If you know you can control something, you won't be afraid of it, because the human organism only fears things it can't control.

Ask a woman who has been raped, and then undergone combat firearms training, if she still fears any big man with a knife. She too will say no, because she has learned situational dominance, and no one is going to get within range of harming her before she has a weapon in her hand, a weapon with which she can shut off the previously terrifying rapist like flicking a light switch, with a mere twitch of her index finger.

Combat pistol master Jeff Cooper was once asked by a student, "When do I know that I've mastered all this?" "You will reach that level," Cooper replied, "when anyone who attempts to harm you is in more danger from you, than you are from him."

In terms of postvention therapy for crime victims caught in a spiraling ascendancy of fear, I think that says it all.

WINNERS HAVE AFTERMATHS, TOO

When you fight your way out of a danger situation, the aftermath can in some respects be more pleasant than otherwise. A guy tried to mug you and you knocked him unconscious, or someone tried to rape you and you squashed his scrotum flat. You've fought, prevailed, and did the socially acceptable thing. You're going to feel like something of a hero, and in many ways that feeling will be justified. It will be warm comfort when you nurse the bruises and scrapes you may have sustained from the encounter yourself.

But other problems await you, problems that will make your victory taste bitter. If the incident is reported, the person you injured is quite likely to sue you. One friend of mine, an accomplished martial artist, shattered a man's jaw in a brawl; he wound up paying $5,000 to an orthodontist for putting the man's teeth back together. Even if the clown who sues you loses in court, you lose in your pocketbook. It can cost you thousands to mount even a minimal civil court defense, while *his* lawyer (quite possibly a bit on the hungry and sleazy side) will be working "free" in return for a percentage of the judgment against you.

If the person you fight back against is killed or crippled, it won't be as easy to live with as you think. When you watch a sickening crime story on the news, or talk with someone near and cherished who was victimized by thugs, a sense of righteous rage washes over you and at that moment, you could slaughter them completely self-righteously.

Only those who've experienced it know how much it takes out of a civilized human being to kill another person, no matter how justifiable the act. In 1981, newscaster Charles Austin of WBZ-TV in Boston, spent a day filming at my Lethal Force Institute. He was planning to build a major story around citizens who were fighting back at criminals with deadly force, and told me that he would interview, on camera, several people who had killed in self-defense.

"Good luck," I told him. "I doubt that even one of them will come through for you." Indeed, the only segment that appeared was the one featuring the school; none of the thirteen people Austin had found, who had lawfully shot criminals, agreed to appear on TV. "I just want it to be *over*," was the apology Austin heard again and again.

It's called postshooting trauma, and it affects even police officers who've had to shoot the most vicious criminals in the line of duty. Similar symptoms appear in crime victims. They include nightmares, depression, withdrawal from society, sexual impotence, compulsive obsession with the cataclysmic incident, and abuse of alcohol and other substances.

The good news is that these symptoms are far less pronounced in people who have prevailed over lawless violence and had to kill or cripple an offender, than in those who have been victimized or crippled—or widowed or orphaned—themselves.

Among crime victims, the symptomology is much more dramatic. You see people locking themselves in, both physically and psychologically, especially the older and frailer victims. They won't answer their doors even for friends unless they've phoned beforehand. They often won't go out at night, even in the safe company of friends. One of my clients came to me after she had already been through "postvention" with rape counselors, and thought she had it together until one night when she drove home from the supermarket. As she reached down to open her car door, she found herself paralyzed with fear. She didn't know why; she only knew that she didn't dare get out of the car by herself. After that, she was referred to me. You almost never see those symptoms in people who have done physically shattering things to *others* in self-defense.

One who kills in self-protection will suffer things like the "Mark of Cain Complex," a feeling that everyone who looks at them can see that they slaughtered another human being. This is reinforced by the fact that most of your friends and co-workers will know about it. Killing has a perverse fascination to it, and many of them *will* be looking at you strangely.

Yet the victims suffer far worse than the unhurt survivors. They wear a "Mark of Abel" if you will, and feel branded as helpless losers. You can see it in their eyes. It is one thing to be remembered as someone who killed a criminal in a savage battle to the death; at least there is something in this culture that allows you to reach back and take pride in that. You were strong. You prevailed. You were a winner.

You have to make your own value judgments. I can only tell you how I made mine. If others of my species endanger people like me, I shall not permit them to bring me down to their level.

I won't hide from anyone who threatens me, in a barricaded apartment like a cornered rat. I won't make a habit of going out at night only when surrounded by friends; only dogs should have to travel in packs. I won't sacrifice my identity in an attempt to disguise myself and fool predators who might be stalking me like those women who deliberately "dress down" to look less appealing to rapists. I will not let the human animals who stalk us in this society make an animal out of *me*.

I willingly accept the possibility of postshooting trauma, something one is largely innoculated against as soon as one understands how it works, because it is far more preferable than being a victim. Victimization is a condition for which there is no innoculation.

I never arrested a man or woman I didn't feel sorry for, and I never drew a gun on a person I *wanted* to kill. I just didn't let that pity stand in the way of doing what I had to do, to protect myself and other innocent human beings from their lawless depredations. I can remember sleepless nights after looking down a gun barrel at another person and questioning my own humanity for being ready to extinguish their lives without an ounce of compunction.

I don't *want* to lose the symptoms of postshooting trauma. When that happens, it will mean that "they" have brought me down to their criminal level, with an absence of compassion and decency that makes them separate from the things integral with what some call the human soul. I accept those symptoms willingly because they are far preferable to the symptoms suffered by the Victims.

Would you rather inspire fear or pity? Would you rather live in fear or know that when attacked by a human predator, he is in more danger from you than you are from him?

It hurts to hurt someone. That's because you are a decent and civilized human being. But it hurts more to have been victimized. It hurts a whole *dimension* more to know that someone you love was killed or injured or violated and made a permanent victim because you were unprepared or unable to keep it from happening.

Decide for yourself whether you can better wear the Mark of Cain or the Mark of Abel. Perhaps the man who said it best was Hal Swiggett, the Texas gun expert who is also an ordained minister:

Swigget wrote once,

No, I'm not recommending the shooting of people, but I do feel everyone of us has a right to defend ourselves and our loved ones whether we are home or traveling. I would rather be hung by a jury for defending my family or myself than to have to face God for not doing it.

46. INTERFACING WITH A LAWYER

The moment has come: A mugger or rapist or home invader has pounced on you and you've fought back intelligently and lawfully, and you've prevailed. The criminal aggressor is on his back now, moaning as he clutches his wounds, or twitching his feet as his life runs out of the bullet hole in his chest.

At this moment, there is good news and bad news. The good news is, he isn't going to try to hurt you anymore. The bad news is that, if you're not careful, he can destroy you even after he's dead. There are different ways that your life can be ruined by street criminals. Most people only think of the obvious: being murdered, brutalized, or stolen bankrupt by criminals. But when you use force to repel such assaults, the other two dangers can still sneak up on you: You may lose everything you own to the attacker or to his estate in civil court, and you may end up in jail yourself.

Far, far too many karate students and gun owners think that if they dump a mugger or rapist, they'll get a pat on the back from the chief of police and a good citizenship award from Kiwanis. Not necessarily. There are a lot of horror stories out there. Consider some of the following:

—A Detroit police officer on an undercover decoy assignment is accosted by a seventeen-year-old with a knife. He draws his revolver, identifies himself as a police officer, and orders the youthful mugger to drop his weapon. Instead, the mugger plunges the knife into the officer's chest. The cop returns fire, killing him. The family of the deceased sues the police department for seven figures; fearing a prejudiced jury (the officer is white, the dead mugger black, in a predominatly black city) the department settles out of court for $90,000.

—Two drug addicts break into the home of an elderly man in New York, savagely bludgeoning him about the head as they scream their demands for money. The old man, who has been mugged before, grabs a revolver from under his bed and shoots one mugger to death. He is charged with murder; the gun was unlicensed, and he has thus "killed while committing a felony."

—In Chicago, a sexual psychopath breaks into a girl's apartment and all but kills her. When her roommate arrives home he goes for her, too. Surprise—she draws a gun from her purse and blows him away. One wonders how many of the eight Chicago nurses murdered by Richard Speck would have mortgaged their souls for a gun in *their* pocketbooks, but this is lost on The System: The roommate has no license to carry a gun, so she is arrested.

The list goes on. Fortunately, there is a lot more

justice than injustice when self-defense cases come to court, but the horror stories continue. To prepare yourself to survive the legal aftermath just as you survived the assault itself, you need the same cold, calculated preparedness and determination.

You also need to know some unpleasant yet basic truths. The American criminal justice system is probably the best in the world, but if it has a fault, it is that the guilty may be favored and the innocent can easily get dumped on.

It's not hard to see how things evolved that way. Both the American system, and the Brithis common law from which it largely derives, are aimed at protecting the Little Guy. In modern American society, that can mean a system that often gives the benefit of the doubt to the criminal who hurts you—in this case, a socially underprivileged Little Guy who can't afford his own lawyer and who is up against the massive power of The State.

When it's your turn to be the defendant, you'll find out a few other things. First, there's a very good reason why ours is called the adversary system of justice. Simply put, each lawyer gets up there and says or does just about anything he can to discredit the other side, to subtly distort reality, and to make his side look righteous.

For this system to work, the lawyer has to take an oath to pursue his client's interests to the best of his ability. There's nothing in the law that says, "If the criminal admits to his lawyer that he killed Joe Smith, the lawyer has to have him plead guilty."

Dozens of criminals are turned loose every day in American courts because smart lawyers skew the appearance of the evidence and the truth, distorting reality in the eyes of the judge and the jury. *They do this knowing full well that their client is guilty.* They justify it on the grounds that they are fulfilling their oath to do all in their power on behalf of their client.

This is why, if a woman is raped, the lawyer for the rapist will make every possible innuendo in court to the effect that sexual enticement and promiscuity on the victim's part were the cause of the attack, not the rapist's depravity.

This is why, if you break a mugger's legs and call the cops on him, his lawyer may encourage him to bring criminal charges against you for assault, or sue you civilly for $30,000 in orthopedic surgeon's bills, plus six or seven figures' worth of mental anguish. To do so, the mugger may, in consultation with a less than scrupulous attorney, find it expedient to say something like, "Hey that dude tried to assault me, and I just took out my knife to defend myself."

Another basic truth: *Anybody can sue anybody for anything. If you don't believe that, ask your lawyer.* Nuisance suits abound. There are a lot of people out there who passed the bar exam but just aren't too good at what they do, and to make a living, they'll take any case that comes along. They may take a case "on contingency," with the understanding that the indigent mugger or rapist won't have to pay a retainer up front, but will forfeit to the lawyer one third or more of what they win by suing the citizen who thwarted their attack.

Let's assume that, while you're reading a book, you hear someone screaming outside. You recognize the voice as your teenage daughter's. You grab a gun and run outside. The attacker has her down; he lunges at you with a weapon in his hand, and you fire. He falls, his spine is severed, and now he's a paraplegic for life. If he doesn't have a long record for rape—or maybe even if he does—he's going to sue you. Paraplegia goes in the hundreds of thousands of dollars in civil court at this writing. The injured person can say that he was having consensual relations with your daughter, that she only cried out when she climaxed, that you came at him with your gun and he drew his weapon only to defend himself, and that you wrongfully shot him. While most states prevent a rape victim's sexual history from being introduced as evidence, *this won't apply to her history of intimacy with the accused*, even if that history is only a figment of his warped imagination.

If you don't realize all this up front, your lawyer is going to explain it to you and you might not want to put your daughter through the ordeal of testifying against this person. So charges are dropped by the district attorney against the rapist for lack of effective prosecution potential. Though everyone in the legal system except the cops will tell you otherwise, dropping the charges helps set the stage for a successful civil lawsuit against *you* by the paralyzed rapist. *Even if he is convicted of rape or attempted rape, he can still sue you for shooting him, and the fact of his conviction will not be admissible evidence in your defense.*

He gets a free lawyer in criminal court, courtesy of your tax dollars, and another free lawyer who works on a percentage of what they, together, rip off from *you* in civil court. *You*, the citizen who earns his or her own living, have to pay for your own lawyers. The court and The State don't pay you back for your defense lawyer, even after you're acquitted of the most ridiculous assault charge against a rapist that you can imagine. It is most unlikely that you'll get court costs and attorney's fees back after you win the civil suit; most courts don't award them, and if they did, the typical rapist probably wouldn't have the money to pay you with anyway.

We aren't talking nickels and dimes here. In real life, if you shoot or maim somebody even though they were the aggressors in a criminal assault on you, you probably *will* be sued civilly. For a homicide, we're talking about $5,000 in legal fees—*to begin with*. A really good trial lawyer (and really, do you want anything less?) will charge $200 to $300 an hour in court, and up to $200 an hour to talk with you and otherwise prepare the case.

I've seen self-defense shootings cost upward of $30,000

in legal fees and court costs. Consider that for appeals and retrials you have to pay the court two dollars per triple-spaced page of transcript of testimony. One of those pages contains about 200 spoken words. The average human being speaks at 60 words per minute. Your trial may last a week or more. *You* figure what that "accessory cost" alone is going to mean to your savings account.

I can't explain why the court system has to work this way. I personally think trials should be tape-recorded, even videotaped, and then transcribed. Not only would there be far fewer misstatements caused by the harried court stenographer trying to keep up with the rat-tat-tat of words, but the nuances of speech would be visible to the superior courts instead of just the cold, emotionless, printed words of the transcripts. Good-quality tapes would cost less than $1.00 an hour to make, would be preserved indefinitely, and could be transcribed by Clerk II personnel at $4.50 per hour or even Kelley Girls for two mills per word.*

A year before writing this book I testified as an expert witness in a landmark civil case involving guns and firearms training. I was on the stand for a day and a half. Each transcript of my testimony was worth $556.50 ($2.65 per page), and even though we won, the only people who've been paid so far are me and the court stenographer. Justice is expensive, and even when you win, it can take forever to collect.

If you have a good lawyer, he'll make all these things clear to you. And he's going to give you an option you aren't going to like; settling out of court in civil suits.

I told you about that cop who shot the mugger who sank the knife in him, and his employers who settled for 90 grand. To the world, it looked like they were admitting that their cop was wrong, and was too dirty to stand up in court and face the consequences of what he did. Sure,

---

*One mill-1/10 of a penny.

lawyers and judges will tell you, "Settling out of court has no legal implication on guilt or innocence," but that's not the way the public sees it in real life, and they know that as well as I do.

The *nolo contendre* plea, in legalese, means that the defendant pleads neither guilty nor innocent to the charge; he merely chooses, for whatever reason, not to contest it. In real life, everybody knows that *nolo* is "a gentleman's way of saying, 'I'm guilty.'" The average citizen sees an out-of-court settlement as the civil court version of pleading *nolo*.

PLANNING LEGAL STRATEGY

I've just spent over 2,000 words telling you the bad news. Now it's time for something more encouraging. You can get out of legal nightmares the same way you can get out of street nightmares. You fight your way out by using intelligent planning, self-control, and appropriate weapons that you're trained to use.

In this case, your primary weapon is your legal counsel. If you want to take karate training, you don't ask the nearest big guy to teach you how to fight; you shop around. If you want to learn guns, you don't buy your uncle's rusty souvenir Luger from WW II; you go to a competent gun dealer and seek training at a qualified firearms training facility.

By the same token, you're out of your mind if you wait until you're really in trouble before, and retaining a lawyer then pick one at random out of the telephone book. If I had the choice of entering a violent encounter with an inexpensive .38 revolver and the phone number of the best criminal lawyer in the state, or going in with a $2,000 combat-customized .45 automatic and taking pot-luck with attorneys at the Legal Clinic Storefront, I'd take the low-priced .38 and the good lawyer every time. I have the training and determination to make the lesser gun do what it has to do, but the lawyer works independently of me, and there's no way I can make up for any deficiency in *his* quality and power.

I work a lot with attorneys. I know the best around. In any state where I travel regularly, I have a good criminal trial specialist lined up, and I have his home *and* business phones on a plasticized 3-by-5-inch card in my wallet.

Lawyers tend to work hard and play hard, which keeps them away from their telephones a lot. My phone privileges, if I get arrested for blowing away or otherwise damaging a dangerous attacker, are limited to one phone call *that connects*. I don't want that call to reach my lawyer's answering service while he's in court on Tuesday, or out sailing on Long Island Sound on Saturday.

That's why my one phone call is going to be aimed where yours should be: at home. One's spouse (or mother or roommate; whoever lives with you generally cares more about you than almost anyone else in the world), what psychiatrists call a trusted other, is going to be free to fight for me or you as soon as we hang up that telephone and get ushered into the cellblock.

My wife has a list. You can call your own attorney and get a list of emergency numbers for when he isn't there. Don't think that it's being paranoid; the lawyer will probably gain new respect for you. If your lawyer won't give you his home number, it's time to look for another lawyer.

When I call my wife, *she'll know what to do, because we've got a plan worked out.* First, I'll give her everything she needs to know. I won't say, "Hey, babe, I just shot a mugger and the cops arrested me." I'll say,

Dee, listen. This is *not* a practical joke. I'm being held at Precinct X of X Police Department, in the custody of Captain X. I've been charged with murder/aggravated assault/maiming (pick one). The location where I'm at now is XXXX North X Street, and the phone number is (XXX) XXX-XXXX.

Honey, this is the only call I'll be able to make to you. Call up the best attorney you can get. *I can't discuss it over the phone,* but I'm innocent, and I need your help so that I can get out of here as soon as possible. You know what to do.

Do you have any questions? In case we get cut off, there's a letter explaining what to do in my desk, third drawer down on the left, with a list of attorneys' phone numbers. OK? I love you. Take care of me. Goodnight.

Notice that no reference is made to the incident itself. Note that I leave at home a list of lawyers' telephone numbers for the benefit of my wife, and if she can't find it, or if she isn't home, I also carry a list of lawyers in my pocket that I'll use in desperation. It's incredible how few people take these simple precautions. Frankly, the practice is usually limited to people who have already been through the nightmare of having to defend themselves forcibly and then faced hassles over it.

Pick your lawyer the way you'd pick your doctor, or anybody else you need on call for services that are vital to your continued existence. Use the same criterion you would use in evaluating police and other emergency services in a community you were moving into, assuming you had a choice. Does the guy have a good record? Does he have a lot of satisfied "customers" singing his praises? Has he been established for a while? Let me tell you a little secret. One of the reasons why lawyers are so hungry to win their cases is that *whether they win or lose goes on their record.* Select your lawyer as carefully as you would select your gun and ammunition if you *knew* a homicidal encounter was sneaking up on you.

PERSPECTIVES

A lot of you will read the foregoing and think, "My God, this man is telling me that it's worse to hurt my attacker than to submit to the attack." *Not true.*

You're reading this book because you're worried about getting hurt by criminals. OK, let's develop a sense of priorities up front. I can't do that for you; no one can do that for you. I can only tell you what my own sense of priorities is, learned from the recognized masters of mortal human combat and forged in moments when my own life and future were on the line.

There is a saying among police officers that "It is better to be judged by twelve than carried by six." The twelve jurors can be persuaded to forgive you for killing your criminal assailant, and if they don't you can always appeal. None of the six pallbearers can make you alive again, though, and there is no earthly appeal from the grave, nor can the court order that vitality be restored to your paralyzed limbs.

I decided a long time ago—my own decision, just for myself, as *yours* must be—that I would rather walk into the courtroom as the defendant, than be rolled in on a wheelchair as the plaintiff in a civil suit, or complaining witness in a criminal trial.

When you are the defendant in a case where you properly zapped a criminal assailant charged with aggravated assault, maiming or mayhem, or murder or manslaughter—you have all sorts of possibilities to shoot for; retrials, acquittals on technicalities, acquittals on the facts, jurors who think you look nice and/or have a more persuasive lawyer, even a declaration of mistrial that the system doesn't think it's worth the money and hassle to retry your case.

Those who hurt you and get caught can get their

freedom back on technicalities. They can't give you back the powers you had before you got hurt or crippled—movement, sexual enjoyment, thought, freedom from paranoid fear. You had those things before, but what they did to you took them away.

Turn the tables and learn from your attackers. You have to understand what the American Way of Court is, and how the Justice Machine works, and understand it as thoroughly as those who prey on people like you, know it. They make it work to their advantage.

You can do it, but better. Unlike them, you won't be lying. You are a moral and law-abiding American citizen, and you will strike your attackers down only when it is legally and morally and technically proper to do so. Nonetheless, you will have to resort to lawyers, as they do, to beat them and to finish your fight.

Your lawyer is as important as your gun or your fist. Pick him or her carefully. Choose an attorney who specializes in such cases, and be wary of any "general practitioner" lawyer who promises to skate you out of a criminal charge or civil suit involving use of serious force. *That is a job for specialist lawyers who have extensive criminal trial practice,* and you should trust your life and your future to nothing less.

If you don't have a lawyer now, contact the State Bar Association or a lawyer referral service in your state and city. Choose carefully. Your future, and that of your family, may depend on the attorney who represents you when all the chips are down on the jury's betting table.

47. WHAT PRICE SAFETY?

It was understood from the beginning that this book would not be tailored for any one socioeconomic class. Viable protection alternatives for America's poor, who are so frequently victimized because their limited funds require them to live in the areas most infested by the criminal predators, is as important as sensible, cost-effective approaches for the Middle American pocketbook. Also included are the top of the line choices in each protective discipline, not so much for millionaires, who can hire the best security consultants and don't need to read this book anyway, but for those middle-class citizens who have already been victimized. Once you come face-to-face with the terror and the agony of being brutalized by criminals, there is a tendency to feel that cost is no object to keep it from happening again.

People who have already been victimized find that a security system pays for itself with the greater peace of mind the very first day. And in terms of hard dollars alone, protection is cost-effective at virtually every level. Good locks are a relatively small investment, yet they last for decades and are an attractive selling point when you put your home on the market. Depending on the system you've chosen, your alarm can be taken with you when you move if it's relatively portable. If you've dumped well over four figures into having your place hard-wired, don't consider it lost funds if you choose to move; a hard-wired alarm system is a top selling point and you can easily raise your asking price. Indeed, it can be a major "impulse factor" in guaranteeing a quick sale of your home, saving you expensive delays at moving time.

Many insurance companies give substantial discounts on burglary protection policies to homeowners with good alarm systems and quality locks. In ten or twenty years, these discounts can easily meet or exceed your initial investment in the security devices.

You eventually will want to dispose of your Mace or any other similar substance when it reaches its expiration date, but after having given you a couple of years of protection for under $10, it certainly doesn't owe you anything. A Kubotan or Mo-Gem should theoretically last forever. If you buy a Kubotan and training manual for $10 and have it to rely on for twenty years, that's a very cost-efficient $.50 a year, or less than $.05 a month, that you've paid for protection.

When you figure in the pet food and the vet bills, a dog can cost you a good piece of change in the long run. But you're getting more than protection. Doctors and psychiatrists agree that pet owners find their animals therapeutically soothing, and some claim that owning one can reduce your tensions and extend your life.

Guns are perhaps the most "investment-grade" component of a home security system, *if* you have wisely chosen top-quality weapons. A Colt Python .357 Magnum bought new in 1956 for $125 can sell second-hand for $350 to $400 if it has been kept in good condition; the identical gun retails new this year for some $500. A mundane Colt .38 Detective Special purchased for $68.50 in 1956 will easily fetch $200 on today's used-handgun market.

Conversely, a cheap imported .22 revolver bought for about $13 in the late 1950s would be laughed at by any reputable gunshop or pawnbroker you tried to sell it to. They *might* give you $5, deactivate it with an arc welder, and turn it into a doorstop or paperweight. Only quality holds its value.

You needn't wait 25 years to get your money back on security items you've bought. A Colt .45 automatic pistol, purchased at retail two years ago and kept clean and rust-free, can be resold today for about the same price. The German shepherd puppy you paid $150 for two years ago, now a well-trained young adult dog with a good disposition and instant response to commands, will easily earn back its purchase price and more if you sell it tomorrow to some frightened citizen who wants canine protection and can't afford to wait for a puppy to grow up.

In many cities, quality martial arts instruction is no more expensive than belonging to a tennis club or exercise spa. The vigorous workouts are superb for muscle toning, weight loss, and general health, quite apart from the defensive skills that will be with you all your life. Far more exciting than jogging or calisthenics, karate or judo or *aikido* gives you a strong incentive to keep up with your training, and they bring a sense of personal discipline beyond what you're likely to get in any other sport or exercise format.

After you drop out of your weight-reducing salon, you're likely to put the flab right back on in a year, but the defensive skills and mental discipline and confidence you acquired in your martial arts class will never leave you. An investment in yourself? Believe it.

Once you get past the initial capital outlay, you will find that quality protection is a remarkably sound investment. Locks and hard-wired alarms are home improvements that enchance your abode's resale value far more, dollar for dollar, than almost anything you'll find suggested in *Better Homes and Gardens*. A finely bred dog can, with care and responsibility, more than pay for itself with its progeny. Quality handguns appreciate in value considerably faster than the Dow-Jones average. The instrinsic value of property insurance requires no explanation to anyone who has been around American society and the

Law of Logical Probability, long enough to become a grown-up.

If the only reason you've been putting off the acquisition of security measures is that it's too expensive, you've been kidding yourself. Take the money out of savings, if necessary. In a personal cash crunch, things like guns and portable alarm systems can be quickly liquidated for most of, and sometimes more than, what you paid for them. Investments that protect you are "savings that can save you."

Don't cast yourself into Jack Benny's old joke. When confronted with a holdup man who snarled, "Your money or your life," Benny would fold his arms, put a hand to his cheek, and say, "Let me think for a minute."

Once you've made the commitment to protect yourself and your family, you will be pleasantly surprised at how cost-effective it all is, even if your total self-protection system is *never* tested by a real-life criminal. When you add in the peace of mind—and when you project just what it's going to be worth if a criminal *does* try to violate you or yours—it may well be the primest bargain you ever laid out money for.

ABOUT THE AUTHOR

Massad Ayoob is an internationally recognized expert on self-defense. His articles have appeared in numerous martial-arts magazines, technical-firearms periodicals, and police-professional journals. He is the author of two classic self-defense manuals, "In the Gravest Extreme" and "Fundamentals of Modern Police Impact Weapons." With eight years' experience as a sworn police officer from patrolman through sergeant ranks, he is presently Director of Lethal Force Institute in Concord, New Hampshire.

We Deliver!
And So Do These Bestsellers.